ART AS ACTIVISM

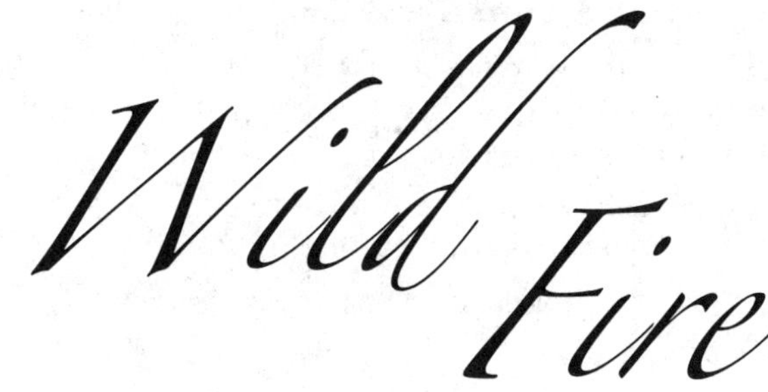

Wild Fire

ART AS ACTIVISM

EDITED BY

DEBORAH BARNDT

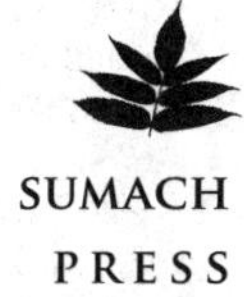

SUMACH
PRESS

Library and Archives Canada Cataloguing in Publication

Wild fire : art as activism / edited by Deborah Barndt.

ISBN-13: 978-1-894549-55-4
ISBN-10: 1-894549-55-4

1. Artists and community. 2. Artists--Political activity. 3. Politics in art. 4. Arts and society. I. Barndt, Deborah

NX180.A77W54 2006 700'.1'03 C2006-900348-3

Edited by Beth McAuley
Designed by Liz Martin

Cover photos: Julia Winckler (Fire Clock) &
Lee Bensted (Flaming Footprint)

Royalties from the sale of this book will go to
the dian marino fund, York University.

Sumach Press acknowledges the support of the Canada Council for the Arts and the Ontario Arts Council for our publishing program. We acknowledge the financial support of the Government of Canada through the Book Publishing Industry Development Program (BPIDP) for our publishing activities.

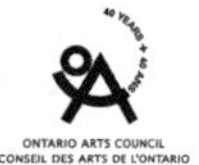

Printed and bound in Canada

Published by

SUMACH PRESS
1415 Bathurst Street #202
Toronto ON Canada M5R 3H8

sumachpress@on.aibn.com
www.sumachpress.com

Contents

Part III: Eco Art

Part IV: Art Heals

Foreword

In contemporary North America, most non-artists, of whom I am one, encounter art in packages, commercialized, commodified and cleaned-up. *Wild Fire* returns us to a more authentic encounter with art in a context of social contention — messier, even disquieting, but exuberant and affirming. These are artists with a sense of place and purpose. This is art that makes you sit up and take notice.

Wild Fire brings together a remarkable collection of stories. The global reach is striking: the artists in *Wild Fire* take the reader on journeys from Nicaragua to East Asia, from Canada to Chile. Perhaps more striking is the intimate and personal lens through which most of these stories are refracted: we see here artists working with communities in triumph and failure, in success and in frustration. But across this range and through the diversity, the binding thread that makes this collection so compelling is the message of the inseparability of art and social change. Art sometimes provokes, sometimes portrays or sometimes precedes social transformation, but it is never far from the heart of struggle. The essays in *Wild Fire* show us how and why.

As Dean of the Faculty of Environmental Studies (FES) at York University, I am intensely proud that this collection represents work of our students, graduates and teachers. That a faculty can attract and nurture such talent and commitment is extraordinary. FES is one of the few institutional settings where art, academia, activism and environmental awareness not only co-exist but are welcomed as mutually reinforcing. In the first decade of the twenty-first century, universities are increasingly becoming businesses, and are run as such. It is harder to find spaces within academia where social commitment, community process and alternative ways of knowing and learning are valorized (or even tolerated). But learning and teaching are not spectator sports, or shouldn't be. At its best, a university can serve a singular social role as a place where analysis and activism are both nurtured, where students and teachers together map a landscape of intellect and art, passion and dispassion. The astonishing work represented in this anthology shows us why it is so vital to keep wedging open those spaces.

— Joni Seager,
Dean, Faculty of Environmental Studies, York University

Acknowledgements

THIS IS A COLLECTIVE EFFORT IN SO MANY SENSES. THE PROJECTS BEING described and analyzed in these pages are collaborative by definition, engaging both human and non-human actors in critical and creative processes of reflecting, educating and organizing. The contributors participated in many stages of the book project: conceiving and framing the project, reading each others' proposals and chapters, naming the book and offering images for its cover, and, most recently, planning the launch with visual and performance pieces. At every stage of this process, as I have sent out emails asking for ideas or advice, there has been a wonderful creative flurry of cyberspace dialogue which has served to inject us regularly with a shared energy and excitement about this project.

More specifically, though, we want to thank Gabrielle Etcheverry for helping to organize the book proposal and the first meetings of contributors and Amanda Montgomery for helping to organize the final meeting and to prepare the manuscript for the publishers.

The two images on the book cover are photographs by contributors: the central image by Julia Winckler is of an old pagan ceremony, the burning of the clocks, which takes place on winter solstice on Brighton Beach in the United Kingdom. Lee Bensted offered the upper right-hand image of a flaming footprint, part of a larger installation called "Passages," that was created at the Burning Man Festival in Nevada in 2005.

I am particularly grateful to Joni Seager, the Dean of the Faculty of Environmental Studies where I teach and where most of the contributors once studied, for writing the foreword for this collection. Joni has brought a new energy to the Faculty, which builds on and promotes the kind of synergy reflected in the projects and chapters of *Wild Fire.*

Once again, it has been a pleasure to work with Beth McAuley of Sumach Press, whose careful editing of these chapters has made the stories sharper and more accessible. A special thanks, too, to Sumach's Liz Martin, who has brought her own artistic flair and activist commitment to the layout and design of the cover and the book. We are delighted that Sumach recognizes the value of making this kind of work known to multiple audiences, as a press that honours the art, activism, and academic reflection that we have integrated in *Wild Fire.*

— Deborah Barndt
Toronto, April 2006

Playing with Wild Fire:
ART AS ACTIVISM

Deborah Barndt

BRING TOGETHER PEOPLE WITH PASSIONS FOR ART, FOR POLITICS, FOR community, people with fire in their bellies, and things are bound to heat up. This book wasn't so much envisioned and planned, as it emerged through a kind of spontaneous combustion. The flames were fanned, however, by three different moments around my dining-room table which connected the contributors.

AROUND THE TABLE: A BOOK IS CONCEIVED (2003)

In the fall of 2003, I invited recent graduates with Masters in Environmental Studies (MES) to a celebratory dinner. As we toasted the completed MES projects (a mural produced on food security, a book produced by Muslim women questioning their misrepresentation in the West, among others), we were struck by how all of them were related to art and activism. The stories told were definitely too rich to sit on a library shelf but cried out to be used by educators, artists, activists. "Let's make a collective book …!" we decided, and the sparks began to fly.

York University's Faculty of Environmental Studies had indeed already laid the groundwork for such a project. Known since the 1960s for its interdisciplinary and praxis-oriented graduate program, FES attracts mature, socially conscious and creative students who want to put diverse ideas to gether in new ways, explore alternative ways of knowing, communicate to a broader public and contribute to environmental and social justice. Built around individualized plans of study, the FES program encourages collaborative learning and university-community links. Courses and student projects often integrate the arts as modes of inquiry and forms of communicating knowledge. This was definitely fertile soil for a collaborative project around art and activism.

I put on the table my own interest in looking at the contradictions engaged in projects, in particular the "creative tensions" often present in alternative art and popular education practices, such as the tension between process and product, between aesthetics and ethics, between cultural reclamation and cultural reinvention, between the spiritual and the political, between the body and the Earth. These resonated with those who were at that first dinner, and I was charged with pulling together a book proposal. Now the heat was on.

I sought proposals from the more than twenty graduates I had supervised since 1993, whose work at the time and since then fit under the rubric of art and activism, as well as from others connected with my courses (Popular Education for Social Change and Cultural Production Workshop) or the VIVA! Project (a collaborative research project on community arts in the Americas).[1] I knew that many of them had continued to use the arts in their activist work once they left the academy. I invited potential contributors to gather around my dining-room table in late March to review the proposals. The response was overwhelming.

AROUND THE TABLE: A BOOK TAKES SHAPE (2004)

One Sunday afternoon in March 2004, thirteen people arrived at my door to read the eighteen proposals submitted and to offer their own visions of this collective project. While we didn't concur on everything, we agreed that the tensions within our work were rich sources of critical and creative discussion.

One tension we shared was our multiple and overlapping identities as artists, activists and academics. Each of these labels evokes strong reaction: feelings of passion and exclusion, of commitment and threat, of stimulation and alienation. Each is contested terrain: none of us could (nor wanted to) pin down a definition for art, for activism or for academic work. But we could identify the tensions within and between these practices. While they may sit uneasily one next to the other, each is critical to our varied practices (though we may identify more with one than with another). Artist, activist, academic: three multi-faceted and sometimes seemingly contradictory identities that can interrogate, challenge and enrich the other.

This tension resonated with my own experiences doing doctoral research in Peru in the mid-1970s when I struggled to reconcile these same aspects of myself, what I called in Spanish *la pensadora* (the thinker), *la poeta* (the artist) and *la política* (the political person who must act). As a graduate student, I was expected to focus on the critical thinking side and cordon off my artistic practice as well as my political activity. As an artist using photographs as research tools, however, I felt images could speak to people in ways that most academic writing could not. As a social movement activist, I was challenged by my Peruvian colleagues to take a stand on behalf of the marginalized majority, to not perpetuate colonial relationships by packaging their knowledge for Western academic purposes and personal gain. I agonized over these contradictions but eventually concluded that these three identities — the artist, activist and academic — would have to co-exist, as each needed the other and I was unwilling to give up any one.

In many ways, the essays in this book challenge conventional understandings of art, activism and academia. We question, for example, the elitism and individualism of conventional art practices and the internalized oppression that most of us suffer from when we say "I can't draw." We question how art has become increasingly separate from daily life, and ever-more commodified as a consumer good in a global marketplace. We are more interested in the processes than the products of artmaking.

Similarly, we question a narrow understanding of activism that frames mass protests as the primary mode of political action. How we think, converse, write, draw, sing, move (in other words, how we tell our stories as well as the stories we tell) can unveil power relations and transform knowledge production and everyday actions. Finally, our arts-based research counters within academia the dominance of rationalist and linear thinking, of text-based knowledge, of purportedly neutral theorizing and of theory disengaged from practice.

Not only do we challenge you, the reader, to reconsider how art, activism and academics are framed and practised, but we also ask you to rethink their interrelationship. Why is there often a divide between academics and artists? Between artists and activists? Between activists and academics? What are the roots of these splits? What can each offer the other? The contributors to this book blur the boundaries between these modes of engagement.

The air was electric that Sunday afternoon in March as potential authors began to make connections between their work and their thinking, as one idea sparked another. In the kind of work we do, the *how* is as important as the *what,* so we fantasized the creation of this book as a rich collective educational process, spinning off dialogues. We also wanted to break through the verbal domination of texts, including images that would bring our stories alive.

Fuelled by the energy of the gathering of thirteen co-creators, we each retreated to our respective corners to take on the somewhat solitary task of writing our own chapters (though three essays were collaboratively written). As these trickled in, were edited and revised, they were again distributed to all contributors, in time for another dinner-table conversation.

AROUND THE TABLE: A BOOK IS NAMED (2005)

In April 2005, six of us gathered to review the final draft chapters, to consider how the pieces spoke to each other and to collectively conjure up a title. Narrative was a recurring theme: all pieces tell stories, indeed are *about* telling stories, yet are not about reifying any story. In fact, the authors here actively interrogate the stories told by themselves as well as by others, what is told, to whom, how, for what and with what consequences. There is a recognition that stories are fragmentary and contradictory. In fact, part of our attraction to art (the multiple forms through which we tell stories) is its capacity to "hold paradoxical truths, like an egg in each hand," as Heather Lash framed it.

Most of our conversation focused on the processes of our artmaking and activism: the risks, the messiness, the surprises. A strong reflexivity runs through the essays, as we question our roles as artists, as facilitators, as theorizers. Power is central to all of these undertakings, and these authors embrace a complex notion of power, one that is multi-dimensional and constantly shifting. The processes described in this book at the same time claim and question power.

What, then, draws us to this messy, unpredictable work? When someone suggested that it was like "playing with wild fire," the metaphor resonated strongly with us.

Playing. Play challenges boundaries, the way things are. It can be a creative way of engaging people, ideas, power. Artmaking can offer a playful response to academia and to political activism. At their most creative, art, activism and academic work are about challenging the old and ossified, about making new. Moving into unknown terrain requires both humility and humour, as Leah Burns suggests.

Several authors refer to a trickster type figure as a model of this daring playfulness, as one who can play with contradictions, can help us laugh at ourselves, one who can potentially destroy or create. Many of the practices explored in these stories involve playing with symbols of power: through phototherapy, culture jamming, adbusting, guerrilla theatre, gigantic puppets, reclaiming the streets movements. Play combines the critical and the creative, challenging what is while allowing us to imagine what could be.

Wild Fire. When we imagine wild fire, we may think of it as a natural force, out of human control. In an interdisciplinary environmental studies, however, we learn to see natural disasters as anything but natural, as shaped by human agency, by social and political forces. We question the nature/culture split, explore the symbiotic relationship between the human and non-human, and consider ourselves as part of, not separate from, nature. We need to embrace the wild and passionate in ourselves in order to make change.

The authors in this book share a passion for life itself, for its diversity and struggles, its endless challenges. A passion that is not only an expression of life but also a way of living. A passion for truth (not as a singular truth but as a search for understanding), for beauty (not as a given but as something historically grounded which we must daily construct), for justice (not as a rationalist adherence to an ideology but as a commitment to being part of an evolving struggle).

Many of the stories in this book unfold in heated life-and-death contexts: whether in Chile of the 1970s or Nicaragua of the 1980s, or more currently in detention centres in Toronto or working with youth in post-conflict Bosnia. They amplify the voices of those threatened by globalization, whether it's the struggle of salmon to survive industrial farming or the struggle of students to resist the corporatization of the university. The art processes described are tools for examining myriad hot issues: from clear-cutting and food security to racism, sexism and war.

Playing with wild fire. Fire is potentially both a destructive and a creative force. And wild fire can suddenly rise up and spread quickly. The work of art as activism can ignite a spark and fan the flames; it both stimulates desire and courts danger. To embrace the passion of art, the intensity of activism and the creation of new knowledge is to play with wild fire. No guarantees, no innocents; we are all implicated. The co-authors of this book have chosen to take the risk. To embrace the contradictions, to plunge into the "uncertain waters," as Petra Kukacka describes this journey. They realize that change often demands dramatic action, fuelled by passions of the spirit, mind and body. Playing with wild fire is part of a transformative process, an openness to change and to being changed.

ART AS ACTIVISM

In challenging narrow definitions of art and activism, we reframe art *as* activism. Whether the modes are verbal or non-verbal, artmaking that ignites people's creativity, recovers repressed histories, builds community and strengthens social movements is in itself a holistic form of action.

The modes of expression are endless. Most important is that they are appropriate to a particular group, time or place. Look carefully within these stories and you will find storytelling, gossiping, chatting, poetry writing, zines, street theatre, guerrilla theatre, theatre of the oppressed, masks, puppetry, drums, horns, meditational chanting, protest singing, community radio, drawing, painting, grafitti, murals, homemade postcards, sidewalk chalk drawing, origami, banners, textile art, sewing, weaving, photo-stories, phototherapy, adbusting, billboard transformation, digital imagery, video, websites. The mediums themselves are not as important as their relationship to the context, the way they are produced and how they are used. The more important questions, then, are the *why* and *for whom* of artmaking.

INTRODUCING OURSELVES AND OUR ESSAYS

Aside from sharing the York University context and similar approaches to art, activism and academia, there is diversity among the authors of this book. Although most of us are women (save for one) and primarily young, we come from diverse origins (from Aboriginal nations on Turtle Island to descendants of European colonies, from Toronto to British Columbia, from Pakistan to Korea, the U.S. to the U.K., Hong Kong to Chile); we are, in one sense, representative of the multi-ethnic and diasporic Toronto context where our paths crossed. Some are trained as artists or consider themselves artists, while others might more comfortably call themselves educators, organizers or writers.

The seventeen essays are grouped around four themes: Art in Social Movements, Art as Activism, Eco Art and Art Heals. In the section one, "Art in Social Movements," Leah Burns reflects on her efforts to engage youth in participatory art processes in "Seriously ... Are You *Really* An Artist? Humour and Integrity in a Community Mural Project." She playfully confronts sticky moments that challenge her own assumptions and reveal inevitable tensions between aesthetics and participation, theory and practice. Heather Chetwynd, in "Releasing Voices, Reclaiming Power: The Personal and Collective Potential of Voice," examines two quite different experiences with voice as an empowering process: meditative chanting in exploratory voice workshops, which releases the physical voice while developing the social voice, and the singing of protest music with Latin American exiles to build community and promote solidarity with political causes.

In "Whose Nicaragua? Popular Communications across Eras, Regions and Generations," Christine McKenzie and I reflect on our work as internationalists working in Nicaragua, myself in the 1980s and Christine in the early 2000s. We compare two distinct experiences, emphasizing how all activist art is shaped by, and attempts to shape, very particular historical, political and cultural contexts.

Gabrielle Etcheverry, in "Ediciones Cordillera: An Exile Community's Role in Cultural Production," revisits the experiences of her parents and their friends, exiled Chilean writers and translators, who created a literary press in Canada that both kept them connected to their political and cultural roots and mapped their struggle to recreate themselves in a new context. Finally, in "The Strawberry Tasted So Good: The Trickster Practices of Activist Art," chris cavanagh raises two key questions: What is art and who is an artist? Claiming that everyone has the power to create, he emphasizes play, trickster pedagogy, the carnivalesque and storytelling as ways to challenge power.

Section two, "Art as Activism," offers experiences and reflections on the processes of artmaking as political in their own right. In "Demechanizing Our Politics: Street Performance and Making Change," Maggie Hutcheson proposes public theatre as a collective demechanization of our commodified culture. With examples ranging from agit prop to utopian performances, from giant puppets representing the plagues of the New World Order to phoenixes rising from the ashes, she challenges dominant rationalist practices of protest to embody the change they advocate, to better integrate emotion and intellect, the personal and the political.

Salima Bhimani, in "Reconstructing Our Culture of *Ilm* (Knowledge): Muslim Women Represent Themselves," invites other Muslim women in Toronto to explore their common struggle against Islamophobia by deconstructing the ways they have been (mis)represented in Western media. She explores how Muslim women can take on the challenge of representing their own more complex stories, reflecting not only a common history of colonialism but also the tremendous diversity in beliefs and practices among Muslim people. Yukyung Kim-Cho in "*Jamming* with Women's Rights Activists in East Asia: A Process of Critical Reflection" revisits her project of exploring the internal contradictions of women's rights movements by juxtaposing interviews, photos, drawing, typography, lines of text and blank space in a process she calls "jamming."

In "Mixing Metaphors: Risk in Art and Activism," Petra Kukacka explores the risks we take as artists and activists. She argues we must engage with "monsters" in "uncertain waters" and that we cannot remove ourselves from the inevitable tensions that are both in the broader social context as well as within the ways we have internalized it.

The third section, "Eco Art," features projects that engage directly with the non-human, and challenge the anthropocentrism of much social movement activism and art. Melanie Kramer in "Garden the City: Activism through Interventionist Art" emphasizes the element of surprise that is central to interventionist art. She reflects on her project that challenged the use of public space in downtown Toronto by drop lifting postcards around the city. The postcards encouraged unsuspecting readers to grow their own food on the rooftops and balconies of their urban spaces.

In "Salmon Tales: Eco-Art Activism," Aileen Penner, Jacinda Mack and Lee Bensted write about their collaborative art project. The production of silk-screened banners allowed each to represent both personal and political stories about salmon in the context of neo-liberal globalization; in the process, they revalue regenerative as opposed to reductionist thought, the sacred significance of salmon as opposed to its commodification. Sau Wai Tai also reflects on a collaborative undertaking in "Confessions of a Community Artist: A Letter to My Fellow Earthworkers." She revisits the collective experience of creating "earthballs" and installing them on the York University campus to mark sites of hidden histories; she reflects on her own struggle to "let go" as a facilitator and to allow other group members to shape the project, while also allowing the Earth herself to speak.

To end this section, Pariss Garramone challenges academic writing practice in "Tellingsmiths: The Work of Planting Trees and the Politics of Memory." She interrogates her own experience of creating an environmental autobiography on forestry work in the form of a zine and reflects on images and metaphors that have been clear-cut from academia.

The final section, "Art Heals," reveals the healing power of creative practices, whether for individuals or communities, an element of art and activism often glossed over in social movements. In "Arts in Detention: Creating Connections with Immigrant Women Detainees," Oona Padgham and other members of the No One Is Illegal group have a conversation about how they use art as a medium of expression with immigrant women and their children in detention. Their insights confirm the healing power of group artwork as well as its capacity for cutting across language and cultural barriers. Equally important is the use of the detainees' art as tools for a broader political project advocating their release.

Heather Hermant recounts her three years of work with youth from the three ethnic groups in post-conflict Bosnia in "Language as Landscape: Navigating Post-Conflict Reconstruction with Bosnian Youth." She problematizes the use of English as a common language, or a "mediating bridge," in producing theatre pieces and a school newspaper, projects intended as healing processes for Bosnian youth.

Stephanie Conway and Julia Winckler put themselves in the picture in "Acts of Embodiment: Explorations in Collaborative Phototherapy." They create an egalitarian therapeutic context in which to share stories and re-enact scenarios for the camera that provide an alternative to the family album and conventional snapshots.

To end the collection, Heather Lash reflects on the process of theatre production with refugees from diverse origins in "You Are My Sunshine: Refugee Participation in Performance." She distinguishes between testimonial work and spectacle and problematizes the role of the animator, in particular one's responsibility as a "witness" to horrific histories.

Most of the contributors to this volume are young and their energy is reflected in the spirit of these essays, giving us all hope. *Wild Fire: Art as Activism* speaks to new activists, artists, educators, students and community workers who are daily crossing borders, blurring boundaries, dissolving dichotomies and embracing contradictions. We hope it will inspire both critical and creative response, deeper reflection and bolder action. And that it will ignite many other sparks that will spread like wild fire.

NOTES

1. See www.vivaviva.ca

PART I

Art in Social Movements

CHAPTER I

Seriously … Are You Really an Artist?

HUMOUR AND INTEGRITY IN A COMMUNITY MURAL PROJECT

Leah Burns

MY VERY FIRST WORK SESSION ON THE MURAL PROJECT WAS A HOT AND sticky Wednesday afternoon in the middle of August. Amidst the heat and a city-wide smog alert, I found myself packed into a small classroom with seventeen participants. They had been directed to collaborate with me as part of their work assignment in an employment and skills-building program for "at-risk youth."[1] Their faces were pretty non-descript, but I had the impression I was being sized up very thoroughly. I had planned to get the group to use collage and Polaroid photos as a way to begin exploring issues of identity through visual imagery. When I explained this, the first reaction I got was, "Man, we just did collage with our other supervisor this morning!" Already a bit nervous, this threw me off even more and I bumbled a little uncertainly as I gave instructions.

As the group settled in and began working, I realized I didn't really know what to do with myself. They were all talking and interacting while I just sort of stood there leaning awkwardly on the supply table trying to recover some confidence. One participant, Cameron, turned to me suddenly and said, "Hey, are we doing this right?" Relieved at having something to do I had begun to walk over and lend a hand, when he proceeded to barrage me with all kinds of questions:

"How old are you?"

"I'm thirty."

"Can you draw?"

"Yes."

"Are you good?"

"I guess it depends on what you think is good."

"Well, are you *really* an artist?"

"Yes, but I don't always work in …"

"So you are an artist."

"Yes."

"No, SERIOUSLY, are you *really* an artist?"

(*slightly exasperated*) "No, I'm just pretending. I'm faking it, but don't tell the staff, OK?"

(laughter from around the room)

Well, I wasn't entirely joking. This interaction, although it put me on the spot, did ease tensions. The humour broke some of the distance I was feeling from the group and I relaxed a bit. But Cameron's question was actually really poignant. I've never been completely comfortable with claiming the title of "artist," largely because of a lot of the connotations and stereotypes associated with it.

The exercise was meant to get the participants thinking about visual representations of their identity, but it also raised questions about my position. I was struggling with issues of identity myself. How should I present myself to this group? How did I want them to see me? Who was I? Why was I there? What kind of background did I have to be able to be in this position co-ordinating or "leading" these people? Sometimes I did feel like an impostor.

My goal as a "community artist"[2] is to engage in creative practices that are relevant to the communities that I live in and interact with. In collaboration with members of these communities, I use arts projects and arts processes as sites for socio-political dialogue and exploration. A large part of this work involves questioning and negotiating boundaries — boundaries which are present in society, in cultures, in the communities I work with and in me. As a white, Western woman with academic training in the arts, I come from a position of privilege, which has shaped my aesthetic sensibilities and methods of production. How does this act as both a resource and a barrier to democratic and inclusive creative practice? How do my own social, political and cultural locations serve to shape the planning, implementation and outcomes of these projects? How might I challenge the limits of my perspectives, to work at preventing them from reinforcing boundaries I wish to bridge? Two essential elements in meeting these challenges are humour and integrity.

Humour

One of the most effective means for subverting dominant paradigms, that I have experienced, is humour. If you can get someone to laugh, you may have not only touched on their sense of the order of things but also disrupted that same sense of "the way things are" by interjecting or pointing out something that doesn't fit. This unruly something pokes fun at assumptions and plays on a sense of irony; its very existence disproves that things can only be one way. By revealing discordant variables, humour can show that we are fooling *ourselves* if we take certain systems of organizing understanding too seriously. "The joke affords the opportunity for realizing that an accepted pattern has no necessity. Its excitement lies in the suggestion that any particular ordering of experience may be arbitrary and subjective. [Many] jokes have this subversive effect on the dominant structure of ideas."[3]

Throughout North American First Nations traditions of philosophy and storytelling there exists the pervading figure of the tickster.[4] The trickster's identity shifts according to tribal culture and story context, but the trickster's role is usually one of humour and subversion.[5] The book *The Trickster Shift* examines the use of humour and irony in contemporary First Nations art in Canada. Editor Allan Ryan explores how contemporary First Nations visual artists take on aspects of the trickster within their work, subverting stereotypes of indigenous peoples and critiquing dominant and oppressive political and social structures. Their incisive and critical dialogue with both dominant paradigms and with one another is at once comical and razor-sharp. Native American author Gerald Vizenor writes about the comic in indigenous literature, "You can't act in a comic way in isolation. You have to be included. There has to be a collective of some kind. You're never striving at anything that is greater than life itself. There's an acceptance of chance. Sometimes things just happen ..."[6]

Humour can be a way of connecting divergent ideas to a collective consciousness of taken-for-granted knowledge. It is based on interaction and therefore cannot be done alone, separated out. This conception of the artist as trickster or jester playing with empathy contrasts with the myth of creative geniuses discovering "original" ideas off by themselves — as if not informed by their environment, their own history and their interaction with others.

INTEGRITY

From August 2002 to January 2003, I co-ordinated a community mural project at a mid-sized, not-for-profit organization in the City of Toronto. The mural process brought to the surface some of my questions about identity, ethics and aesthetics in relation to my goals as a community artist. The young people I was working with (although all categorized under the problematic label "at-risk youth") represented multiple nationalities, cultures, classes, racial backgrounds, genders, sexual orientations and abilities.[7] Working as a group, we encountered and interrogated many assumptions about identity and arts practice. As a team of people with diverse backgrounds, experiences and living situations, we had a wealth of different perspectives and insights to share. Our differences offered both points of interest and enthusiasm, as well as points of tension and conflict. In our efforts to communicate effectively and to engage these tensions, during the mural project, humorous moments often became valuable points of interpersonal connection and consciousness-raising.

FoodShare, the not-for-profit organization we all worked for, focuses on food security and works towards community mobilization and education around food issues. The goals of equity and diversity are also an intrinsic part of the organization's mandate. As the mural co-ordinator, I had taken on the responsibility of creating a large-scale painting that represented FoodShare's values, appealed to its staff, volunteers and other members, and acted as an educational tool about its programs. I had also taken on the responsibility, as a community artist aiming for an equitable and inclusive collaboration, of facilitating a creative process that recognized and respected the group of young people I was working with, this meant that their ideas of what the mural should look like or what it should represent also needed to be incorporated. Balancing out these two areas of responsibility was often a tricky negotiation between ethics and aesthetics. The organization wanted a skillful painting in a representational style that showed some of the activities it engaged in. It also wanted me to provide an opportunity for participation to a group of youth who had not previously had access to arts training or arts production. Could I facilitate both the creation of a "high quality" final product and a collaborative process with integrity?

THE POWER GAME

One day I was working in the classroom space with the youth participants. My intention in this particular session was to initiate some discussion around issues of power: what was power, were there different kinds of power, how could it be represented visually? If we were going to create images that promoted goals of equity and diversity, we needed to think about how power was symbolized within images and compositions so that we didn't unconsciously reproduce hierarchies or oppressions in the mural.

Another of my concerns was that although the organization wanted the youth group to participate in painting and designing the mural, it was staff that ultimately had the final say. "We want it to look professional," one person told me, "you might have to go in at the end and fix things up." To me this seemed to be a bit of a mixed message. I wanted to be really explicit about these power dynamics and to hear what the team thought about it.

After introducing these issues to the group, I asked them to participate in a short theatre exercise as a way of getting started. They were pretty reluctant, "another stupid exercise, what is the point?" They all got up, however, and helped me make a space in the centre of the room with a table, a bottle and a few chairs in it. The exercise, called "The Power Game," was based on a drama process from Augusto Boal's Theatre of the Oppressed.[8]

First, I asked for a volunteer to go into the space we had cleared and arrange the chairs, table and bottle so that one of the objects appeared to be the most powerful. Then one volunteer was asked to go into the space and take a position so that he was the most powerful thing in the arrangement and to stay there and hold his pose. One after another everyone took a position in the space, each successive person trying to take the position that had the greatest power. Some tried to get to the highest point, some took an authoritarian pose (hands on hips and a stern expression), or pointed at the group as if directing them. One person sat down facing the scene, propped up his feet and held out a newspaper as if he was reading and ignoring the whole thing. As the last person to join the composition, I stood back and pretended to be observing and taking notes about everyone on a pad. I then asked who they thought appeared the most powerful. Natalie immediately said, "You are."

I replied, "OK, so why do you think it's me?"

She responded, "Because you are making us do this exercise."

"Oh! Good Point," I laughed.

I had forgotten how I embodied power both inside and outside the role play. I was part of a hierarchical system within the organization. Even if I didn't always feel like I had authority, it was clear, to the participants anyway, that I was placed higher within that system than they were. Whether I recognized it or not, it manifested in many ways. I could determine what the objective of a session would be and what activities we would pursue. In trying to get the participants to think critically about how power was represented visually, they opened my eyes to a new consciousness about myself. It had to be acknowledged that although the organization's goal was equity and mine was collaboration, in many ways we were still reproducing hidden hierarchies. So what did this mean in terms of the images we were creating for the mural, would they reflect these realities? Was collaboration possible between people in disparate power positions?

The exercise wasn't a flop; it had opened up dialogue about power though not in the way that I intended. Natalie's point was an even stronger and more relevant example than any I had thought of. Using a humorous comment as an opening, she had challenged some of my assumptions as co-ordinator and some of the power dynamics within the group. We did go on to look at how the poses used in the exercise represented different kinds of power and different ways of seeing or expressing it. We also got into a really useful discussion about how decisions were being made about the mural. They explained that they were glad I was being explicit about process, but they were not happy with staff having the final say and censorship rights over the mural content. They wanted to be part of those negotiations.

When I create artwork for public display, I am contributing to an ongoing cultural conversation that communicates not only information about the artwork's content but also information about its form and aesthetic — in other words, what art is and what art looks like. When I create artwork in collaboration with others, I am entering the conversation from a different location, one which emerges out of a dialogue that negotiates with similarities and differences to determine what our contribution will be and how it will be shared.

You can take the artist out of the ivory tower, but can you take the ivory tower out of the artist?[9] I recently read this line in an article about community arts practice and it put me in mind of my interactions with the youth participants. I have done all kinds of theorizing about what art is, the importance of process, the need to be open to reassessing what is "good" art; but when it comes to actual practice, especially in collaborative situations, incorporating those theoretical ideals isn't easy.

PRIMING SURFACES

It arced up and out, a sleek white line flying through the air then landing, gracefully, in a sticky trickle clinging to my ponytail and running part way down my neck. I looked up and nearly caught another splotch in the eye. "Hey guys, it feels like I'm painting under a flock of seagulls. What are you doing up there? Seems like you might have too much paint on those rollers."

After a month and a half of trying to get the team motivated, drawing and visualizing imagery for the mural, I reckoned that doing something more physically engaging and immediately tangible, like priming the mural wall and panels, might help to kick-start some momentum. The hot, humid weather had been sapping energy, and trying to do finicky design work sitting at a table inside the classroom seemed to be making everyone drowsy or impatient.

The day before, I had asked the group to bring in clothes that were OK to get dirty. Most had forgotten, others simply didn't have clothes to spare (a reality I had not considered), so we innovated. Decked out in garbage-bag overalls and shopping-bag-covered shoes, the crew assembled in front of the wall. While they were getting ready, I had set up the drop sheets, rollers, paint trays and brushes. "OK, let's get started," I called out. "Grab a brush or a roller. You can work on a panel or you can work on the wall."

Pretty soon it was total chaos. Paint was flying everywhere. People were dripping it on each other's heads. Paint trays were tipped over and several people, unknowingly walking into the spills, left tracks across the floor. I zoomed around from person to person trying to give pointers. I had assumed that this task would be relatively simple. My notion that this would get energies up, develop a sense of teamwork and inspire people to start imagining possibilities for the mural was partly accurate. They were laughing and interacting, but I was caught between wanting them to feel engaged, needing to economize on paint and feeling responsible for getting the task done with some semblance of professionalism. Ultimately I had to step back and join in their laughter, chuckling at myself running around covered in paint and at my swishing, plastic-bag-attired crew. I had been in such a hurry to give everyone a "hands-on" experience that I had neglected to check in and see where they were at in terms of skill and comfort levels with the medium.

The situation recalled to me the tension I felt as a teenager house-painting with my dad, half listening, eager to get started. Surely he realized I wasn't completely stupid. I knew how to dip the roller in the paint and move it across the wall; it was just a matter of getting the entire surface covered. "Come ON, just let me do it!" I realize now that any surface is impacted by the accumulation of gestures that move across it. My dad was concerned with the kind of impression he left. Part of the reason for being methodical in the painting process is to be frugal with materials, but one also wants to avoid cracking and peeling later on which may be caused by various particles falling into the paint or by an uneven application.

Formal techniques although restrictive aren't inherently negative or uninspiring. It is the way in which they are shared or taught that can be limiting, if, for example, they are presented as rules to be adhered to, rather than skills to choose from based on particular needs or goals. Learning ways of facilitating skill development without smothering creativity is one of the biggest challenges in arts education and community arts practices. In the case of the mural, I needed to take more time to prepare the group, acknowledging the material circumstances (the amount of paint we had and the kind of surface that would best support the mural we intended to paint on top of it) and demonstrating certain methods of roller/brush work that would best suit this particular context.

This sticky situation, instead of increasing frustrations, offered a playful moment in which the participants were able to enjoy one another's company and at the same time recognize that our painting strategy might need to be rethought. The participants smirked as I stood there looking quite dishevelled and said, "Um … OK you guys … maybe we need to organize this differently." The episode was both comic and ironic. The irony was that in my attempt to be inclusive, I had not recognized that we were all coming from different places and skill sets. I had assumed that this task was basic enough, that anyone there could jump in and do it — and they could, easily, if given a bit more guidance. As someone with training in the visual arts and in building-renovation, I had made assumptions, based on my own experience, about what knowledge my co-workers had access to. The same conditions applied to theorizing about the appearance and meaning of art. If I gave the staff and the youth participants some background on the debates about high and low art, before rushing in and asking them to come up with design ideas, their analysis of mural content and style was very sophisticated. Yet, again, their perspectives raised issues I hadn't even thought of.

It hadn't gone according to plan. There'd been lots of false starts and dead ends. I couldn't say that the project embodied all of my theoretical ideals in exactly the way I had imagined, but the process, despite all its crazy messiness and perhaps because of it, had initiated many new friendships and deepened older ones. A lot of learning and teaching transpired between those of us who worked on the mural and those who witnessed its production and provided much needed support in other ways.

Since it was completed, FoodShare estimates that over 10,000 people have seen the mural as part of the daily tours or weekly conferences and training sessions at the Field to Table warehouse. The United Way brings close to 1,000 people a year to tour the warehouse as part of its staff and volunteer training. All tours to the warehouse stop in front of the mural, where the FoodShare story is told using the mural as the guide.[10]

Humour can engage difficult issues in a way that is provocative without being antagonistic. It can ease tensions and offer connection even between disparate subjects. This is not to say that confrontation is necessarily negative or unproductive, or that humour is inherently positive; a joke might also be used to create conflict. Rather, it is an acknowledgment that we do not always have to be serious when addressing serious issues. Comic interventions may be powerful, thought-provoking and simultaneously disarming. Shared laughter can be a way of emptying a moment, not of conflict or challenge, but of the intensity that can sometimes be manifested in bodies and interpersonal or group dynamics when encountering difference.

I have been asked to speak on many occasions about my experiences working on community arts projects. The question I am asked most frequently is: What is the best way to deal with the conflicts and contradictions that arise when facilitating a collaborative, creative process? Of course, there is no perfect answer. Every context, community and project is different and requires processes of communication constructed to suit its particular needs. What I have found to be effective, however, especially in the role of co-ordinator when others are looking to me for leadership, is always working to maintain honesty, humility and a good sense of humour.

> You can't act in a comic way in isolation. You have to be included. There has to be a collective of some kind. You're never striving at anything that is greater than life itself. There's an acceptance of chance. Sometimes things just happen ...[11]

NOTES

This essay is dedicated to the members of the August 2002 to January 2003 Focus On Food Program. Additional thanks to Zahra Parvinian, Mary Lou Morgan, Debbie Field and all the other incredible staff and volunteers who worked at FoodShare's Field to Table Centre during my tenure there: Akemi, Ben, Delsie, Edwin, Kate, Lauren, Lynn, Mario, Rachel, Vera, Yvonne and many others.

1. The label "at-risk youth" is meant to denote young people engaged in or emerging out of contexts or life experiences that are particularly challenging and which may put them at risk of failure to thrive within dominant social and cultural structures. Many of the participants in the program described in this essay had problems with this label. They felt it carried negative connotations and that people treated them differently as a result. It was not an identity or a descriptor that offered a sense of empowerment and most did not want to be associated with it.
2. The title "community artist" or "community arts" is itself contested. The title is most frequently claimed by those who engage in arts practices within communities as paid professionals. There is, however, a rich history of creative arts traditions to be found in grassroots communities around the world where those participating do not identify or benefit from the professionalization of this "career field." As community-based arts practices have gained legitimization and support through cultural policy and arts funding bodies, the definitions — of what qualifies as community art and who qualifies as a community or community artist eligible for financing and official recognition — have often become more exclusive.
3. Mary Douglas quoted in Allan J. Ryan, ed., *The Trickster Shift: Humour and Irony in Contemporary Native Art* (Vancouver: University of British Columbia Press, 1999), 5.
4. "The trickster is a figure found in oral cultures the world over, [as well as] North America. Among [trickster] names used in Canada, are: Glooskap, Nanabojoh, Weesakejak, Napi, Raven, Hare, Coyote. Half hero, half fool this figure is at once like each one of us and like none of us." Lenore Keshig-Tobias in Ryan, ed., *The Trickster Shift*, 6.
5. Gerald Vizenor in Ryan, ed., *The Trickster Shift*, 4.
6. Ibid.
7. Out of respect for their privacy, the names of all the participants described in this essay have been changed. The experiences described were shared, but the perspective from which the stories are told is mine. It is one version and, like the other layers, memories, interpretations and relationships engendered by this mural project, it offers a site/sight of potential and limitation.

8. Theatre of the Oppressed (or T.O.) focuses very explicitly on the socio-political issues and contexts faced by its participants. The drama functions as a forum. Analysis of cultural assumptions and structures of power that promote oppression are played out through the creation of images and the enactment of scenarios. Augusto Boal's theatrical pedagogy aims to use theatre as a form of consciousness-raising and transformation. "[Theatre] should help us learn about ourselves and our times. We should know the world we live in, the better to change it. Theatre is a form of knowledge; it should and can also be a means of transforming society." Augusto Boal, *Games for Actors and Non-Actors* (New York: Routledge, 1992), xxxi.

9. Nina Felshin, "Introduction" to Nina Felshin, ed., *But Is It Art? The Spirit of Art as Activism* (Seattle: Bay Press, 1995), 2.

10. Debbie Field, "Report Letter from FoodShare Executive Director to Toronto Arts Council," September 12, 2005.

11. Gerald Vizenor in Ryan, ed., *The Trickster Shift*, 4.

CHAPTER 2

Releasing Voices, Reclaiming Power:

THE PERSONAL AND COLLECTIVE POTENTIAL OF VOICE

Heather Chetwynd

MY VOICE HAS BEEN A SOURCE OF JOY, SELF-ESTEEM, CONNECTION AND power. IT HAS allowed me the opportunity to inspire, motivate, calm and energize, helping me to bond with others and to experience a deep spiritual connection. Recognizing the profound influence that voice and song have had on my life led me to research and experiment with voice, sound and song. In this chapter, I reflect on the immense potential power of voice to strengthen our sense of both personal and collective power.

Our voices are such intimate musical instruments. Resounding throughout the physical body, our voice can lead us to experience our thoughts, emotions and physical sensations as one. The sound, and all it carries with it, lives in our whole being. Our thoughts are embodied, creating a bridge between conscious and unconscious awareness, experience and knowledge. Our voices become powerful tools for connecting the different ways we know and perceive the world.

The vibration of our voice enters us not only through the ear, but through the entire body. Even a deaf person experiences many aspects of the sound of a voice. As a result, we both listen to and feel our own voices and those of others. When we experience the body through sound, we have a sense of being *grounded.* When we are grounded, we can feel our own energy and power. We feel stable, focused and strong.

Perceiving the world through sound, our attention shifts away from sight, the sensory perception favoured in the Western world. Through the eye, we have a fixed viewpoint of the environment: light travels in a straight line and vision is unidirectional. We are unable to look inward and include ourselves in the picture. In contrast, perception through the ear is multi-directional — sound travels through and around matter. We perceive it as creating a sense of inner and outer awareness both inside and outside of the body, helping to bridge the feeling of separateness.

The biological function of the ear is to achieve balance, allowing the brain, eyes and body to co-ordinate movement. Consequently, as we tune into our environment through the ear, we create "a rhythmic form of communication"[1] with the environment and other people, something that can be felt in the body, "moving" us both physically and emotionally.

The vibration of our voices moves within our bodies and simultaneously throughout our physical environment, passing into and through all that surrounds us. We can yield to the intimacy of its touch, allow ourselves to be moved by its rhythm or attempt to block its invasiveness. Our judgements play a critical role in how useful our voices become as potential tools for bonding across difference, for developing trust, openness, community and solidarity.

Whether chanting slogans in a demonstration, lulling a baby to sleep, singing a hymn at church or crying ourselves to sleep, the voice has a power which we can either open to and build upon, or close out and resist. Our voices are potential vehicles for exploring the self, connecting with our spirituality, breaking down our sense of separateness and building collective power.

EXPLORING VOICES: CHANTING AND TONING PRACTICES

My interest in voice led me to organize voice exploration groups to explore "alternative" forms of vocalizing. In this space, we experiment with a variety of vocal practices, ranging from highly structured chanting to free-form vocalizing. My experience is that structured repetitive chanting parallels listening to a melody played on one instrument, tending to draw people into an inner peace and a sense of oneness. In contrast, the unstructured exploratory nature of free-form vocalizing can be likened to a full orchestra, playing with many elements, moving energy, creating drama and ending in an often unexpected resolution.

Chanting, whether it be shouting slogans or repeating mantras, draws on the powerful influence of repetition. Physiologically, the repetition of sound tends to mask other sensory input and highlight the so-called right brain functions,[2] moving us into a more sensorial, affective state. Repetition "comforts listeners by bringing them to a state of receptivity."[3] When we sing or say simple repetitive phrases, words or syllables, chants are "planted like seeds in our conscious mind, and through repetition and acceptance they send their roots into our unconscious minds."[4]

In contrast to chanting slogans, meditational chanting requires focus, a silencing of the mind and attention to listening. This practice stimulates energy and increases our awareness of harmonics, or overtones — a series of high frequencies created above any single tone.[5] Under normal conditions, harmonics are difficult to perceive, but chanting can increase their volume, making them easier to hear. Listening to high frequencies can improve our listening ability by causing a voluntary opening of the inner ear, a desire to listen rather than ignore certain sounds.[6] Many sacred traditions believe that overtone singing strengthens our connection to spirit by focusing our listening, moving the singer to a new level of communication and another state of consciousness. While there are many measurable physical responses created by harmonic chanting (changes in heartbeat, respiration and brainwaves),[7] its ability to heighten listening offers an interesting potential for improving communication skills.

The structure of meditational chanting can be contrasted with the unstructured, sometimes chaotic and emotional experience of free-form vocalizing. Often referred to as *toning*, these vocal expressions of emotion include spontaneous moans and cries as well as organized collective crying (known as *wailing* and *keening*), and *free-form toning,* a form of sounding during which the mind follows the voice rather than vice versa. The purpose of toning is to release emotion and resonate the physical body and energetic fields[8] in order to restore balance. We can liken a healthy being to a well-built, finely tuned piano, toning "tunes" different parts of the body, bringing their vibratory levels back into "pitch" and releasing energy blockages.

LIBERATING VOICES: COLLECTIVE VOICE EXPLORATION

When I first introduce free-form toning into my workshops, participants often feel inhibited. Toning requires us to let loose, follow our vocal urges and leave our judgement of sound behind. I often compare toning with making love — with overcoming self-consciousness, letting go of conscious control and just following where the body leads us. Our tendency to repress ourselves vocally comes from the idea that certain sounds are "unclean" or "bad." When we let go of that idea, all sounds (including those which commonly have negative or sexual connotations) can be very purifying.

In my facilitation, I make a point of marking the transition from day-to-day life into a space of non-judgement. We can then allow all sounds to flow regardless of their meaning in society, neither censoring our own voices nor attributing social meaning to sounds coming from other participants. This frees up participants who have censored and negatively judged their voices to start to appreciate them and allow themselves to be heard. One woman, for example, concluded: "There is no wrong way to do it, and no matter what comes out of your mouth, it's perfectly fine ... I like it because I just play, play with my voice. And in the end I feel that my voice is important to the group."[9]

Through this process of collective voice exploration, I have observed how releasing the physical voice helps people develop their social voice. In society, we are taught when to speak, which tone of voice to use, how loud we can be in given situations and when it is acceptable to cry or laugh. These rules change according to ethnicity, gender, age, cultural context, and so on. In the process of internalizing such cultural expectations, particularly amongst marginalized groups, there is the danger of being silenced. Breaking this silence through voice exploration becomes part of challenging social and political structures and taking power.

Women participating in my voice exploration workshops, for example, often express the desire to lower, strengthen and *embody* the voice.[10] Many consciously associate what they perceive as their high, weak or disconnected voices with low self-esteem and being silenced as young girls. In contrast, they often perceive the male voice to be loud, potent and silencing.

Raising our voices, either physically or socially, is often experienced as a risk, particularly for those who feel their voice manifests a sense of powerlessness or oppression. When we raise our voices, we challenge our perception of weakness, challenging those who have power over us and claiming our own power. Collective exploration is one way to share the experience of risk-taking, and this strengthens the bond between the participants, creating a sense of both individual and collective power. Through voice exploration, these women often find that they are soon able to make more "noise" in their daily lives and begin to feel that people listen to them more.

> I felt that I didn't really have a voice … The work enabled me to be more expressive of who I was. It gave me an opportunity to focus on myself, my internal voice, through the [physical] voice, so then I could express that as well verbally.[11]

> I've noticed a progression in a loss of inhibition … The biggest change I notice is that I am speaking louder and clearer, and am not afraid to speak up ... [I have] less of a fear of calling attention to myself with sound.[12]

Collective exploration of the voice in a safe environment can help us both embody and release the voice and, as a result, begin to reconnect to that power and express it through our collective voice as social power. In this sense, the recovery of the physical and personal voice is part of the social process of empowerment. If we take the silencing of voice as a metaphor for repression, and if we agree that there is an interrelationship between the physical and social bodies, then it follows that freeing the voice can help to free us as individuals, and sharing this experience can be a part of the process of social transformation.

In my experience of collectively exploring the voice through chanting, overtone singing, voice games and free-form toning, I have found that nearly everyone is left feeling uplifted and energized. I create activities to develop an intimate, trusting relationship within the group which leads to an atmosphere of openness and willingness to experiment. Voice games relax the participants and introduce a playful, exploratory environment. Unstructured toning (which is also a very powerful therapeutic tool)[13] encourages the expression and release of emotional tension. Chanting and overtone singing create a state of intense listening, highlighting a sense of being both inside and outside of oneself. Occasionally, a group which really clicks experiences a coming together of emotion and energy, creating what can be best described as a sensation of spiritual communion. Participants feel grounded, uplifted and empowered both personally and collectively.

PROTESTING VOICES: SONGS IN SOCIAL MOVEMENTS

As we move out of our small groups and into larger settings, we continue to experience the connecting capacity of voice through song. In social action settings, we sing to counter oppression and strengthen identity. This becomes clear when we see how genres develop around specific political struggles, racial and cultural groups and social classes. Music has an important role in people's efforts to claim and make history and to challenge current power relations.

> Most, if not all, revolutionary struggles and social change movements have been accompanied and inspired by a distinct music ... It must be no accident that churches and armies have their own distinct music in much the same way that the Sandinistas in Nicaragua, anti-apartheid groups in South Africa, or the contemporary women's movement have anthems.[14]

Singing enhances our sense of community, deepens commitment, restores faith and develops a sense of power, fearlessness and protection, often moving people from apathy to engagement. Collective singing creates a communal space where people share common sentiments and goals while still acknowledging difference, making it a powerful tool for building coalition and solidarity.

Singing can provide us with a deeper understanding of ourselves and the world. As cultural products which grow out of the history, social norms and belief systems of a culture, songs can reinforce our own cultural identity while also allowing us to explore the identities of others. Even if we don't understand the lyrics, songs can help us develop a visceral and emotional relationship with a cultural genre, an experience which nurtures empathy and a desire to learn more, both of which are key to developing critical consciousness.

This was very much my experience. In the 1970s, when many political exiles were arriving in Canada from South America, I was drawn by the emotional intensity of Latin protest music. I joined a band and began to sing of their exile, pain and resistance. Although I sang of other people's realities in an unfamiliar language, this new music touched me deeply. I connected personally to the spirit of the music which stimulated me to repeatedly reflect on the content and meaning of the songs. Over time, I developed a strong emotional and intellectual connection to the cultures and struggles of the Latin American peoples and was moved to participate in many ways to support them.

This movement from awareness to voluntary engagement in any process of change seems to depend upon our sense of conscious responsibility and the meaning a situation has for us — in short, it depends upon *need, feeling and connection.* Expressing feelings in song encourages active engagement in struggle by integrating emotional and intellectual understanding.[15] The connective and emotive properties of our voices play an important role in *emancipatory learning*, defined as "a process of coming to know *for* and about one's self and about one's self-in-relationship to others and to a larger community."[16] The critical word in this definition is for: we learn *for* ourselves, implying that we attribute personal meaning to this knowledge which can motivate us to act upon it. We move into a spiral of emancipatory learning that moves back and forth between exploring the forces that shape our lives and taking action to change them.[17]

It is easier to engage ourselves in processes of change when we feel supported. Singing with others is a collective act of support which raises energy, nurtures our sense of power and encourages commitment. It helps us to develop and maintain an openness to new ideas and a positive attitude. Musicians in the Civil Rights movement, for example, reflected on the power of music to create feelings of collective and individual power and a sense of invulnerability.

> We would stand up and march out of the church ... singing and singing, and that music kept us together, and kept us less afraid. It's like an angel watching over you. You know you are in trouble, you know you are going to get your butt beaten ... you know you might even get killed, but the sound, the power of the community, was watching over you and keeping you safe.[18]

Whether singing in church, chanting on the street, crying alone or toning collectively, we can use our voices to experience communion, relief and balance, and deepen our knowledge and strength. As vibration, rhythm, tones and lyrics move out of our lungs, into our ears and through our bodies, we draw on multiple ways of knowing and experiencing. The physical voice is an expression of our social voice and through its use, we either reinforce or shift our sense of power.

NOTES

1. Music and sound therapist, Don Campbell, speaking at the "First International Conference on the Healing Nature of Sound," Epping, New Hampshire, October 1993.

2. Jeff Volk, *Of Sound, Mind and Body: Music and Vibrational Healing* (Epping, NH: Lumina Productions, 1992), video.

3. Kay Gardner, *Sounding the Inner Landscape: Music as Medicine* (Stonington, ME: Caduceus Publications, 1990), 203.

4. Randall McClellan, *The Healing Forces of Music* (Rockport, MA: Element, 1991), 60.

5. Harmonics are present in all natural sounds, which are really multiple sound waves. What we perceive to be the pitch is generally the slowest frequency, the lowest sound and the wave that has the most energy. All the other sound waves are multiples of the slowest frequency and these are called the harmonics.

6. See, for example, Alfred Tomatis, *Education and Dyslexia* (Fribourg, SWITZ: AIAPP, 1978); John Beaulieu, *Music and Sound in the Healing Arts: An Energy Approach* (Barrytown, NY: Station Hill Press, 1991); Paul Madaule, *When Listening Comes Alive: A Guide to Effective Learning and Communication* (Norval, ON: Loulin Publishing, 1993); Don Campbell, *Music Physician for Times to Come: An Anthology* (Wheaton, IL: Theosophical Publishing House, 1991).

7. Jonathan Goldman, *Healing Sounds: The Power of Harmonics* (Shaftesbury, Dorset, UK: Element, 992), 64.

8. Goldman, *Healing sounds*, 137.

9. Sandy (pseudonym), interview by author, Toronto, ON, December 1993.

10. Carol, Carmen, Ruth, Leslie, Sandy (pseudonyms), interviews by author, Toronto, ON, December 1993.

11. Jasmine (pseudonym), interview by author, Toronto, ON, December 1993.

12. Ruth (pseudonym), interview by author, Toronto, ON, December 1993.

13. Given the often primal experience of toning, I have occasionally had participants move into deeply emotional states. I always make it clear from the beginning that I am not a therapist and recommend that anyone moving into such a state withdraw from the activity. Free-form toning is very conducive to uncovering repressed memories but such work should be done with qualified therapists.

14. Susan Belyea, "Theorizing Women's Music" (Research paper for master's degree, York University, 1989).

15. Moon Joyce, "Singing for Our Lives: Women Creating Home through Singing" (MA thesis [draft version], OISE, 1993).

16. Gwendolyn Kaltoft, "Music and Emancipatory Learning in Three Community Programs" (PhD diss., Columbia University, 1990).

17. Ibid., 2.

18. Civil Rights activist Cordell Reagon, quoted in Pete Seeger and Bob Reiser, *A History of the Civil Rights Movement in Songs and Pictures* (Markham, ON: Penguin Books, 1989), 77.

CHAPTER 3

Whose Nicaragua?

POPULAR COMMUNICATIONS ACROSS ERAS, REGIONS AND GENERATIONS

Deborah Barndt & Christine McKenzie

In the summer of 2001, we find ourselves working together to design and facilitate a popular communications workshop in Pearl Lagoon on the Atlantic Coast of Nicaragua. At the time, Christine is a graduate student and Deborah is a teacher in the Faculty of Environmental Studies; the workshop is part of a York University project supported by the International Development Research Council.

Deborah is returning twenty years after organizing similar workshops for the Nicaraguan Ministry of Education, focused on the Pacific region, during the period of the Sandinista revolution. Christine is embarking on six months of fieldwork, facilitating the production of community radio and a newsletter with a natural resource management project in the Pearl Lagoon basin.

Our shared experience sparks a dialogue about the distinct contexts that shaped the work in two different moments in history, two different regions of the country and across our two distinct generational experiences and perspectives.

Context is Critical

Deborah (1980s): Imagine, Christine, my first experience in Nicaragua was shortly after the birth of the revolution, when you were nine years old. I found myself with a solidarity delegation of Canadians in the Plaza of the Revolution in Managua, celebrating, along with 200,000 others, the "victory over ignorance," barely one year after the Frente Sandinista de Liberación Nacional (FSLN or Sandinistas) led a triumphant insurrection against the forty-year-old Somoza dynasty. Large murals on commercial-free billboards offered public-art homages to the Nicaraguan Literacy Crusade, the first major political and pedagogical project of the new revolutionary government. "La Crusada" gathered the energies of the entire population for five months to teach 400,000 peasants to read and write. The 100,000 young teachers, or brigadistas as they were called, were primarily students from urban areas, who were also "taught" about the hard realities of the countryside by living and working by day with the peasant families they taught by night. The literacy campaign had multiple objectives: to lower the illiteracy rate (it dropped from 52 percent to 13 percent), to prepare historically marginalized people to contribute to building a new economy, to build links between peasants and urban dwellers, and to construct participatory democracy and an active citizenry. It was probably one of the most massive and successful educational events in history.

In the 1980s, the battle was clearly an ideological struggle, as Nicaraguans sought the support of ordinary North Americans. They attempted to counter the negative U.S.-dominated media coverage by inviting delegations to see for themselves the bold initiatives of land reform, health campaigns, peasant and workers organizations, neighbourhood defence and a peoples' army, as well as the showcase its adult education program. Yet they were constantly constrained by the pressures of an ongoing contra (counter-revolutionary) war and deepening poverty.

Nonetheless, popular culture was honoured through oral histories, poetry workshops, mural projects and grassroots theatre. Art was for everyone, central to a cultural (as well as economic) democracy. Canadians went south and Nicaraguans came north through exchanges of educators, musicians, poets, writers and popular theatre practitioners that have influenced many educational and arts projects in Canada today.

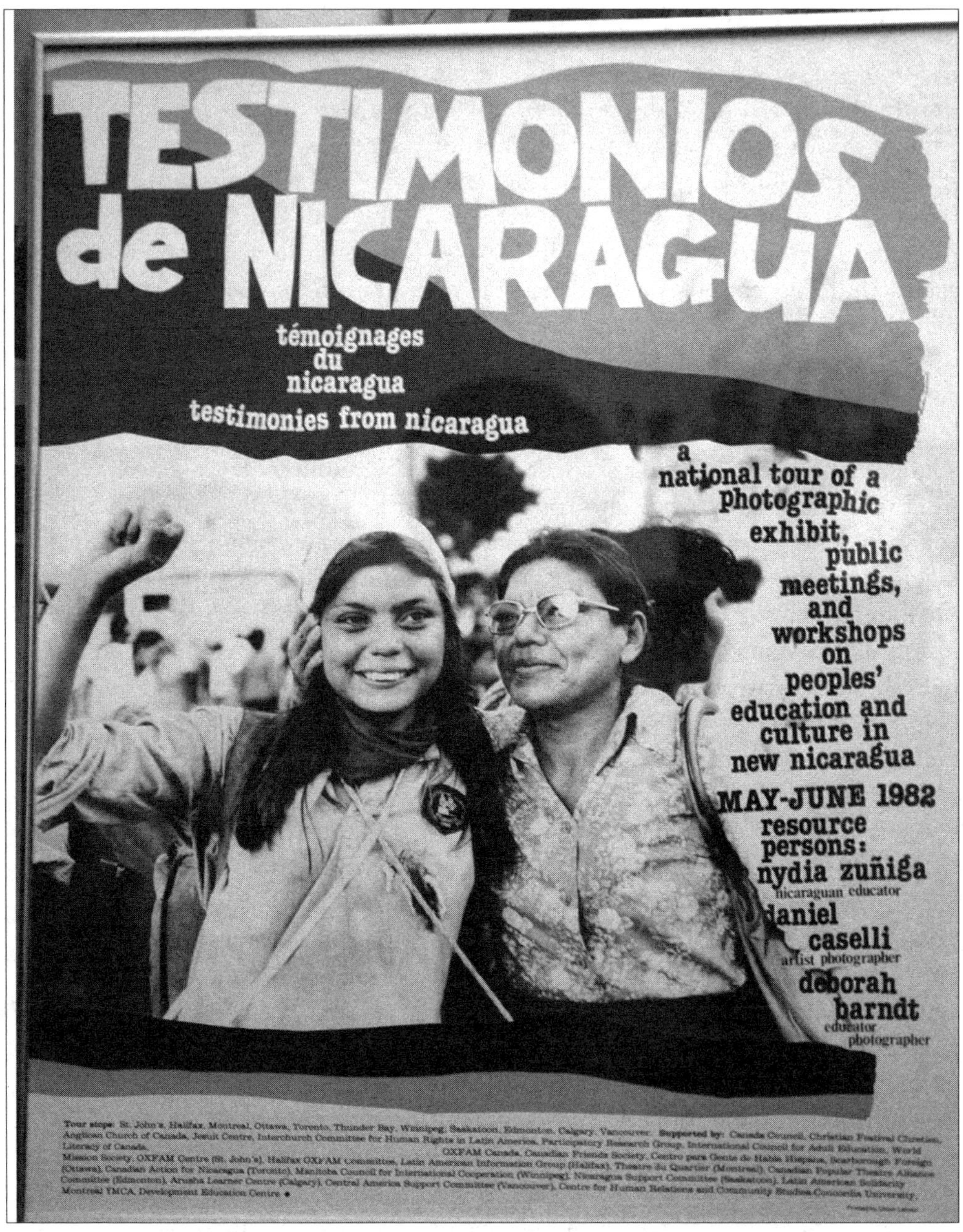

Poster from 1982 Canadian Testimonios tour in solidarity with Nicaragua.

Christine (2002): When I went to Nicaragua in 2002, there were not as many other internationalists around as there were during the revolutionary era, but still the experience was profound. Certain disorienting moments, once percolated for their significance, bring greater clarity. After the initial popular communications workshop with you, Deborah, I invited community members together to conceptualize kick-starting our collective radio and newsletter production. This meeting was rich with connotation.

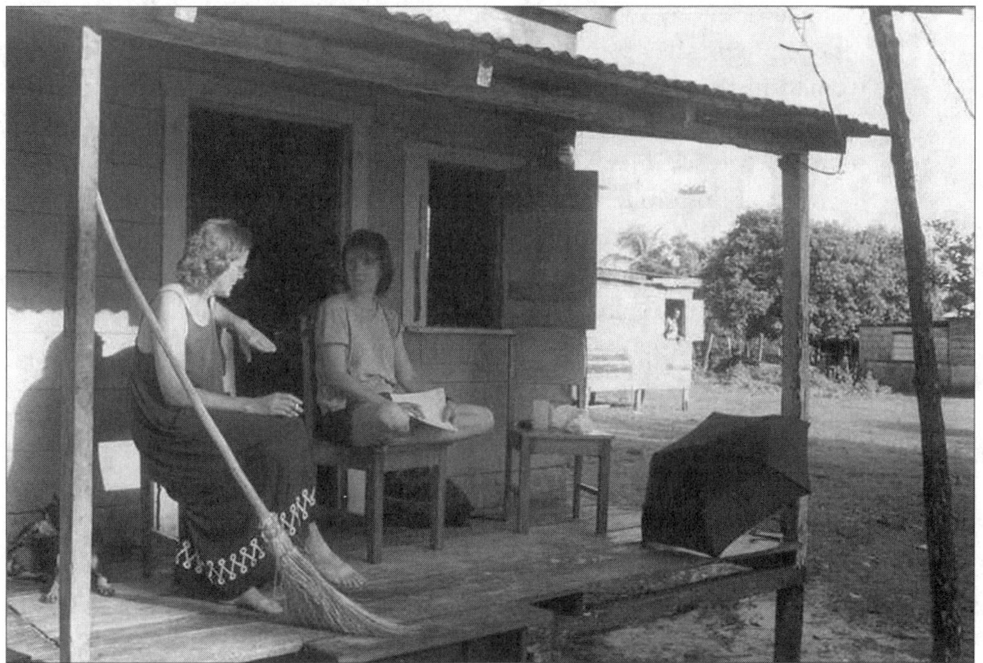

Christine (right) with Bernice Kozack in Pearl Lagoon, Nicaragua.

Meetings about community issues were familiar, but I was not. The project began in 1994, through the Atlantic Coast Documentation Centre (CIDCA) as a means to learn about and advocate for community-based resource management. It was an initiative where "professional" and "community" researchers together investigated what natural resources existed and determined how they could be best used to ensure self-sufficiency.

I gave an overview of why I had been invited to facilitate the popular communications process, with community people creating messages to generate dialogue about and work towards solving the issues that they face.

I talked about how as a student I wanted to do participatory research and was not an expert, but that we would work together, based on their needs and interests. We began to explore issues of importance. Overall, it was going fairly well.

Then a woman breezed into the meeting late, and attention turned to her. It was clear that others saw her as a leader. She said directly that if we wanted community media that we needed infrastructure equipment — a CD player and so on. Now people got *really* animated. They started listing off equipment they could use for the project. Just as straightforwardly, the woman instructed me to buy this equipment for them. I explained that there was no budget for this and that I personally did not have this kind of money. My disclaimer was met by looks of disbelief.

Most of this group were youth, born on the periphery, in the final moments of the Sandinista project. Based in a history of colonization, Atlantic Coast Miskitos, Creole, Garifuna, Sumo and Rama ethnic communities have a history of exploitation both internationally as well as internally by the Spanish-descent mestizos from the Pacific region.

The popular education materials of the Literacy Crusade did not escape this paradigm. Originating from the Pacific and depicting culturally inappropriate mestizo themes and images,[1] these materials met with limited success in raising critical consciousness and political support for the Sandinista vision in Atlantic Coast communities. Not only was the revolutionary spirit not inspiring for everyone in these communities, many fought in the contra war *against* the Sandinistas, and many lost family members in that struggle.

The political moment had shifted since the early 1980s, and this project was embedded with the contradictions of interventions by the Moravian Church and foreign companies,[2] as well as by the inequitable costs and benefits inherent in neo-liberalism and tied aid.

POPULAR COMMUNICATIONS: IN OUR OWN WORDS AND VOICES

Deborah (1980s): Yes, I was working in a different moment when Nicaraguan popular education and communications inspired movements worldwide. For example, we brought Nicaragua's vice-minister of adult education to a popular education conference in Toronto in 1981. Intrigued by the photo-stories we produced with immigrant workers in ESL classes, he invited me to Nicaragua to train new literacy teachers in popular or grass-roots photojournalism. In both 1981 and 1983, I worked for the Ministry of Education, supported by the International Council for Adult Education and financed by the Canadian International Development Agency. I saw these projects as opportunities to contribute to solidarity efforts in a moment when the Nicaraguan revolution was being fiercely discredited by Washington-influenced Western media.

The training of popular photojournalists had a specific goal of producing a magazine for new literates, especially rural workers migrating from one harvest to another. The magazine, *Caminemos* (or *Keep on Walking*), was to keep them learning by reading photo-stories based on their own lives. A team of seven teachers took photos and gathered stories (historical and contemporary) that were both practical and political. That year the coffee harvest arrived six weeks early, so the ministry pushed us to get the magazine out immediately to 150,000 migrating farmworkers. Working feverishly, we edited, printed and distributed it in a record two weeks. Only a revolutionary state could generate such a response.

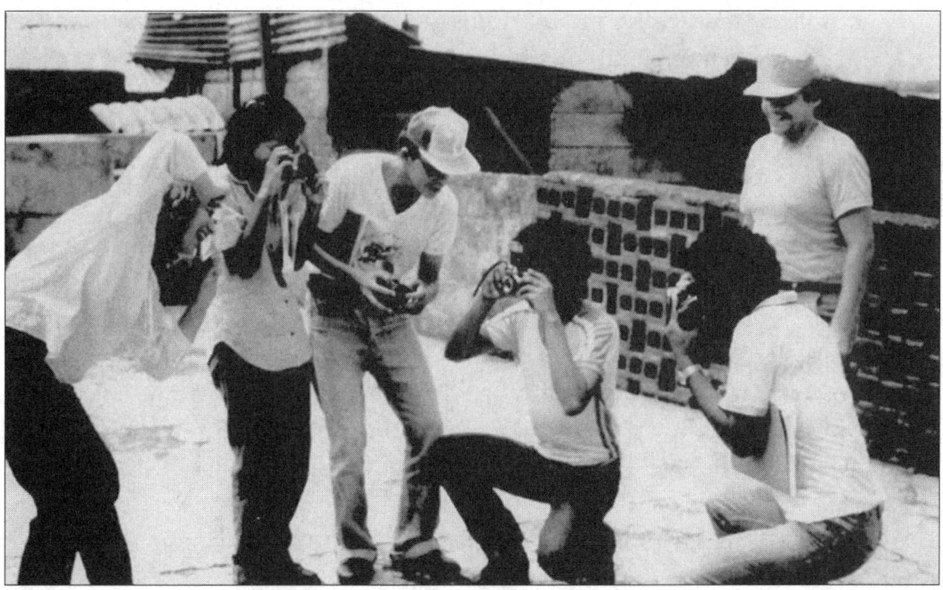

Deborah (left) with Nicaraguan photographers-in-training.

In 1983, I co-ordinated regional training workshops in the areas most affected by war. Working with a team of Nicaraguans, we introduced popular communications as a practice that challenges hegemonic media; draws its content from the daily lives of the marginalized majority; engages literacy students in participatory research of their issues and collective production of their learning materials; and develops their skills in interviewing, drawing, photography, theatre, mask-making and silk-screen production.

The popular art tools created in the midst of war and poverty challenged dominant art and media, as the process also developed the participants' confidence in producing their own communications and learning materials. This participatory production of literacy texts, however, never really moved beyond the three pilot sites (in the Pacific region) to become a widespread practice and, not surprisingly, didn't reach the Atlantic region. So your work in participatory production represented quite a new practice, no?

Christine (2002): Well, it was new in some ways. Many remembered the Literacy Crusade's unsuccessful presence on the coast. Popular communications fit well within the community-based resource management project that had been ongoing for several years, while still being a related process. Community members met weekly as a committee for reflecting, sharing of news/gossip, planning production and raucous socializing. The process of identifying, analyzing and questioning themes related to natural resources, such as shrimp farming and encroachment on agricultural lands, took place at these meetings and beyond. Exploration of these themes was expressed in many forms, from poems to puzzles, to discussions, dramatizations and drawings, with local community members sometimes sending contributions from a distance. The content for the weekly radio program and the quarterly newsletter informed each other, emerging from multiple voices in the communities. In this way, the radio audience became a transmitter as well as a receiver of information, a tool for dialogue.

ROLE OF THE OUTSIDER: AN UNEASY COLLABORATION?

Deborah (1980s): One of the common tensions that we had to deal with emerged from our position as northern educators or researchers in a context shaped by centuries of unequal North–South relations. While most

Nicaraguans in the revolutionary years were able to distinguish between the individuals coming South and the governments they represented, there was often uneasiness about who we were and what we brought to the revolutionary experiment. Often identified with the funds desperately needed, our technical support was both welcomed and resented. I struggled with this contradiction, sometimes questioning my right to contribute to the building of a nation which was clearly not my own. Most often, it was I who was being transformed. How I perceived my role as an outsider and how others perceived it were constantly changing; such questioning, I believe, is a necessary and ongoing process.

As an ESL teacher in Toronto at the time, I was blown away by the commitment and creativity that mobilized the country around the task of literacy. Photographs I took of these creative projects became part of solidarity education in Canada, cross-country photo exhibits and books.[3] The Nicaraguans saw my primary role in the 1980s as educating fellow Canadians about the revolutionary vision and practice.

By the 1990 elections, however, it was clear that Nicaraguans were tired of both war and poverty; over 50,000 young soldiers and civilians had been buried from the Contra war. Economic strangulation by U.S.-led boycotts made it hard for Nicaraguans to continually resign themselves to a life of "rice and beans." Even though the Sandinistas garnered 41 percent of the vote, the UNO — a coalition of liberal and right-wing parties — won the elections on a promise of economic relief in the form of aid from the U.S. Visiting Nicaragua a year later, I was deeply saddened to find the colourful revolutionary murals whitewashed and the literacy texts we had produced burned (USAID was producing new ones). The revolutionary period had been relegated to a paragraph in high school history texts.

Christine (2002): I see my Western-educated middle-class white woman standpoint as a problematic Rorschach test. This standpoint is the imperialist framework I have been taught by the world, with which I fill in the details of what I do not understand.

Expectations of my role in the community fluctuated between a desire for me to work alongside community members and for me to give directions. When we were unsure of what should happen next, extra weight was given to my words, despite my limited understanding of the context.

As a researcher from within an academic institution, I strove to be a specific intellectual,[4] using my skills of knowledge production and organizing *for* the people, knowing I could not be *of* the people as an organic intellectual would.[5] I saw my role as one to enable conditions where the organic intellectuals[6] of the community would take the forefront.

I feel this met with varying degrees of success and reinforced for me what Escobar calls the "impasse of development," in which participatory development measures (for me characterized by the presence of outsiders, among other things) are ineffective in imagining an *alternative to* development, and instead continue to reproduce more "development alternatives" within the current paradigm of inequities.[7]

PROCESS/PRODUCT

Deborah (1980s): I don't think we can ever completely step outside of that paradigm in projects like CAMP-Lab, even as we critique it and imagine alternatives. But popular communications can challenge hegemonic practices of development and mainstream media with its emphasis on the process of building grass-roots power while producing products for specific local uses.

In the early 1980s, we encountered the classic tension between the process of developing consciousness and skills in local communities and the need to produce literacy materials that would help build a nation in the face of war and poverty. Aimed at cultural development and not mere cultural expression, the process engaged new literates and their communities in gathering stories, valuing their histories, representing struggles and strengths using their own forms of art and following their own rhythms. The transformation from passive to active citizens was as important as the transformation of stories into texts, posters and theatre. It was to contribute directly to the development of a participatory democracy after decades of dependency.

Christine (2002): As a team, we struggled to reconcile the dichotomy between showcasing professional products and privileging the mentorship and learning that happened in the process of developing the programs.

One of the highlights of the project was the weekly trip to the radio station in the next community. Members of the group would take turns acting as the host, some would do live interviews with community members or be DJ, while others would come to cheer from the sidelines. Some weeks it was quite an entourage, nervously rehearsing on the way there and enveloped in an air of celebration as we made our way back.

It was a kind of spontaneous "audience survey" that took place from people's front porches. In the small communities everyone knew each other and were quick to speak their minds: "You talked good." "You should get people to explain more about why they are cutting trees for the cows ... was interesting." "You playing too much country music — that is for old people!" These were some of the comments shouted to us as we passed by.

Community people judged the surface appearance of our production, but the deepening of critical questioning, analysis and awareness behind the scenes was no less significant. Within the radio production community, the orientation was more towards high quality production than community capacity building. We constantly wrestled with the tension of where to put the emphasis — a professional radio documentary or one in which technically untrained community participants exercised their right to speak about issues important to their lives. At times, it was a struggle for everyone to feel proud of our own product and not to see it as "less than" those whose work followed the larger, dominant global communications trends.

It was a process of recognizing the ways in which we are colonized by what is seen as beautiful and artistic within these forms; we worked to reframe radio production in the local context, as part of our personal transformation and to offer an alternative example.

An Ongoing Dialectic

Deborah (2005): A common thread of our experiences — across time, space and generation — is the notion that any alternative art or popular communications is both shaped by and can help shape the specific historical, geographic and political context within which it unfolds. The content, forms and use of the tools we were involved in producing reflected the geographic and cultural settings, the historical and political moments they were embedded in.

This work is always done within layers of contradictions and complex power relations. Take, for example, the broader context of Nicaragua negotiating the tension between self-determination and dependence in the face of U.S. neo-liberal hegemony; the colonial legacy of the Pacific region's domination of Nicaragua's Atlantic Coast; the differences within those regions (ethnic, class, gender); and, finally, the contradictions within our roles as outsiders purporting to promote democratic practice — if not in communities at least in the production of media and communications. Our identities, just as those of the people we engaged with, are multiple and shifting. The contradictions (North/South, Pacific/Atlantic, teacher/student, etc.) will not disappear, so we must learn to name them, hold them and engage them, both critically and creatively.

Christine (2005): Looking across time is necessary, yet it is equally important to analyze each conjunctural moment to try to understand what was happening and how that shapes what is currently possible. The revolution and the literacy crusade touched the whole country, and its messages resonated in different ways, depending on geographic location, identity, political affiliation and religion, among other factors. It is the complexities of these movements that reintegrate to shape another day and another story.

NOTES

Deborah dedicates this chapter to her parents, Bill and Laura Barndt, 91 and 90 years old respectively, for modelling intergenerational dialogue, and for sharing their own processes of being politicized by solidarity work with liberation struggles in the Philippines and Central America. Christine dedicates this chapter to friends and collaborators from Nicaragua's coast who shared their wisdom and inspiration.

1. Valerie Miller, *Between Struggle and Hope: The Nicaraguan Literacy Crusade* (Boulder, CO: Westview Press, 1985).
2. Edmund Gordon, *Disparate Diasporas: Identity and Politics in an African-Nicaraguan Community* (Austin: University of Texas Press, 1998).
3. Deborah Barndt, *To Change This House: Popular Education under the Sandinistas* (Toronto: Between the Lines, 1991).
4. Quintin Hoare and Geoffry Smith, trans./eds., *Selections from the Prison Notebooks by Antonio Gramsci* (New York: International Publishers, 1971). Gramsci refers to a specific intellectual as one who occupies a specific intellectual position in terms of his/her conditions of class position, life, as an academic researcher and in relation to

the politics of truth. The specific intellectual through his/her position takes on "not a battle on behalf of truth, but a battle about the status of truth, and the economic and political role it plays." In this way, the specific intellectual works from and with his/her location, while aligning with other struggles.

5. Pablo S. Bose, "Critics and Experts, Activists and Academics: Intellectuals in the Fight for Social and Ecological Justice in the Narmada Valley, India," *International Review of Social History* 49, S12 (December 2004), 133–157.

6. Hoare and Smith, *Selections from the Prison,* 132. Gramsci refers to an organic intellectual as one from within the community or within an oppressed group who plays a role in knowledge production for those interests.

7. Arturo Escobar, *Encountering Development: The Making and Unmaking of the Third World* (Princeton: Princeton University Press, 1995).

CHAPTER 4

Ediciones Cordillera:

AN EXILE COMMUNITY'S ROLE IN CULTURAL PRODUCTION

Gabrielle Etcheverry

ATTEMPTING TO WRITE ABOUT SOMETHING YOU'VE BEEN PART OF OR KNOWN about all your life is much more difficult than it seems. This was the somewhat difficult position I found myself in while reflecting on art and activism among members of the Chilean community in Canada. It felt much like the now clichéd line about asking a fish to describe the water that surrounds it. Not that this is the first time I've written about the artistic production of this (my) community. It has in fact been a major source of my personal academic interest for some years. But the analytical language and thinking that accompanies so much of academic work has always allowed me to view and write about this part of my life from a safe and comfortable distance. More specifically, the post-colonial theorization that has most greatly informed my engagement with this subject has sometimes had the effect of muddying the "water" surrounding me, even though the post-colonial framework directly engages with issues of hybrid identities, exilic subjectivity, and those peoples and cultures that exist interstitially, or "both within and astride the cracks and fissures of the system, benefiting from its contradictions, anomalies, and heterogeneity."[1] This is not to say that academic language and epistemologies are not useful, but they alone cannot give full accounts of the embodied experiences and knowledg*es* of our exilic communities and socio-political practices.

So, please, let me introduce myself. Perhaps that is the best place to start. I am the daughter of Chilean writers and translators who left Chile for Canada in the early 1970s in order to escape Augusto Pinochet's military regime. They were not the only ones. Many other Chilean writers, students, mechanics, housewives, engineers and so on would come to Canada (in our case, Ottawa) for the same reasons. One of the many remarkable things that happened among this fledgling community as it adapted to its new country was the rapid construction of social and political organizations. Many of my childhood memories originate in the social and political events and meetings organized by these groups, such as *peñas* (traditional Chilean social gatherings or parties), poetry readings and protests outside the Chilean embassy, all of which helped to provide me at least with a sense of having a large extended family in Ottawa. Many of us (children of exiles) like our parents, were acutely aware of the distance between ourselves and our blood relations in Chile, and the community ties that were established during the first years of exile helped to mitigate many of the feelings of pain and loss experienced by this separation.

Creating an Artistic Language

A major organization to emerge out of this period was the Chilean Association of Ottawa, which served as a quasi-organizing committee for a number of other community groups. Among them was Ediciones Cordillera, a collective of Chilean writers and editors who, through the Association and other means, were actively supported by the Chilean community and were able to publish a number of books by Chilean and Spanish-speaking writers living in Canada. While my academic interest in Chilean and Hispanic publishing in Canada in general was born out of my parents' involvement with this small publisher, my focus has tended to be on the modes of cultural/literary production available to and created by this group, rather than on its close ties to the Chilean community as such. But through my research and lived knowledge of this aspect of Chilean cultural life in Canada, I have become increasingly aware of the important ties between the community as a whole and the literary production of some of its members. Moreover, much of this production would not have been possible without the community's support.

The linking of politics and art was very much in keeping with the early modern Latin American conception of art practice in which politics and art could not easily be separated into discrete categories. Such a conception of art tended to disrupt the traditional dichotomies of "high" and popular art, aesthetics and ethics, as well as individual and collective artistic creation. The ethos of "art for art's sake" that prevailed in a number of modern European artistic movements was often (and, in some cases, still is) inappropriate in the Latin American context, where political and economic realities have come to inform artistic subjects and aesthetics.[2]

This was also the case in Chile during the era of Salvador Allende, the democratically elected socialist president whose term of office (1971–73) was cut short by a coup and Allende's death on September 11, 1973. Much of the political organizing and strategizing by supporters of Allende's political party, Unidad Popular, was focused on the collective creation of popular art forms, such as mural art, which often incorporated lines and verses by one of Chile's best known poets, Pablo Neruda. While poetry is often considered a form of "high" art or culture, Neruda's poetry on social and economic struggles in one of his most famous works, *Canto general*, could easily be folded into other, more popular[3] art forms. This blurring of the boundaries between elite and popular art forms was also extended to the practices of artistic creation themselves, in that a diversity of social actors (such as artists, labourers, educators and students) were now represented in the various artistic collectives and brigades that emerged during this period.

The increased need for a new artistic language with which to express the changing social reality in Chile brought about the organization of the Committee of Artists and Writers, whose own "Declaration" stating the importance of the popular arts was incorporated into national policy by the Unidad Popular when it came to power in 1971.[4] Thus, even though the primary objectives of the exile organization, the Chilean Association of Ottawa, were social and political, the support of artistic endeavours that would invariably enrich these goals was part of a greater social project that had begun in Chile at the beginning of the Allende years.

Las Ediciones Cordillera

Some of the main goals of the Association's organizers and members were to raise awareness of the political situation in their home country, work in solidarity with other displaced groups (the El Salvadoran and Palestinian communities, for example), and fundraise for social and economic justice groups as well as political organizations in both Canada and Chile. By the beginning of the 1980s, the Association would take on the additional task of supporting Ediciones Cordillera through the financing of their first publications. Established in 1979 by a group of exiled writers living in Ottawa, this collective was run by an editorial committee made up of the founding authors, and sustained through multiple forms of financing under the "umbrella" of the Chilean Association of Ottawa as well as through private donations.[5] Cordillera's earliest publications were financed through community and individual efforts. Having also organized Saturday school classes in Chilean culture and language for the children of their community, the Association (with the agreement of the Saturday school teachers who were also Association members) donated the teachers' wages to Cordillera for the publication of its first books, *Las Malas Juntas* by Leandro Urbina and *Teoría del circo pobre* by Hernán Castellano Girón, works of prose and poetry respectively.[6]

Other forms of funding included the use of proceeds from community events such as *peñas* and the Latin American Children's Fund, a non-profit organization whose mandate was "to collect material aid in Canada and send it to Latin American organizations that are attempting to alleviate poverty … in those countries" as well as to "support community and cultural activities for Latin Americans in Canada."[7] This organization was made up of not only Chilean Association members but also of many other Latin American exiles and refugees, as well as Canadians involved in solidarity work with Latin America. The Latin American Children's Fund and private donations supported another one of Cordillera's publications, the first bilingual anthology of poetry by refugees from El Salvador living in Canada, *El Salvador People's Poetry*. This anthology was published in 1982 and was presented in Toronto at a benefit for SALPRESS, an independent news service from El Salvador.[8] Publishing projects such as these reflected the importance placed on international solidarity by Cordillera and members of the Chilean community, and, like so many of its other literary projects, it also highlighted the importance of the arts in building political solidarity.

As mentioned earlier, the Association served the additional purpose of providing the recent exiles with a sense of community in their new, and vastly different, environment. Association meetings and events also became social spaces for recent exiles to gather and share news from home. Cultural events like poetry readings and book launchings were not seen as separate from community or political events as such. In the early years of exile, as now, various cross-sections of the Chilean community would contribute to, as well as participate in, literary events by bringing wine and food, helping with publicity or selling books. On another level, the literature created by members of this community also voiced the shared experiences of many exiles (Chilean or otherwise) and helped to articulate the "hybrid" reality they had begun to inhabit. According to Linda Hutcheon, nostalgia was highly visible in the "explosion of ethnic writing in those years" from 1972 to 1984, and moreover,

> there was very little irony in first generation (and even some second-generation) immigrant writing in Canada … What existed instead was a strong strain of nostalgia and an almost elegiac tone in the writing: there was an almost overwhelming sense of loss — the loss of what was left behind (often not by choice).[9]

Those immigrant and exiled writers and publishers who saw themselves as "being in the middle of two different spaces, no longer being among the meanings and values of the former, original space, but not giving allegiance to the new one"[10] were able to very publicly express the feelings of nostalgia and loss many other community members were feeling. The following poem by the Chilean-Canadian poet Gonzalo Millán illustrates the feelings of dislocation that are common to the experience of exile:

> HOCKEY
>
> Canadian death
> glides toward me,
> swiftly on the ice
> like a hockey-player
> wielding
> his wooden scythe.

I don't even know how to skate.
I play soccer, I tell him.[11]

The "death" in this instance is that of the immigrant in relation to an alien world. By invoking the contrapuntal symbols of two different "national" sports (hockey and soccer) as contrasting symbols of life and death, Millán not only expresses a dislocation from both these activities, he is also re-fashioning their traditional meanings by placing them together in the context of rupture or dislocation, or a hybrid space.

The feelings of nostalgia found in the early texts produced by Cordillera and other immigrant or exiled publishers also tended to articulate the feelings of loss and disbelief towards the social and political elements of the military coup and its aftermath. Unlike traditional, Western literary ideals that tend to privilege genre and form over content (with the attendant assumption that these are divorced from social or political contexts), immigrant writing often "proclaim[s] the socio-cultural or socio-linguistic to be literary," and "brings into the picture aspects that by official norms are of extraliterary (i.e., documentary or sociological) relevance and that, rehabilitated, are incommensurable."[12] The "socio-cultural" or "socio-linguistic" was central to the early poetry and prose by exiled Chilean writers, where "the political theme … is also closely linked to the theme of nostalgia, since the politically committed texts often dealt with the state of things in Chile, and … tend to focus on former times and spaces."[13] Consider, for example, a section of another poem by Gonzalo Millán, "Fragment 48":

The river flows against the current.
The water climbs up the waterfalls.
The people start walking backwards.
The horses walk backwards.
The soldiers unmarch the parade.
The bullets leave the flesh.
The bullets enter the barrels.
The officers put away their pistols.
The current flows back through the cords.
The current enters into the outlets.
The tortured stop shaking.
The tortured close their mouths.
The concentration camps are emptied.

The missing appear.
The dead rise from their graves.
The planes fly backwards to their carriers.
The rockets climb towards the airplanes.[14]

Through these representations of the social and political reality of the Chilean community and the experience of exile and immigration, members of this community were also able to identify themselves and feel some comfort in this self-recognition in an otherwise alien symbolic environment. In this sense, the community figured prominently not only in the production of these texts but also in their very spirit.

A number of researchers from exile communities have begun to document the types of cultural production employed by exilic groups in their adopted nations. The work of Hamid Naficy (an exile himself) on the television and film production of the Iranian exile community in the United States is particularly useful for framing my own experience and knowledge of the modes of cultural production among my community. This "interstitial mode" of cultural production employed by a number of exile communities can potentially provide a range of alternatives for writers, publishers and audiences alike, since this mode of cultural production often breaches the gap between producers and consumers. Exilic literary production in this case shares an important feature with the exilic cinema that Naficy has documented and interpreted so well:

> the expected imbrication of exile and politics … goes beyond the inscription of political content or of mimetic, autobiographical, and theoretical criticism within the films themselves … Because it involves inserting politics at the point of the film's origination, as well as of its reception, the exilic mode of production offers, by the fact of its existence, a powerful criticism of dominant film practices.[15]

While exilic literature (and "minority" literature in general) has often been seen to suffer from its marginalization from dominant production practices, exiled Chilean writers have been able to establish audiences both in Canada, Chile and abroad. In May 2001, the National Library of Canada and the National Library of Chile signed an agreement that would lead to the creation of Proyecto Adrienne, a joint project to collect the works of Chilean writers and artists living in Canada following the military coup by General Augusto Pinochet in 1973, and to return these cultural products to Chile. Named after Canadian Governor General Adrienne Clarkson, who was instrumental to the signing of the agreement and who is a writer and journalist herself, Proyecto Adrienne represents official recognition from both Chilean and Canadian governments of the effects the military coup had on demographics and cultural production in both countries.

Until its demise in 1997, Cordillera would publish an average of one book per year[16] for a total of approximately seventeen books,[17] including the anthology of Chilean poetry in Canada that includes the poems by Gonzalo Millán excerpted in this essay. There is some correlation between the period of Cordillera's operation and the duration of Pinochet's dictatorship (the national plebiscite was held in Chile in 1988 and democratic elections would soon follow), given that a number of exiles returned to Chile in the early 1990s. This change in Chile's political situation also had the effect of lessening the need for the Chilean community abroad to work towards raising awareness of the injustices of the Pinochet regime, since many of these would soon be dealt with openly by successive national governments and activist groups within Chile itself. Thus, at the same time that some of the exile community members moved back to Chile or elsewhere, the need for political organizing was now diminished by Chile's return to democracy, no matter how problematic this return might be, changing the dynamic of the Chilean exile community considerably.

Over the course of its existence, Cordillera's writers would also be supported through government grants, but much of their work could not have been published or continue to be a viable literature without the help of the community, as is the case for the Chilean literary activity in Canada that continues today. And, even as the community links and feelings of nostalgia have lessened with the passage of time, second-generation Chileans in Canada like myself continue to be intrigued and inspired by our Chilean roots and our parents' stories of resurgence.

NOTES

1. Hamid Naficy, "Between Rocks and Hard Places: The Interstitial Mode of Production in Exilic Cinema," in Hamid Naficy, ed., *Home, Exile, Homeland: Film, Media, and the Politics of Place* (New York: Routledge, 1999), 134.

2. Oriana Baddeley and Valerie Fraser, *Drawing the Line: Art and Cultural Identity in Contemporary Latin America* (London, UK: Verso, 1989), 9.

3. Although the terms "popular" and "mass" art or culture are often confused, popular is used here to denote the traditional concept of art and culture "of the people," which has more similarities to folk art, for example, than mass/commercially produced cultural items and forms. In Latin America, popular art forms have often taken an explicitly political or revolutionary stance since the days of the Mexican Revolution at the beginning of the twentieth century, with the works of Diego Rivera and David Siquieros. In the case of mural production in Chile during the Allende era, as in Nicaragua during the revolutionary periods there, these art forms were not only explicitly political in content but also in their form of production, whereby students, labourers and peasants would work together to produce large-scale murals, often with the use of industrial or easily accessible materials that most of the population would have had some experience with.

4. José Balmes and Catherine Humblot, *Chile: Brief Political Imagery, 1970–73*. Retrieved 11 December 2003 from www.abacq.net/imagineira/index.htm.

5. Jorge Etcheverry, "La aventura de la Editorial Cordillera," in Luciano Diaz and Jorge Etcheverry, eds., *Alter Vox* (Ottawa: Verbum Veritas and Split Quotation, 2002), 83.

6. Ibid.

7. Ibid., 85.

8. Ibid., 84.

9. Linda Hutcheon, "Critical Perspectives on Writing Ethnicity in Canada (interviewed by Rosalia Baena)," in Rocio G. Davis and Rosalia Baena, eds., *Tricks with a Glass: Writing Ethnicity in Canada* (Amsterdam, Holland, and Atlanta, GA: Editions Rodopi B. V., 2000), 293–294.

10. Jorge Etcheverry, "Chilean Poetry in Canada: Avant-garde, Nostalgia, and Commitment," in Joseph Pivato, ed., *Literatures of Lesser Diffusion/Les littératures de moindre diffusion* (Edmonton: Research Institute for Comparative Literature, 1990), 300.

11. Gonzalo Millán, "Hockey," in Naín Nómez, ed., *Chilean Literature in Canada/ Literatura Chilena en Canadá: A Bilingual Anthology* (Ottawa: Ediciones Cordillera, 1982), 70.

12. Francisco Loriggio quoted in Travis DeCook, "The History of the Book, Literary History, and Identity Politics in Canada," *Studies in Canadian Literature* 27, no. 2 (2002), 71–87.

13. Etcheverry, "Chilean Poetry in Canada: Avant-garde, Nostalgia, and Commitment," 300.

14. Gonzalo Millán, "Fragment 48," in Nómez, ed., *Chilean Literature in Canada/ Literatura Chilena en Canadá*, 58.

15. Naficy, "Between Rocks and Hard Places," 131.

16. Number of copies issued ranged from 1,000 for the earliest publications to 500 copies for the more recent ones.

17. This figure has been reached through an examination of various bibliographies in the articles referred to throughout this essay but does not represent a comprehensive list of publications.

CHAPTER 5

The Strawberry Tasted So Good:

THE TRICKSTER PRACTICES OF ACTIVIST ART

chris cavanagh

DIAN MARINO[1] LIKED TO START THE ACADEMIC YEAR FOR THE NEWLY inducted graduate students of the Faculty of Environmental Studies (FES) with a twist. The Master's program is a self-directed one, with students negotiating a plan of study to suit their unique needs. Lacking a prescribed curriculum, the program proves challenging for those accustomed to conventional structures of learning. And, with playful glee, dian took aim at convention with this tale of an archer who had once been a soldier and who had spent many years studying to become a master of his discipline. This master archer happened upon a village in which he saw hundreds of arrows each in the bull's eye of hundreds of targets. Demanding to meet the master archer more skilled than he, the archer meets a young girl who patiently explains her method: "I take my arrow and I draw it back in the bow and point it very, very straight. Then I let it go, and wherever it lands, I draw a bull's eye."

Both storytelling and the choice of story are trickster tactics designed to disrupt expectation and to open possibility simultaneously. This playful pedagogy is nothing new, and it holds an important key for practitioners of community art. For art is powerfully bounded by regimes of inclusion and exclusion (e.g., who does art and who does not? what is art and what is not?) that the vast majority of people live with quite unconsciously. In this essay, I offer some thoughts about the power of common sense to hinder learning and I challenge how educators and artists (myself included) use, teach and make art in the context of struggles against oppression.

Disrupting Expectations

I don't know how to draw. A startlingly common refrain from adults. For surely few four-year-olds make such claims. Which makes me very curious about when it is that we learn such things. Everyone can draw — anyone who can hold or grip a pencil, pen or crayon, can make marks on paper, canvas or wood. Having taught in numerous art programs for children, I have often witnessed a common willingness to draw, paint and sculpt without the provisos about their lack of ability. Ahhh, but with adults the retort is fast in coming: I can't draw *well.* I've seen people go to great lengths to persuade me of their aversion to drawing. And yet, given that images are one of the most powerful means of communication in our very, very visually biased culture (if you *see* what I mean), it is unwise to take this pervasive (even "common-sense") attitude of incapacity at face value. Whether one can draw or not, visual art is used by all people to communicate and make sense of their world.

Popular education[2] (as well as much post-structural theory) recognizes that there are many means, including art, by which people communicate and make meaning of their world. Verbal language remains the predominant form of communication. And, given the pervasive and global nature of the advertising industry, television, cinema and the Internet, visual media are a close second. Some might argue that visual media are, in fact, the number one means of communication, but I'm going to stick with language.

As I've learned from Antonio Gramsci[3] and dian marino, there are powerful bulwarks of common sense about art embedded in both our individual and collective consciousnesses. For example, we might tell a child that her fingerpainting is lovely art, but we "know better" than to suggest she do more than stick it on the family refrigerator. We might call it art but our common sense, as we've learned it, dictates that it is not *art.* And yet the pleasure (even joy) of creating, the pride of product that can be seen in a child for having created something meaningful and communicative is often self-evident. Many an artist has striven to reproduce that childhood experience, that experience of creating before the personality has been overlaid with all the many rules, rituals, habits of thought and behaviour that are the norms of our social world.

What is the relation between the common childhood experience of creating art and the dominant social-global notion of art? Not that I plan to answer this question very thoroughly. I'll leave that to the scholars, and I'm no scholar; but it doesn't take a scholar to witness the difference between the world of art (deserving of galleries, museums, schools, training, investment of wealth and so on) and the world of the common individuals who fancy they can paint more than a wall of their house.

The Trick of Common Sense

While there are many good reasons to distinguish between the drawing of an untrained, untutored individual and that of a professional artist, there are also some detrimental common-sense notions about creativity that hitch a ride on these distinctions. For common sense is not, as *common sense* would have it, always a positive thing. Gramsci was the first major twentieth-century political/cultural theorist to recognize the formidable power of common sense in processes of social change. Struggling to understand how and why the Italian working class could act against their class interest (as Gramsci's Marxism explained it) and support the Fascists, he theorized that there was a pervasive "common sense" that the Fascists were able to tap into and rely on to persuade and coerce the population to support them. This common sense included notions of Italian nationalism and pride, notions of what constituted good leadership, what ought to be feared vis-à-vis political and economic change and so on; and it was more powerful than the emerging class identity of the majority of workers and citizens who were increasingly oppressed by economic hardship. As Gramsci reflected on this common sense, he theorized that it was contradictory, composed of both good sense and bad sense. But this contradiction is cleverly disappeared by the common sense belief that common sense is *all good*. Common sense is like the Great Oz (as Dorothy learns in the *Wizard of Oz*) telling us all to "ignore the man behind the curtain." And all are eager to agree. Where's Toto when you need him?

And so, of common sense, we can make a simple equation: common sense = good sense + bad sense (plus a dash of nonsense). It is *good sense* not to step out into moving traffic. It is *bad sense* to assume that cars are the single best means of urban transport (transit fares just went up again in Toronto) and it is *nonsense* to think that cars are determined to leap off the road and mow one down (as I once worried as I tried crossing a busy street while under the influence of a particularly powerful psychedelic).

In our Euro-American, post-Enlightenment Western world we live with powerful common-sense notions of art that act to exclude the vast majority of people from the identity of "artist." The "artist" (regardless of whether we're talking of painter, director, dancer, writer and so on) is the heroic, lone individual who has struggled "against all odds" to learn her/his craft and, presumably, has something to say. The popular appeal of the saying "it takes a village to raise a child" is, perhaps, almost common sense (triggering complicated and contradictory feelings about child-rearing in our nuclear-family dominated world). But compare the ease with which people grant this saying legitimacy in the context of art and artists. Isn't it equally true that "it takes a village to raise (create?) an artist"? And yet it feels to me like we are a far cry from admitting any such thing. Scholars (as well as a minority of critical thinkers) might say, "of course"; but the majority of our citizenry still respects, if not worships, the specially gifted artist who does something it cannot. This last powerful exclusion is the unique challenge facing the educator who is committed to resisting oppression and who desires to inspire the use of the fullest range of communication, including art.

One of the principle functions of art is to disrupt expectations. The common-sense notion of "I cannot draw" may be true when our scale of drawing includes only Pablo Picasso, Jan Vermeer, Frida Kahlo, da Vinci and Artemisia Gentileschi. But if we were to include on our scale the drawing of a child to whom we would not dream of saying "that's nice, but you don't know how to draw" (such is good sense), then, of course, we can all draw. Not that it is all "good" drawing according to whatever scale of high and low art one might abide by, but it *is* communicative. This is what the popular educator seeks to facilitate: the accessibility of the full range of communicative means for the participant in learning. This accessibility is not about forcing anyone to adopt that means (it is, however, tendering — with critical consciousness — the opportunity of its use) and, should that opportunity be taken, there is the possibility of an increase in the capacity of that learner to communicate and to act in the world for her/his benefit. When we operate, as popular education does, with an understanding and ethic that sees the individual as existing in dynamic social relation with others, then there is the possibility of acting with others against the unjust use of power used to benefit the few at the expense of the many or, put more simply, to resist oppression.

It is important to recognize that the common-sense regimes of exclusion and inclusion work in concert with powerful material allies, economic/political actors that permeate our world. The predominance of commercial art (including advertising, film, television and the Internet), for instance, acts as a formidable force in popular consciousness. As the popular educator promotes collective production of art (not to diss individual production but, rather, to act with the fullest range of practice, individual and collective) he/she must take on the overwhelming context of art as part of global economic relations. dian marino wrote:

> Drawing and graphic imagery are being used to "educate" us on a large scale … Processes such as drawing have political ramifications, and often these relationships are lost in the shuffle to describe a "new" technique. Our corporate reality is educating us, focusing our attention and actions to suit the political economy of profit. If education is not neutral, then neither are the visuals embedded in that process. Klaus Mueller details the political ramifications of language patterns, indicating that working-class people are often hampered with "restricted" language structure that operates as a major obstacle to reflective and action-oriented responses to problems. An elaborated language pattern facilitated the middle and upper classes' maintenance of a political economy that supports them. The use of visualization processes such as drawing can, then, help working-class people make a language work for them.[4]

A popular educator's responsibility to facilitate access to the full range of means of communication necessitates a critical consciousness. dian's words as well as this essay are only a beginning, a mild scratching of the surface of the history and practice of art in everyday life. Popular education values equally the process and the product of learning and creativity. One at the expense of the other can lead to imbalances that could well come back to haunt us, consequences that undermine the capacity of people to resist oppression.

Trickster Pedagogy

A popular educator must facilitate both engagement in democratic dialogue and disruption of oppressive behaviours, ideas and structures. One very powerful means of disrupting the bad-sense notions that prevent people from drawing or painting is to play. Playfulness, much more than a simple pleasure, can also be a very effective means for challenging the "power over" relations that act to shut down our creativity. When creativity is quashed, people are more vulnerable to being kept in line with dominant "common-sense" behaviour. Playfulness exists along a wide continuum of behaviours, from infants engaging their world almost entirely as a game or puzzle to adults engaging in sports to city populations frolicking in carnivals. The popular educator wishing to use art as a means of communicating and teaching critical thinking in learning situations needs to engage playfulness. It is this playfulness that encourages a necessary atmosphere of light-hearted risk-taking that is essential to the creative process. I once spent a week teaching "wizard school" (a summer arts program at the Mississauga Living Arts Centre) for twenty ten-year-olds. The Harry Potter novels, of course, provided the leitmotif and the kids created an imagined world as visceral as the novels' fictional castle.

The "playful" educator is acting in the very old role of trickster and thus has a wealth of trickster practices and traditions from which to draw. Trickster pedagogy[5] ranges from facilitating "simple" techniques of drawing (that can demonstrate to the non-artist a previously unknown ability to make meaning with images) to the disruptive insurgency of banners and giant puppets made for and used in public protest. And, of course, there is the ubiquitous trickster tale. From the stories of the Hasidic tales of the Baal Shem Tov[6] to the Sufi tales of Mullah Nasrudin[7] and the koans of Zen Buddhism,[8] and from the antics of the Native American Coyote[9] to the adventures of West African and Caribbean Anansi,[10] a wealth of teaching stories abound. Nasrudin was once asked which was more important, the sun or the moon. After thinking a moment he answered, "The moon is more important because the sun comes out in the day when it is already light, but the moon comes out at night when it is dark." A university professor seeking wisdom from a Zen master watched as the Zen master poured a cup of tea to overflowing. The professor pointed this out and the master responded, "Yes, this cup, once full, can receive no more tea. And you, who come to me so full of your own learning, what room is there for more?" There are many layers to these seemingly simple tales.

Raised to the level of the social-political world this trickster pedagogy becomes a dynamic, singing, dancing, outpouring challenge to the prosaic hegemony. The carnivalesque, as Bakhtin said, is "free and unrestricted, full of ambivalent laughter, blasphemy, the profanation of everything sacred, full of debasing and obscenities, familiar contact with everyone and everything."[11] The carnivalesque inspires a deep (and perhaps mostly unconscious) fear in the hegemonic coalition of ruling-class interests. It is, he points out, way too unruly and grotesque for the comforts of common sense:

> The grotesque ... discloses the potentiality of an entirely different world, of another order, another way of life. It leads men [*sic*] out of the confines of the apparent (false) unity, of the indisputable and stable. Born of folk humour, it always represents in one form or another, through these or other means, the return of Saturn's golden age to earth — the living possibility of its return.[12]

Balancing the world of small-group pedagogies with the dynamic energies of broader actions for social change is also a trickster skill. It is important for the facilitator of community art to decide (or discern) the purpose of the artwork. If it is only being used to have a dialogue by other means than talking, then it may not be very important to evaluate the aesthetic of the works produced — messy, contradictory, clashes of colour and collage may not be considered "good" art, but they can yet act as powerful contributions in a group dialogue. The quality of a piece takes a back seat to its communicability. If, however, the artwork is intended for public display (for viewing by more than the workshop participants — community members, organizational colleagues or fellow residents of a city, for example), then the aesthetic can become more important. This question of aesthetics, especially in a world dominated by Euro-American mass media, must also be engaged with critical consciousness. Dominant (even hegemonic) notions of "proper" aesthetics must be contested in light of our globalized and disaporic post-colonial world.

I would like to conclude with two pieces of advice for the educator who dares to engage the tricky terrain of art for social change. The first is from dian marino: "Be passionately aware that you could be completely wrong." The second comes from the tricky world of Zen storytelling:

> A man was walking across a field when he noticed a tiger stalking him. He ran, the tiger chasing after him. He came to a cliff, caught hold of a wild vine and swung himself over the edge. The tiger sniffed at him from above. Terrified, the man looked down and saw that, far below, were jagged rocks that would as surely be his doom as was the tiger above. Just then, two mice, one white and one black, began to gnaw at the vine. It was then that the man noticed a strawberry, fat and ripe, on the cliff wall near him. He knew that if he grabbed the strawberry his grip on the vine would not last long. He plucked the strawberry and ate it. The strawberry tasted so sweet.

NOTES

1. dian marino was a visual artist, environmental educator and professor in the Faculty of Environmental Studies at York University until her death in 1993.

2. "Popular education" is a practice, theory and philosophy that is explicitly aimed at resisting oppression and unjust uses of power. Popular education, heavily influenced by the work of the Brazilian educator and philosopher of education Paulo Freire, privileges the experience of the learner as the starting point for the learning experience. Recognizing that any person engaged in learning already has an abundance of experience, popular education seeks with respect to draw out that experience and subject it to critical scrutiny, exploring contradictions, seeking new knowledge when necessary and appropriate, and increasing the capacity of the learner in the context of their community to name their world, resist injustice and change their life and their community for the better. Popular education aims to connect individual and community experience and knowledge of the everyday with the social, economic and political domains of life. Popular education is a participatory and democratic practice that employs many traditional methods of learning as well as many non-traditional methods including popular theatre, drawing, mural making, song, poetry and more.

3. Antonio Gramsci (1891–1937) was an Italian writer, political theorist and leader in the Communist Party of Italy. As a journalist and editor, Gramsci paid particular attention to popular culture. Arrested by the Fascist police in 1926, Gramsci spent the next eight years in prison where he continued to write political theory attempt-

ing to understand Italian political life and revolutionary social/political change. Gramsci completed thirty notebooks known as the *Prison Notebooks*, which have been translated into many languages.

4. dian marino, *Wild Garden: Art, Education and the Culture of Resistance* (Toronto: Between the Lines, 1997), 70.

5. "Trickster pedagogy" is a concept I have been developing to examine the use of trickster stories (including jokes and riddles) as a means of teaching and learning. Tricksters can be found in all cultures. They come in many guises, including clowns, fools, jugglers, tramps, clever (and foolish) animals. They include Jack (as in the Giant Killer, and T-Jean, the specific example I grew up with in Acadia), Mullah Nasrudin, Coyote, Anansi (a spider), Molly Whuppie, turtle and tortoise, Br'er Rabbit, Herschel Ostropolier, Nanabozhoo, Wesakeechak and many, many more. Trickster tales typically are used to instruct from the point of view of what not to do. But there is also much more to it than that. Some good starting points for exploration include Paul Radin's now classic *The Trickster* (New York: Schocken Books, 1972), and Lewis Hyde's more contemporary *Trickster Makes This World* (New York: Farrar, Strauss and Giroux, 1998).

6. See Martin Buber, *Tales of the Hasidim: The Early Masters* (New York: Schocken Book, 1947); Martin Buber, *Tales of the Hasidim: The Later Masters* (New York: Schocken Book, 1948); and Dan Ben-Amos and Jerome R. Mintz, trans./eds., *In Praise of the Baal Shem Tov* (Bloomington: Indiana University Press, 1970).

7. See these three books by Idries Shah, *The Pleasantries of the Incredible Mulla Nasrudin* (New York: E.P. Dutton, 1968); *The Exploits of the Incomparable Mulla Nasrudin* (New York: E.P. Dutton, 1972); and *The World of Nasrudin* (London: The Octagon Press, 2003).

8. Nyogen Senzaki, *The Iron Flute: 100 Zen Koans*, trans. Ruth Strout McCandless (North Clarendon, VT: Tuttle Publishing, 2000); Steven Heine, *Opening a Mountain: Koans of the Zen Masters* (New York: Oxford University Press, 2002); Hau H¯o¯o, *The Sound of the One Hand: 281 Zen Koans with Answers* (New York: Basic Books, 1975).

9. Mourning Dove, *Coyote Stories* (Lincoln: University of Nebraska Press, 1990); Barry Lopez, *Giving Birth to Thunder, Sleeping with His Daughter: Coyote Builds North America* (New York: Avon Books, 1977); and William Bright, *A Coyote Reader* (Berkeley: University of California Press, 1993).

10. Philip Manderson Sherlock, *Anansi, The Spider Man: Jamaican Folk Tales* (New York: T.Y. Crowell, 1954); Martha Warren Beckwith, *Jamaica Anansi Stories* (New York: American Folklore Society, 1924); Emmanuel V. Asihene, *Traditional Folk Tales of Ghana* (Lewiston, NY: The Edwin Mellen Press, 1997).

11. Mikhail Bakhtin, *Problems of Dostoevsky's Poetics* (Minneapolis: University of Minnesota Press, 1984), 129–130.

12. Mikhail Bakhtin, *Rabelais and His World* (Bloomington: Indiana University Press, 1984), 48.

PART II

Art as Activism

CHAPTER 6

Demechanizing Our Politics: STREET PERFORMANCE AND MAKING CHANGE

Maggie Hutcheson

January 2003: On Toronto Public Transit

It is just two months before the Americans begin to bomb Baghdad and everyone is watching the negotiations in the UN Security Council with baited breath. Some hope that war might be prevented still prevails at this time, along with deep foreboding. A group of Toronto activists have chosen to use the phoenix, a mythical bird that rises from the ashes of destruction, as a metaphor for the widespread opposition to the war that continues to grow. The back room off my kitchen is taken over by plastic sheeting, clay, old newspapers and paint, and a consistent stream of people drop in to help make five large and brightly coloured phoenixes, each rising up out of flames. Hoping to inspire reflection on the diverse forms of resistance that can be employed to resist war, we script examples of recent actions from across the globe above each figure.[1] We also make fifteen fiery flags with the phoenix image on each of them. Everything gets finished just in time for the next big peace demonstration, and we send out a flurry of emails encouraging people to join our lively contingent.

I take the streetcar alone to Nathan Phillips Square on the Saturday morning, carrying two of the puppets and a handful of flags. This streetcar ride is unlike any of my previous experiences on public transit. Everyone wants to talk about the phoenixes. "What do they represent? Who made them?" Once I start to explain, conversations flourish all around me, and not only with me but among other strangers; about how people are feeling as they witness the build-up to war, about friends and family in Iraq, friends in the United States and their experiences since 9/11. An old man gets another stranger to take a photograph of him and me together with the puppets, and a couple of teenagers decide to come along to the demonstration. The streetcar driver wishes us well and tells us that he's sorry not to have the day off to join in.

The demonstration is large and vibrant,[2] but at the end of the day I find myself most excited about my time on the streetcar. Clearly, public opposition to this war is widespread, but I have yet to experience such interactions while carrying a placard or banner. What was it about our creations that made the reception different this time?

I first began doing political street performance, using giant puppets and other pageantlike imagery, in 2002. That year, as an educational initiative for the Toronto Mobilisation for Global Justice,[3] I organized a series of puppet-making workshops in the hopes that a group of us could make something for the upcoming protests against the G8 when they met in Kananaskis, Alberta, later that spring.[4] The 14-foot-tall (4.5-metre) Gaia puppet (a figure symbolizing the Earth) that we made over two months in an old garage was driven across the country that June, making a number of appearances at different demonstrations after that. The following year the group continued to work together and grow, eventually becoming Paperfire, an arts collective for social justice.

Since 2002 I have continued to create giant puppets and have begun to perform modest street-theatre pieces, both with and without Paperfire. What is it that continues to draw me away from traditional protest and towards these kinds of theatrics? Does it simply feel good to get such positive reactions from the public? Or is it because dressing up in wild costumes and performing different roles is often a lot of fun? These are undeniably partial reasons for my continued interest in street theatre! But I also have a hunch that performance lends itself uniquely to bringing social justice struggles into the public sphere, offering contributions that extend beyond those offered by traditional protest politics in Canada.

South African writer Njabulo Ndebele has suggested that if we rely too heavily on the traditional language of politics that our art, our imaginations and, ultimately, our ideas will suffer as a consequence.[5] While any effective protest is itself a well-staged performance, whose organizers are conscious of their principal actors and audience, performance has the potential to offer a particularly fluid vocabulary with which to think, to communicate and to push for radical social change. I have come to think of making theatre in public as a form of collective demechanization. Just as popular theatre animator Augusto Boal uses physical exercises and silly games to "demechanize" the bodies and minds of participants before engaging them in Forum Theatre,[6] public performance can serve to demechanize our perceptions of public space, our imaginations and our very sense of what constitutes "the political." This potential for demechanization makes me very excited about public performance, in all of its diverse forms, as an activist practice.[7]

At the same time, even brief exposure to street performance has revealed its limitations as a dialogical tool, leaving me with difficult questions about who speaks, about the ever-troubled relationship between activists and corporate media and about how to effect change successfully. In this chapter, I share some reflections on street performance as an activist practice, using examples from anti-war performances that I participated in between 2003 and 2004 to fuel the discussion.

Demechanizing Public Space

No space is truly "public" in the ideal sense of the word. Public spaces are always owned or controlled by someone, are usually designated for some particular use, and are never free of power relations. Whether it's a street, a university, a government building, or a mall, each space has its own rules, clientele and hierarchies. What distinguishes public performances from other forms of community theatre, therefore, is not that they are actually equally accessible to everyone but that they draw an unintentional audience, an audience that did not pay or even gather to see (let alone participate in) a show.

Whatever form they take (be it the projection of video images on the façades of buildings, the instigation of conversations on public transit or a dance at a busy intersection), all street performances, to varying degrees, make visible both the issues they seek to raise awareness about and the well-concealed rules of public space and social conduct. By engaging in excessive (i.e., abnormal) behaviour, performances reveal the possibility of different ways of "being" in each space they occupy. Activist performances outside of the theatre have the potential to reveal the rules of society to be socially constructed (and therefore alterable) but they also expose the specific public spaces that they are performed in as socially constructed, carefully controlled and, most importantly, alterable. While much activist performance in urban centers has specifically addressed the increased privatization and corporatization of public space in recent years, even performances that aim to stimulate public dialogue about other issues (such as war, police brutality, AIDS or racism) reveal the rules of the spaces they are in.

March 2003: Dundas Square

When the parade begins, the sound of the drums is shaking the street, the horns are playing a raucous rendition of "We Shall Overcome," and the Dancers of Death are leading the procession, followed by the Plagues of the New World Order, and then by Gaia, the phoenixes and the smaller wire-frame birds that we've helped people to make throughout the Toronto Social Forum. All weekend we've encouraged people to sign up to wear a puppet or carry a flag in Sunday's parade. People were hesitant at first, shy to play or be noticed. But now there are about seventy of us with flags, costumes and masks heading out into the street to join the much bigger anti-war march. We've rehearsed together over the past hour and, when Gaia gives the signal, the little birds surround the Dancers of Death and the Plagues until they melt down to the ground, trembling. Each time this is repeated we all cheer and the drums get louder, picking up the tempo. The giant puppets bob up and down to their rhythm in an awkward dance, and the people carrying the birds make them soar above us in the wind. After we've joined the thousands of people gathered at Dundas Square, we continue to move as a contingent, unable to hear anything above our own drums and horns. When my friend Logan puts his arm around my shoulder and, grinning jubilantly, yells, "It's good!" I know exactly what he means.

Demechanizing Imagination

The peace parade that came out of the Toronto Social Forum is an example of a kind of performance that goes beyond the critique of existing social conditions to offer a (fleeting) glimpse of what a radically altered society could look like and *feel* like. While the phoenix actions that Paperfire originally staged are probably best described as agitprop (simple imagery designed to mobilize people around a particular idea),[8] pageants, parades and renegade festivals are often enactments of social alternatives, what Jan Cohen-Cruz refers to as utopian performances. Carnivalesque and playful, they "merge desire with reality by staging themselves in streets … transforming would-be spectators into participants."[9]

Hakim Bey calls the space that is fleetingly created by performances like these the "Temporary Autonomous Zone" (TAZ), and suggests that the creation of such spaces is an ideal tactic with which to drive a wedge in the cracks of what can seem like all-encompassing state power and surveillance. Referring to events like Reclaim the Streets Festivals and Subway Parties (always arising spontaneously for the spectators who become participants in them), Bey suggests that the TAZ is an elusive "microcosm of that 'anarchist dream' of a free culture," a moment which must vanish as soon as it is named, represented or defined.[10] While the TAZ cannot substitute for real long-term change, Bey proposes that, despite its fleeting nature, the TAZ can permanently shift the consciousness of those who have experienced it. In other words, by participating, even momentarily, in the "better world that is possible," we may come to see just how possible it is and or be better able to envision that world.

It is partially the contingent element of such moments, the "non-ordinary" nature which Bey argues gives the TAZ meaning, that distinguishes performance from traditional protest. There is no easy category of public behaviour within which to place political carnivals (although the media often uses words like rioting or vandalism to discredit them) that look and feel different every time they are performed. Unlike traditional protests (the footage and photographs from which could often have been taken in any place at any time), these events are ideally rooted in the place they disrupt and the people who participate in them. When a TAZ is created, everyone within it becomes a participant in the performance. Breaking down the boundary between the traditional theatre roles of actor and spectator, the TAZ blurs the lines between reality and theatre. Public space, society and our sense of "realistic possibilities" are exposed to participants as cultural constructions (performances), while their participation in what could be thought of as theatre makes it, in fact, a reality.

But aren't these extraordinary events eventually subsumed into a repertoire of unremarkable public behaviour? And just whose utopia is created in such moments? Who participates in events like Reclaim the Streets? Who participated in the Toronto Social Forum parade and what did they feel about it? Utopian performances and the TAZ cannot be romanticized. As Cohen-Cruz makes clear, one group's performance of utopia may be unappealing, ridiculous or outright oppressive to others who find themselves subsumed by it.[11] Just as the questions *Who speaks? For whom? Under what conditions?* and *At what expense?*[12] must inevitably arise in any democratic undertaking, they arise when looking critically at any performance. Performance that welcomes participation is never liberatory or progressive by virtue of its form alone.

March 2003: In Front of the U.S. Consulate

The bombs have begun to fall in Baghdad and everyone I speak to seems to be experiencing a sudden and desperate sense of impotence. We weren't successful in preventing the war and since it's begun, the celebratory images that Paperfire has been performing with seem trite and of a different era altogether. How can we respond now? Along with other local artists,[13] Paperfire decides to perform something more sombre in an attempt to focus public attention on the death and destruction that have become a reality. How do we do this? Hesitant to contribute to what we consider a pornography of suffering on the part of the media, we decide to wear simple "death masks," painted masks of black and white papier mâché with white tulle veils, and to move in mechanical unison up and down Bay Street in front of the U.S. consulate. The group agrees to remain silent and to stay focused regardless of public reactions. We hope to provoke emotion in our audience, to provide an alternative to the media-driven fascination with events in Iraq that leaves us strangely devoid of feeling for the war's actual impacts on people's lives.

In the two hours that we perform the piece, we experience a range of visceral reactions from people on the street. One man spits at us, others step aside warily and avoid eye contact as we pass. Some people recoil from us but stop to watch nonetheless, usually silent for at least as long as we are in earshot. We move up and down each side of the street, remaining focused and never speaking. We stick around until 6:00 P.M. because we hear that a local TV news station will be coming down to cover any action at the consulate. We finish our performance under the bright lights of the network but don't make it on to the news.

Demechanizing the Political

Our performance at the consulate was created during a period of personal and global mourning; only a piece that acknowledged the gravity of the situation seemed appropriate at the time, ruling out carnival or satire. The grief and anger that we were able to express (and, hopefully, to evoke in our audience) through this performance bring to light another demechanizing element of street performance. This performance, like many vigils and other actions that were staged around the world in March 2003, allowed us to integrate our emotion with our intellect, our feelings with our political beliefs. The Autonomous Movement in Argentina has developed a new saying: "Our Dreams Don't Fit on Your Ballots." In this case, our emotions didn't fit on a placard or a banner. Cultural animators recognized long ago that activism that denies the personal (and emotional) will be ineffective in the end, as would a politics that abandoned a systemic analysis in favour of pure emotional release. Julie Salverson writes: "Ultimately, neither feeling nor thinking alone will take us far toward re-imaging and realizing a different world."[14] Street theatre allows us talk about politics in ways that acknowledge emotion. The lines between "the political" and "the personal" can be called into question when we embody our emotions in our activism. At the very least, in this case, bringing emotion into the picture fed our own conviction that we had to continue to act against this war.

Jan Cohen-Cruz writes: "I used to feel optimistic about education as activism. I believed that if people only knew what was going on, they'd do something about it … But I realized that people often have the information, in all its emotional glory, yet knowledge alone rarely leads to action."[15] I believe that we need to engage with political issues holistically, in ways that integrate emotion and lived experiences with broader political analyses. While there are many examples of grassroots activism that stems from lived experience (examples in which the situation affords no alternative but to take action), it seems to me that traditional protest culture in Canada no longer makes these connections.

But does bringing emotion into the picture go far enough? Our performance in front of the American consulate would likely slip somewhere between Cohen-Cruz's categories of witness and integration. It was not direct action. It did not physically disrupt the American war machine or Canadian corporations that would profit from the war. It simply tried to cast a different light on events that were very much already in the public eye in the hope that this would inspire continued action against the war. Cultural responses to political situations always run the risk of remaining at the level of catharsis rather than stimulating action.[16] While I believe that publicly highlighting the tragedy of war was an important project at the time, I have since thought about how our performance could have gone further. As a member of the Aids Coalition to Unleash Power (ACT UP) once said when asked about the motivations for ACT UP's now infamous die-ins for AIDS victims: "We have to do more than celebrate when so many of us are dying."[17] A prolific group, whose unique combination of guerilla theatre and direct action succeeded in forcing American politicians and drug companies to respond to the HIV epidemic,[18] much can still be learned from ACT UP's approach to public performance. ACT UP was not afraid of media attention for fear that its message might get distorted. Instead, by staging theatrical occupations of offices and other public spaces, it successfully manipulated the media into shaming those in power sufficiently to force action.[19] ACT UP's successes show that well targeted and focused public theatre can be used to create both discursive and material change.

A number of critical questions still remain for me about public performance as a means to create change. Who can afford to take the risks in public spaces that effective performances may demand? Is some of the demechanization that I have talked about less than profound for people who experience oppression in public space on a daily basis? I've only written here about the demechanizing impact that street theatre can have on those who participate in it. How have our audiences experienced these performances? How can we make dialogical street theatre considering the fleeting nature of these interventions? How can we make theatre that is effective direct action, despite the difficulties involved in relying on the corporate media to convey our messages?

These are questions I continue to struggle with. As autonomous movements, anarchists, socialists, feminists and social justice activists continue to work to develop horizontal, less prescriptive visions of revolution, languages with which to express these ideas also need to develop. New ways of thinking and speaking about social change should inform our activist practices, just as these practices will continue to shape further ideas.

NOTES

1. One example was the story of train engineers in Glasgow, Scotland, who had refused to participate in the transportation of arms. A photo of the particular phoenix that bore this story made it through many hands to the engineers themselves who were really tickled that their action had received such press!
2. Toronto's anti-war protests in 2003 continued to grow, despite the bitter cold of that winter. On February 15, a global day of protest against the war, 80,000 people marched in Toronto.
3. A Toronto-based anti-corporate globalization coalition that spearheaded a number of demonstrations and educational events between 1999 and 2003.
4. A figure that represented for us the devastating impacts of corporate rule on both biodiversity and cultural diversity.
5. Interview with Eleanor Wachtel, *Writers and Company*, CBC Radio, 30 January 2005.
6. Julian Boal used this term in a Creative Alternatives workshop on Forum Theatre in May 2004.

7. The terms "public performance" and "street theatre" are used to refer to a diverse spectrum of actions designed to attract public attention. In *Radical Street Performance: An International Anthology* (London: Routledge, 1998), Jan Cohen-Cruz identifies five different categories of street performance: agitprop, witness, integration, utopia and tradition.

8. Cohen-Cruz, *Radical Street Performance*, 167.

9. Ibid.

10. Hakim Bey, "TAZ: The Temporary Autonomous Zone," in Stephen Duncombe, ed., *Cultural Resistance Reader* (New York: Verso, 2002), 117.

11. Cohen-Cruz, *Radical Street Performance*, 168.

12. Tobin Nelhaus and SusanC. Haedicke, "Introduction" in Nelhaus and Haedicke, eds., *Performing Democracy: International Perspectives on Urban Community-Based Performance* (Ann Arbor: University of Michigan Press, 2001).

13. Leah Houston was a key instigator of these discussions and this action in particular. The masks used were made by Clay and Paper Theatre, our puppet-making gurus.

14. Julie Salverson, "The Mask of Solidarity," in M. Schutzman and Jan Cohen-Cruz, eds., *Playing Boal: Theatre, Therapy, Activism* (New York: Routledge, 1994), 158.

15. I am referring here to the marches and rallies that still come to mind when protest is referred to in Canada. Current protest rituals in Canada seem to have become a caricature of themselves, no longer rooted in a living culture.

16. Stephen Duncombe "Introduction," in Duncombe, ed., *Cultural Resistance Reader*, 6.

17. As quoted by Alisa Solomon, "AIDS Crusaders Act Up a Storm," in Cohen-Cruz, *Radical Street Performance*, 47.

18. Eric Sawyer, "An ACT UP Founder 'Acts Up' for Africa's Access to AIDS," in Benjamin Shepard and Ronald Hayduk, eds., *From ACT UP to the WTO: Urban Protest and Community Building in the Era of Globalization* (London: Verso, 2002), 88.

19. L.A. Kauffman, "A Short History of Radical Renewal," in Shepard and Hayduk, *From ACT UP to the WTO*, 38.

CHAPTER 7

Reconstructing Our Culture of Ilm (Knowledge)

MUSLIM WOMEN REPRESENT THEMSELVES

Salima Bhimani

ARTISTS, ACTIVISTS AND ACADEMICS HAVE PLAYED IMPORTANT ROLES within Muslim societies. Whether it has been through the mystical poetry of Rabia al-Basri, the miniature paintings of Persian artists or through the architectural genius of Muslim architects who provoked thought and reflection on the Divine mysteries, the stories told through art within Muslim societies cannot simply be reduced to art for art's sake. They animated the political, spiritual and philosophical concerns and aspirations of the time. In fact, the integration of the artist, academic and activist was not foreign to past Muslim civilizations. Many Muslims were artists, philosophers, scientists and spiritualists all rolled up into one. Great literature spoke of the alluring qualities of Muslim women who were educated in many disciplines. In her book, *Scheherazade Goes West*, Fatema Mernissi speaks about such archetypes.[1] Mainstream Western narratives about Muslims' historical innovative engagement of civil society silenced such history. Recent movements, however, have helped us reconnect with the past, inspiring us to tell our stories with creative agency in the present.

The space that lies at the intersection of artist, activist and academic is a powerful place, as it can be the womb where knowledge, invention and action give birth to mechanisms that allow movement towards the enhancement of humanity. Coming from this tradition, as an artist, activist and academic, I locate myself as a change maker engaging the tensions of my various identities. As artist, activist and academic, I have challenged the silenced, Eurocentric, Islamophobic, sexist and racist history of myself, my religion, my cultures and of our human ancestry, shifting the power that often marginalized me as a Muslim racialized woman. I use these identities as tools with which I can challenge hegemonic and dominant knowledge about Islam and Muslims permeating mainstream society.

SETTING THE STAGE

Many people, many Muslims included, think that September 11, 2001, changed the world forever. Somehow the acts of violence committed by those few people who call themselves Muslims shifted the dynamics of the geopolitical world stage and created a rift between the religion of Islam, its followers and the rest of the world. Such simplistic analysis and present mindedness have misplaced the historical memory of Islamophobia and Muslim civilizations and, in the process, give more fuel to the debate of the clash of civilizations between the "West" and "Islam."[2] In the process, Muslim women have once again surfaced as the unquestioned markers of a dehumanizing and anti-just Islam.

As a Muslim woman of colour, my struggle against both external and internal Islamophobia became more crystallized as I, along with others in the world, viewed the horrors of September 11 being replayed on TV screens. It did not present a new phenomenon, but only added to a deeply rooted historical dynamic. It reasserted my conviction that there was a need to share with intellectual and analytical honesty more about who Muslims are, about the history of Islam and about the present-day reality in countries where Muslims makeup the majority as well as those countries where Muslims are the minority. It reminded me about the limits and the potentials of the debates that have occurred so far, and accentuated the need for deeper dialogue in the present moment.

Just like many of the world's "isms" (e.g., sexism, racism, anti-Semitism), Islamophobia has evolved through a combination of faith-based conflict, political strife, colonization, nationalist responses to current geopolitical issues, and the ongoing struggle for Muslims to shape their identities and place in the world, while staying connected to their religious ethics and cultural heritage. Muslim women have played a particular role in this respect, as they have been central to the discussion and to often one-sided arguments about how the Muslim world is irreversibly backward. Dominant discourses contend that principles of democracy, equal rights and justice are foreign concepts for Muslims.[3] The imposition of ideological, political and other social structures by foreign dominating parties within Muslim countries has caused tensions and rifts among Muslims worldwide. Even more systemic barriers are faced by Muslims in non-Muslim countries where their religious identity has become yet another reason to be discriminated against.

Consequently, it would seem that Islam's fourteen-hundred-year-old life has indeed been one of struggle with those it has engaged with, particularly with Christian civilizations. However, the histories of Muslim civilizations are rich with evidence of mutual sharing and engagement with "others."[4] Even today, if we unveil the richness and pluralistic lives of Muslim people around the world, we begin to encounter relationships of respect and mutuality, as much as we may find the opposite.[5]

> ***Islamophobia:*** The use of power by a dominating group, individuals or systems against the religion of Islam and its followers to deny and/or create barriers to access, opportunities, rights, freedoms and equitable and fair treatment. It is also the fear and hatred of Muslims and Islam.

The Project

The process of addressing Islamophobia has been my life-long project. However, in the year 2000, I decided to examine Islamophobia and its particular effect on Muslim women through participatory, inclusive, cultural production processes that would help us address our silence, alienation and subjugation, particularly around how we are perceived. *Majalis al-Ilm* (Sessions of Knowledge) was a method I created of bringing together women of difference to participate in dialogue and discussion. These sessions were inspired by *Majalis al-Hikma* (Sessions of Wisdom), which were sessions of participatory dialogue held during the tenth century of Islam by the Fatamids who encouraged the journey of searching for deeper knowledge and wisdom through dialogue and discussion.[6]

As an artist (dancer, actor, artistic director, playwright), it made sense to allow the *Majalis's* (sessions) to creatively provoke dialogue and also allow for the creation of new narratives through various forms of artistic representation. The *Majalis al-Ilm* brought together a diaspora of Muslim women by promoting the *Majali*s as an opportunity for Muslim women to address issues affecting them and, in the process, respond to the misrepresentations of Islam and their lives. The women received the invitation to participate in this project through email and word of mouth. Those who were interested contacted me and once they had more information about the goals and objectives of the project, they were able to decide whether or not they would participate. All of the sessions were held in Toronto. There were four in total, and I also met with the women one on one for more intimate conversations.

The idea of the *Majalis al-Ilm* was grounded in participatory, women-centred art and rooted in the Muslim traditions of dialogue and engagement of civil society. The group focused on two objectives: first, to allow our distinctive narratives to be voiced in a way that would honour our varied selves by using an anti-oppression approach and by challenging stereotypes and limited theories; second, to examine the power of visual images in the print media and their impact on how Muslim women are represented.

What does all of this have to do with the relationship between the artist, activist and academic? In my own process of reclaiming my identity and place in the world as a Muslim woman of colour against Eurocentrism, Islamopbobia, sexism and racism, my personal and collective work has focused on confronting, reclaiming, creating and representing the lives of Muslim women as active, intellectual and creative members of their local and global communities. This has involved unlearning those myths historically told by others and embedded within the narratives about Muslim women's lives. It has also involved creating new stories, both visual and textual, that more accurately reflect our lives. The images of Muslim women as veiled, beaten, locked up and alienated from public life have played as much of a role in characterizing a particular kind of Islam and Muslim as have textual narratives (whether disseminated through media outlets or academic texts). A more honest and multi-faceted representation of Muslim women and their life experiences involves retelling stories and producing more complex images.

The myth-making has presented a monolithic and "grey" Muslim woman — one who is, sad, passive, uneducated, religiously enslaved to a patriarchal God, dominated by violent men and voiceless in societal affairs. Thus, embarking on a journey to reveal Muslim women who don't fit this description may seem like the logical course of action. However it is not so simple. The diaspora in which Muslim women exist and the plurality of who we are does not allow for such a dichotomous representation. In fact, what is needed is a representation of the spectrum of voices and experiences that can speak to the diversity of more than half a billion women worldwide. Certainly, even with the best of intentions, we could never represent *all* Muslim women. What can be done, however, is to give people an opportunity to hear, see and experience the multi-dimensionality and multi-reality of Muslim women, opening a possibility for dialogue to discover more than what has been known in the past.

The idea for the *Majalis al-Ilm* was to engage the diaspora of Muslim women about why the misrepresentations existed and what we needed to do to create more realistic representations of our lives. The process had four phases: (1) to talk about the myths, (2) to unlearn them, (3) to create new stories and knowledge, and (4) to disseminate our productions.

Some questions that arose for me as the facilitator of this process were: How do we represent difference, while maintaining a common goal? How can visual images tell a different story about Muslim women than what we are exposed to most commonly in the mainstream North American context? As women from most communities, Muslim women represent a wide spectrum of views and positions. Yet there has been an over-representation of particular Muslim women — often either as "oppressed" or as a liberated secular women. Rarely do we hear from Muslim women who are religiously committed, socially active and consciously living their lives.

It quickly became evident that, although we shared a common religious identity, our differences of religious interpretations, cultural background, class positions and life histories made it difficult to talk with one another. Heated debates often took place over gender roles, American foreign policy and religious interpretations of Islam. One of the women even considered leaving the project. She expressed difficulty in understanding how her "version" of Islam, her own life history and practices could be placed next to the story of someone who was starkly different from her. Would her Islam be watered down by another version placed next to hers? This brought forth the challenge of how women align themselves *within* difference and not simply tolerate one another. What does it mean to come from diverging personal, political and spiritual positions? What does this tell us about our own histories as Muslim women? I saw this as an opportunity to probe deeply into why there is difference, as opposed to debating legitimacy.

Through the use of various techniques such as role play, historical mapping, mind maps, small and large group discussions, I engaged the women in an exploration of various themes I had chosen prior to our meeting. We also engaged in the creation of artistic representation of our discussions. We also used photography as a medium to create alternative visuals of these women, in contrast to images found in mainstream media.

One of the greatest lessons was that the colourful tapestry of each community and individual was the result of processes that have taken course over time. No one's claim to authenticity could diminish the "other," as we decentralized dominant discourses by allowing the breadth of voices and perspectives to be heard. By not working from the premise of legitimacy or authenticity, we shifted the focus to a more anthropological exploration of our lives, placing us all in the centre of history making. If our common goal was to challenge hegemonic and monolithic messages about our lives, then our differences had to teach us about the ecology of how individual and community identity is shaped by engagement with every aspect of local and global society.

We also engaged in teasing out where our identities gave us privilege and where they placed us in marginal positions. As an educated woman coming from a middle class background, I had to acknowledge that these identities have given me access and opportunities that otherwise I might not have had. At the same time, my gender, race and religion have often put me in marginal positions (i.e., living within a white, Anglo-Saxon, male-dominated society). Coming from a Shia (a minoritized *Tariqa* [path] within Islam) background, I was also significantly marginalized within the Sunni-dominated *Ummah* (the larger Muslim community). This kind of honest self-analysis, exposure to and acceptance of our multiple positions and roles in relation to one another complicated our understanding of who we are as Muslim women and what stories we needed to tell about our lives. This kind of work *within* difference challenged our own assumptions about moral or religious superiority, reminding us that we are all products of engagement, resistance, subversion and even assimilation of cultural processes. If our ultimate goal was to create alliances and to commit ourselves to presenting Muslim woman with will, agency and the ability to affect change, then we were doing that, even if at times the process was painful.

The artistic creations took shape over two phases. The first phase was during the sessions making diagrams, maps and photographs; the second when we were writing the rest of the book by putting discussions together, working with photographs and designing the book. The art became an important reflection of our layered interactions and discussions, and spoke to our tensions, struggles, joys and intellectual thoughts.

The Power of Images and Muslim Women's Representation

Images can be powerful tools for relaying messages, ideas and stories about the objects presented. Although interpretations of images are left to the observer, the ideologies that permeate the context in which the picture is being viewed filters the meaning that is extracted. Thus, pictures can reinforce particular characterizations, many of which are stereotypical, racist, sexist and Islamophobic. In the case of Muslim women, their images have been used in the West since colonial times to validate the so-called backwardness of Islam.[7] Whether it's the depiction of the veiled woman or the sexually alluring harem woman or a comparison with women from the West, the dominant message has reduced Muslim women to one dimensional passive characters dictated by the whims of their male counterparts. Their reality has been tightly interwoven into particular religious interpretations that establish male superiority. They rarely exist on their own terms, projecting self-consciousness, a strong identity and life analysis.

Dominant images that are readily accessible and immediately stimulating have done as much damage as narratives, if not more, in how our life stories have been told. Through a culture jamming approach, we decided to subvert mainstream media messages through adbusting. Adbusting provided a method through which we could politicize our commentary on existing images, while attempting to create new ones. Each woman (including myself) was asked to bring in an image from a major print media source. We placed all the images on the floor and took note of what we were observing and what we deduced as being the key messages. We then began to deconstruct, in detail, each part of the image, making connections to the text accompanying the image. Throughout this process, I shifted the conversation to lead us into a hands-on process of suggesting ways to change the image or to openly critique and expose the insidious and detrimental subtext to how Muslim women were being understood and depicted.

Through this approach, we decided that our resistance and our intellectual and political engagement had to be present in the response. This medium became liberatory for us in that we realized that taking back our power to be seen and heard in ways that we agreed to, needed to begin with the articulation of a critical analysis of the dominant representations of Muslim women. Adbusting was a way to engage and respond directly, rupturing the inherent power and authority given to such images. It allowed us to establish our autonomy and not only to change the visual depictions but to transform the very stories that are dominant in our culture.

When such processes become opportunities to speak out against and to challenge dominant discourses, it is imperative to recognize the tools that allow us to do so. As academics, activists and artists, we were able to draw upon the necessary intellectual tools and knowledge to engage in analysis. We also engaged in producing new knowledge that could in turn inform academia. Art becomes a powerful medium with which to create new representations in textual and visual depictions. Thus, the womb in which art, activist and academic intersect allows for such projects to be born.

The project of *Majalis al-Ilm* was more about the process than about the end product. Through a participatory women-centred art-based project, we engaged in something that was unique and had to be shared. The culmination of this project was a book that was published in 2003. As the sessions were coming to an end, I approached the women and talked to them about finding a way to disseminate our process and discussions, as I felt strongly that these were insights that the mainstream public should hear from Muslim women. The women were open to any medium and left it up to me to decide how the *Majalis* would be shared. I decided that a book that was accessible, interesting to look at and engaging would be the best way of getting the information out. The book that was published in the end is called *Majalis al-Ilm: Sessions of Knowledge: Reclaiming and Representing the Lives of Muslim Women.*

A community book launch was held involving all the women who participated in the project. As this had been a personal, political, intellectual, spiritual and artistic journey for myself and for the women participants, it was important to have an event that affirmed our communities, honoured the incredible work being done and inspired what could be done. The book launch reminded us all of the potential power of collective process through which we, as marginalized groups and individuals, can effect change if not be the leaders of it. As it is written in the Qur'an (4:133): "O ye who believe! Stand out firmly for justice, as witnesses to Allah, even as against yourselves, or your parents, or your kin, and whether it be (against) rich or poor."[8]

NOTES

1. Fatema Mernissi, *Scheherazade Goes West: Different Cultures, Different Harems* (New York: Washington Square Press, 2001).
2. Karim H. Karim, *Islamic Peril: Media and Global Violence* (Montreal: Black Rose Books, 2000), 1.
3. The Aga Khan in a recent article in the *Toronto Star* spoke about the congruency between democracy and Islam. Haroon Saddiqui, "Selling a Canadian Idea to the World," *Toronto Star*, 28 April 2005.
4. For more on this topic, refer to Maria Rosa Menocal, *The Ornament of the World* (New York: Little, Brown, 2002).
5. An example of a Muslim leader and community working closely with "others." Saddiqui, "Selling a Canadian Idea to the World."

6. Salima Bhimani, *Majalis al-Ilm: Sessions of Knowledge: Reclaiming and Representing the Lives of Muslim Women* (Toronto: Tsar Publications, 2003), 7.

7. Linda Steet, *Veil and Daggers: A Century of National Geographic's Representation of the Arab World* (Philadelphia: Temple University Press, 2000), 23.

8. Bhimani, *Majalis al-Ilm: Sessions of Knowledge.*

CHAPTER 8

Jamming with Women's Rights Activists in East Asia:

A PROCESS OF CRITICAL REFLECTION

Yukyung Kim-Cho

Welcome to this jamming session. This is a low-key jam about the jam I did with women activists in East Asia and my reflections on women's rights activism as I experienced it in South Korea, in Canada and at international conferences over the last thirteen years.

THERE ARE TWO TYPES OF JAMMING. ONE TYPE OF JAMMING IS AN OPEN musical performance where anybody can join in and play a piece of improvised music without a written score or conductor. I am an enthusiast of jamming for any type of music. I love the open concept, the freedom and the thrill of the space, and that no one knows how the session is going to begin or end. A second kind of jamming is a verbal and visual session that explores the imagination and opens up space where participants' thoughts can meet, reflect, challenge, question and trigger spoken, written and visualization activities.

My jamming sessions involved in-depth interviews with thirty women activists based in Hong Kong, Taiwan, South Korea and Japan and the self-publishing of my jamming book. In producing my jamming book I used the voices of the participants (interviewees), my reflection on each

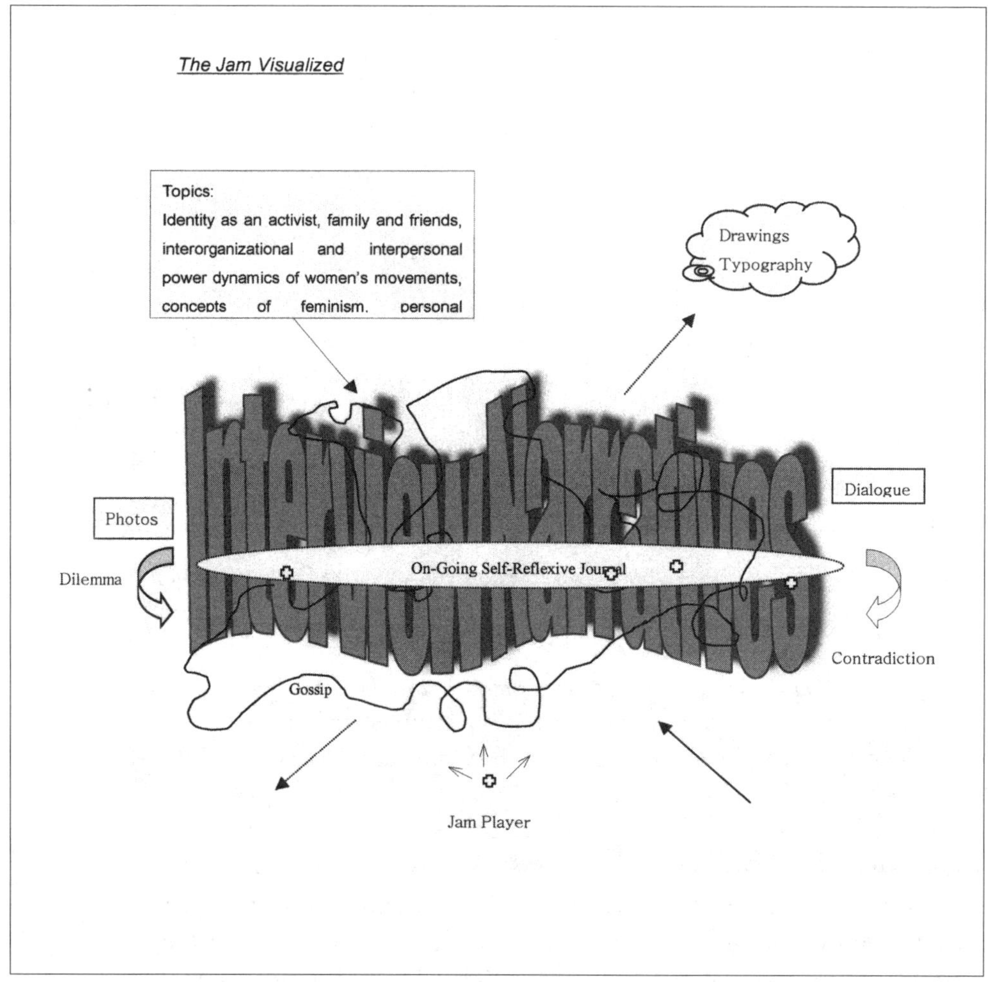

interview, the women's unspoken words during the interviews and my observations of women's activisms in East Asia and the dynamics of their international work. The overall jamming process was to challenge the various power relations and inspire critical reflection within the internal dynamics of women's rights movements in East Asia.

The first stage of jamming sessions was with individual activists. I had one-on-one interviews with the women that lasted one to one-and-a-half hour each. These interviews included casual discussions, chatting and drawing and, with Chinese speakers, the writing down of Chinese characters to help with conversation.[1] Jamming is a useful tool for grassroots participatory research on women's rights activisms because it allows us to explore the unspoken yet critical topics of our activism.

The second stage of jamming, the production of my book, involved drawing, photography, typography, juxtaposition of texts and photos, using musical metaphors as well as working with the narratives from the in-depth interviews to highlight some of the critical moments and key issues addressed.

Women Activists and Feminist Activisms

My observation over my thirteen years of involvement in feminist activisms in South Korea and Canada and from attending international women's conferences is that feminists and women activists live with ironies and contradictions in both their work and personal lives. For instance, it is a complicated matter for some women's rights activists to identify themselves with feminism when the language of "feminism" is from the West and is often perceived as being Western-oriented, un-co-operative, unfriendly, selfish, a bit odd and individualistic. It is a great challenge for these women to orient their own personal behaviours and beliefs towards women's advancement, equality and peace. Many women activists in East Asia who jammed with me denied that they were feminists or part of the women's movement. This shows how the notion of feminism is perceived and not accepted in East Asia, even among many women who would be easily considered feminists in the West. Some women may work on women's employment equity issues or on behalf of marginalized women's rights but they do so without a gender analysis.

Women activists who are involved in the public struggle against sexist hierarchies and unjust power dynamics organize legislative movements, run public education programs, hold campaigns on gender discrimination and demand better social services for women and children. However, within their own movements, the very same women are players in another kind of power hierarchy and oppression. Biases against class, race, sexual orientation, location of residence and competition among organizations and issue-based groups are manifested within women's activisms at the organizational and individual level. For instance, tensions among members and lack of understanding became an issue between the counselling

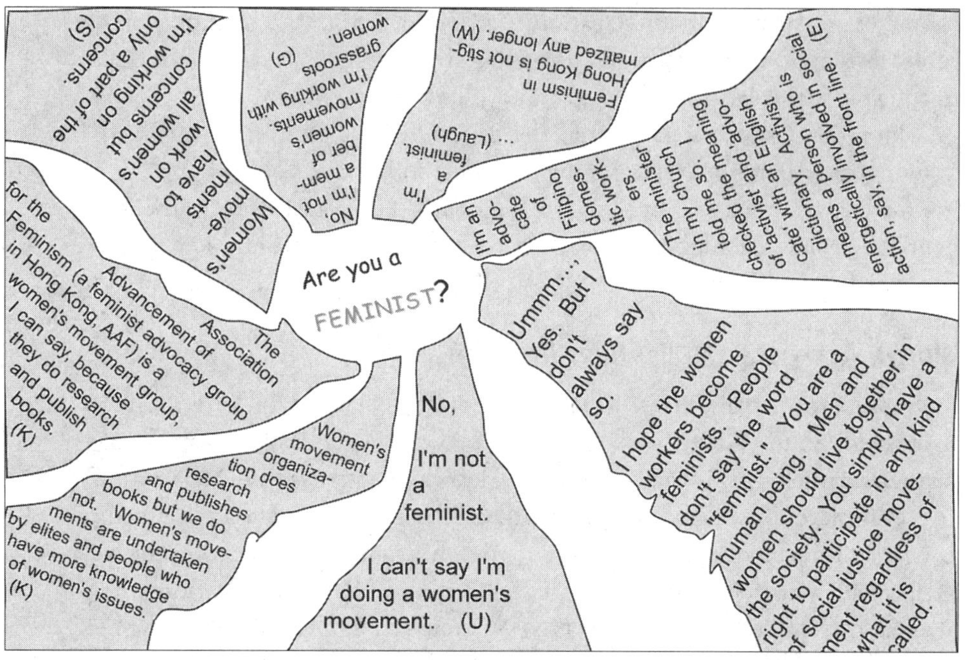

Are You A Feminist?

deparment and the rest of the employees in an organization that ran a women's hot line in Korea.

Ageism, racism and homophobia are often found in the women's movement in the country where the Confucian culture of hierarchy is very strong and the understanding of diversity is sadly lacking. I observed from the international East Asian Women's Forum and its preparation process that state relations, political orientation and nationalism affect cross-border feminist/womynist (non)co-operation among mainland Chinese, Hong Kong and Taiwanese women's groups.

Many women activists say they compromise their own individual human rights when they work within women's rights movements. They are asked to make personal sacrifices and to work with some urgency and insufficient resources in order to reach the short-term collective goals of these organizations. One question that has been raised repeatedly among women activists I've come across in East Asia and Canada is, How can we mobilize a real feminist/womynist movement that may be oriented towards achieving materialist outcomes but through a feminist/womynist method and process that includes, for all the women involved, the pleasure of learning from their involvement in the movement? Fortunately and unfortunately, I found this to be a common concern, particularly for many of the young women activists.

Chatting, Gossiping and Improvising

The jamming session addressed and discussed a *jammed* situation and by doing this revealed tensions about power and identities, differences in perspectives and priorities, and dilemmas in a group dynamic. The entire process provided the participants, including me, with a "smooth space,"[2] a casual and flexible space where we could share "nomadic thought(s)"[3] that kept moving in the changing environment. The jam helped us to pose questions about the issues of internal power dynamics within women's activisms as a way to reflect on them with other women involved in women's activisms.

In jamming, I shared a feminist/womynist way of doing research and presenting ideas. In this way, women's rights activists' subjective voices were revealed, and rather than drawing conclusions from what was said, I asked challenging questions. Through this experimental project, I was able to explore the power of visualization in communication and the interconnectedness[4] of feminist activisms.

Two elements of the jam session I introduce in this chapter are gossiping and chatting. These play an important role because they challenge hegemonic relations that are often built on modern logocentric discourses: discourses carried out mainly with logic that are recognized by the formal sphere of life. Discourses that do not follow the standardized logic were regarded as useless and unimportant by modern scholars and thinkers, especially male scholars. However, in real life, gossip has been a favourite way of transmitting information, although it has been associated with unexamined truth and, problematically, deemed to be women's stereotypically troublesome behaviour. I agree with Mary Leahh that the logocentric structure of scientific knowledge has regulated women's bodies and belied complex relationships between consonances and dissonances of meanings.[5] Practising gossip with and about East Asian women activists in my jamming project has helped to reclaim the subjectivity of the participants, including myself, and has challenged problematic binaries and boundaries within and around us.

When I was able to relax into the interview and identify an element of what a participant said about internal power dynamics within women's activisms, I commented on it and raised additional points or questions. This helped the participant relax and allowed her to let her real self come out. We then started chatting more enthusiastically and soon began to gossip about a hierarchical or dominating individual, someone or a particular organization that the participant did not like or whom she thought was unfair to others. After we discussed this, I asked the participant a more personal question. For example, I asked if she uses the same problematic behaviour with others whose socio-political position may be lower than hers.

GOSSIPING WITH JOYCE LEE

Me: Do you think hierarchical culture is significant in Taiwan?

JL: When we have a meeting, if the chairperson, who is usually older than the majority of the staff, participates, people will pay attention. If it's only staff, they don't care. Of course, of course, of course ... All leaders have power.

If some people are already dominating others, I won't join the group. If the leader dominates, others don't feel like joining. Equal participation is important. For example, Lydia was quite dominating in the Fourth East Asian Women's Forum this time. Those young people who worked for the Forum were all from her organization. How can others join? People might complain that only Lydia's organization will remain working for the Forum. We want to join, but we can't.

Me: You mean there is no room in there?

JL: No room, because she already dominates and takes up all the space. I think women should change this kind of behaviour, otherwise we are the same as men.

After a series of wild chatting and gossiping like this with women's rights activists in East Asia, I sat down at home in Toronto, listened to the record-

#

Yes. Your question about international relations is also relevant to the English language issue. In Korea, without this language ability, we can't talk about international relations. Therefore, everything becomes a meaningless question for people who don't have English language ability. In U.S., the distinguished Third World feminist theorists are all Indians.

. Yes!

Why? Because they speak English.

. That's why people in Korea jokingly say 'I wish Korea had been a British colony.'

Exactly! It tells us that the pressure of learning English is so significant that people even joke about it. I don't think everybody should learn English. I think only those who need English should. But in this internet world, it may not be true to say that.

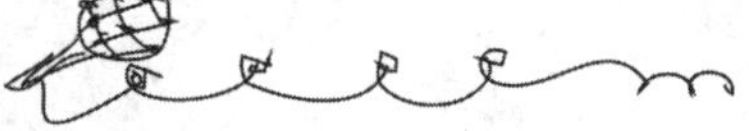

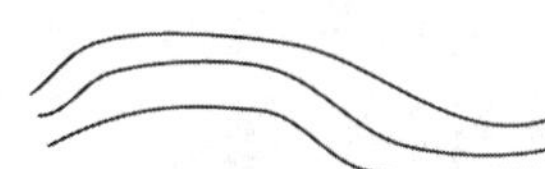

Yes, although I couldn't read Chinese, I was bilingual. I became a bridge. We gained a lot in the women's movement. The Hong Kong women's movement has done a lot, pushing for legislation, gaining clout in the Hong Kong government, and so on. I learned a lot from this work and I found Hong Kong activists' behaviours very different from that of Anglo-Saxons. We don't have meetings on Saturday night because it's private time. In Hong Kong, they don't care.

<! You really have a "white" cultural identity. You use "we" for Anglo-Saxon people or westerners, and "they" for Hong Kong Chinese people. Even though you are biologically Chinese, you place yourself on the side of Anglo-Saxon westerners. ...>

But three years later, I saw myself as a poor worm having to work too hard with no personal life. I felt miserable, not even human, suffering from the workload, the unnecessary hierarchy and the tension in the women's organization. This made me cry in the middle of the night in my little apartment near the office, with a bottle of Soju (the cheapest and strongest Korean alcoholic drink).

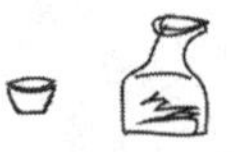

Even leaving the horrible workplace was not easy. I had to be patient for nearly one year. During the last year, I was very cynical. I barely managed to carry on the given work before me, but I was neither creative nor reflective. I was simply an employee, not an activist.

Suh-Jin: If somebody wants to interview me as a member of women's movement, it's painful to me, because I don't do the women's movement now. I'm more interested in my personal matters ...

Jamming with Women's Rights Activists in East Asia

Bits and Pieces

ings and conducted the second series of jamming with the transcripts, my memories and imagination.

Our thoughts like to improvise. Jamming is, in terms of improvisation, a very appropriate metaphor for the way we live, learn, communicate and work. Many other people naturally think and act this way too. Our thoughts are scattered and unorganized; they can go anywhere and do not follow a particular direction or schedule. It is mainly modern academia and the dominant culture that tries to tame our thinking or structure our written and spoken communication into a specified format of introduction-body-conclusion. Such a structuralist culture has trapped our grassroots and nomadic thoughts, inhibiting our expression.

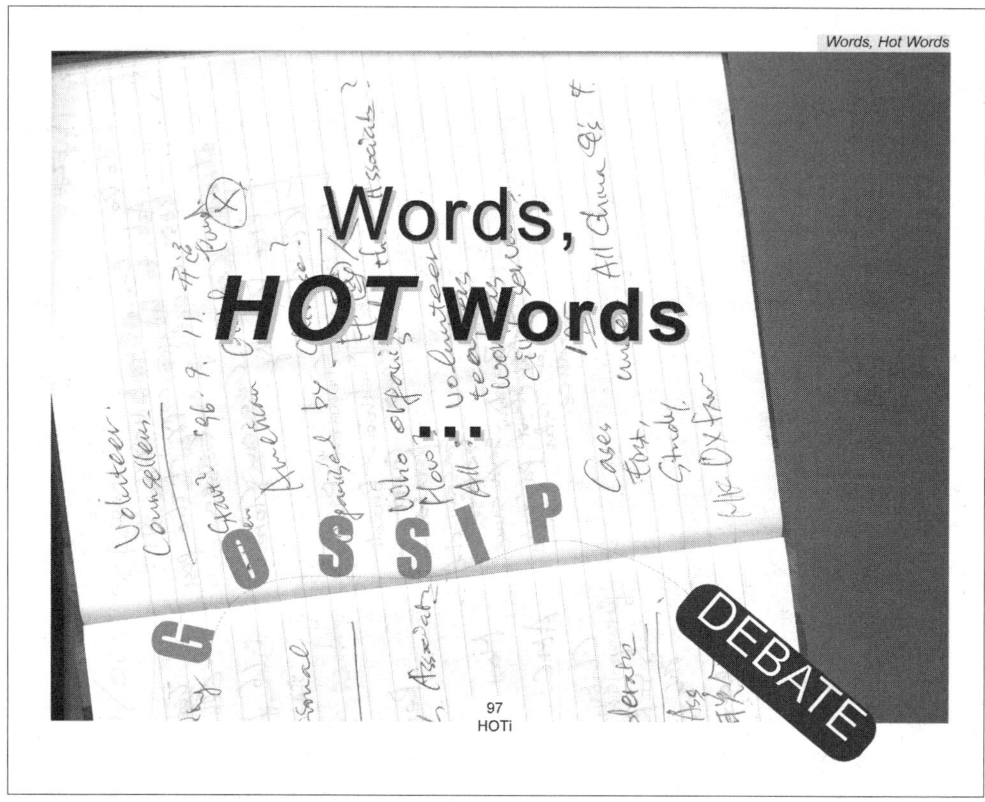

Words, Hot Words

JAMMING AS A GUD

During this year-long process of the jamming with other women, I imagined I was a "Mudang." Mudang is a Korean Shaman-like figure who facilitates the Gud, a Korean Shamanist ceremony held as part of the traditional folk culture. Mudangs are supposed to be a bridge between people and God. The Gud tradition has been severely criticized as an uncivilized and illogical practice that should be eliminated but, from an alternative perspective, it can be seen as a community festivity, involving art and teamwork. By dancing and chanting, the Mudang, who is usually a woman, takes on the role of inviting people into a space where logic and science cannot explain what is happening. Korean cultural studies scholars such as Gang Hyun Ju suggest that treating Gud as a superstition is a Western-oriented imperialist view.[6] He argues that this ceremony is, in fact, an opportunity for women to liberate themselves. I wanted my role in the project to be a catalyst, like the Mudang's role in a Gud, to stir up the world of women's movements in East Asia and make their once-silenced voices come out and hang out with others.

My jam project was a journey of critical but playful talking, thinking and sculpting with my fellow activists as well as my own multiple subjectivities (through voices, words, photos, drawings and other images from actual and imaginary events). On this journey, I saw a lot more than I could show on the pages of the jamming book I produced. The dimensions of my jamming went beyond the text and included various forms of signs, metaphors, subtexts and absences. My reading audience, therefore, can only get a general impression of my work, because it can never be exactly or truely transcribed. This jamming process is a form of cultural production that engages the politics of visualization and its wordless voices and power.[7]

According to Deborah Barndt: "Cultural work is about affirming differences, digging deeply into the roots of our diverse cultural identities, and in the process of unearthing who we are, connecting with others who are also unearthing themselves. This breaking of new ground creates the conditions for new forms."[8] She adopts Lucy Lippard's framing of her vision of "new art" to suggest that cultural work includes the processes of mapping, naming, telling, landing, mixing, turning around and dreaming. "Naming" is particularly important for women's art/cultural work, as it involves naming "who we are as well as who I am, reclaiming the power to name, and to rename as we shift and change, seeing ourselves differently. It allows us to explore who we are and to create new names in the process."[9] Barndt points out the individual and momentary differences in naming while emphasizing the participatory and collective aspects of cultural work.

I would like to use this theory to explain what happened through my jamming project. The participants and I could name a number of complicated problems we faced through our movements and tried some mapping to see where we were in various East Asian cultural and political contexts. Some participants named and mapped the same issues and circumstances differently from others, but sometimes they changed their views during the jam.

*T*uning ...

Kim Joyce

Nuri

‹Nuri's internal voice or others' voice in her memory›

Tuning

In my jamming book, I included the written and visualized voices of women activists whom I met in East Asian countries. I decided not to use a uniform layout for each of them, as each woman brought a unique voice to the project. I didn't want to frame such diversity as an "assembly line." Through this para-verbal jamming of photography, drawings, typography, blank spaces and written words, I believe that I, the author, as well as my reading audience will find a supplementary mode of expression and space for our own interpretations and reflections. For us, jamming through visuals and metaphors as well as text certainly plays a counter-hegemonic role, especially since verbal expression in English is more limited to us than in our first language.

Engaging in our daily life as a continuous dialogue with ourselves and with others, from which we problematize our everyday lives, is a way of critical and creative living and learning. Life is a continuum of drafts and jamming. My jamming book is a draft that will continuously evolve. So will my jamming projects. As an integrative feminist activist, at least a wannabe, committed to popular arts-informed research on feminist activisms, I am excited about planning my next jamming session. Because I jam at every moment in my daily life, as many women do, handling more than one thing at a time and moving between the different tunes, my jamming project will continue to evolve.

NOTES

This chapter is based on the Master in Environmental Studies project at York University, "Jamming with Women's Rights Activists in East Asia," completed in 2001. The published version is available at the Toronto Women's Bookstore or through the author at ykimcho@pancakehouse.org. I dedicate this chapter to the women writing for women's rights in East Asia, to the participants of my Jamming sessions, and to Nuri Kim, my mother.

1. This project was carried out in English except for a few jams with Korean women for which I used my first language, Korean. I used my knowledge of some Chinese characters to help communicate with women who spoke Chinese as their first language.

2. G. Deleuze and F. Guattari, *A Thousand Plateaus: Capitalism and Schizophrenia* (London: Athlone Press, 1988).

3. Michel Foucault, *The Archaeology of Knowledge* (New York: Random House, 1972).

4. Donna E. Alvermann, "Researching Libraries, Literacies, and Lives: A Rhizoanalysis," in Elizabeth A. St. Pierre and Wanda S. Pillow, eds., *Working the Ruins: Feminist Poststructural Theory and Methods in Education* (New York: Routledge, 2000), 114–127.

5. Mary Leahh, "Feminist Figurations: Gossip as a Counterdiscourse, " in St. Pierre and Pillow, eds., *Working the Ruins*, 223–236.

6. Gang Hyun Ju, *Social History of Gud: Life and Customs in Korea* (Seoul: Woong-Jin Press, 1992); Sue Nam Kim and Hwang Sue Shi, *Pal Do Gud* (Gud in Eight Provinces) (Seoul: Daewonsa Publishing, 1989), 24–25.

7. See, for example, Deborah Barndt, "Zooming Out, Zooming In: Visualizing Globalization," in *Visual Sociology* 12, no. 2 (1997); Stuart Hall, *Representation: Cultural Representations and Signifying Practices* (Thousand Oaks, CA: Sage, 1997), 13–74, 223–290; Jo Spence, "Questioning Documentary Practice? The Sign as a Site of Struggle," in *Cultural Snipping: The Art of Transgression* (New York: Routledge, 1995), 97–108; Liz Wells, "Thinking about Photography: Debates, Historically and Now," in *A Critical Introduction to Photography* (New York: Routledge, 1997), 11–54.

8. Deborah Barndt, "Cultural Work: Reclaiming the Power to Create," *Arts* 7, no. 2 (Winter 1995), 27.

9. Ibid., 25.

CHAPTER 9

Mixing Metaphors:
RISK IN ART AND ACTIVISM

Petra Kukacka

… the crocodile rushed up alongside the canoe, and its beautiful, flecked golden eyes looked straight into mine … I tensed for the jump and leapt.

— Val Plumwood, in Simone Fullggar, "Desiring Nature"[1]

What charms, cradles, beguiles us in writing is the wall,
 `the obstacle to overcome
Much as the splash and gleam of water for the diver …

Fascination of the eye. Reverie of the ear.
To see no more, hear no more, wait no more.
Dive down …

— Edmond Jabes, "To Enlarge the Horizons of the World"[2]

Art and activism, at their core, are deeply true to life, requiring that every day be a new experience rather than time spent in anticipation of the next experience. Our lives, the act of simply *being*, require a constant engagement with the indeterminate limits of living. This, of course, is paradoxical: to engage with the unknown, to ceaselessly peer into the darkness, is to perpetuate one's exposure to threat.

Engaging in that paradox, following it out into the open, endless depths of what lies beyond our comprehension, messes up the milieu, unpacks the unpackable and drags us further into the darkness, mesmerized, not quite seeking, but encountering. Engaging with our monsters — no longer containing them in the back of closets, in deep, impenetrable forests and at the bottom of lakes and oceans — is the pinnacle of human experience. We find that reality is not a second-hand experience; it is not a handmaiden to a pre-ordered course for being that creates alienation rather than relation among all things, animate and inanimate. Reality is engagement with "what is found there," the fillament of the day: that chair, that person, that remark, arriving just in time to colour that story and allow it to take off.

When we engage with *les animaux dangereux* we derail the steady course set by a pre-determined logic. We turn to monsters to reject this order, yet this is not at all a light or easy turning away, as monsters are, by definition, threatening. Nevertheless, this turning away is the only way to remain in pursuit of resistance and accompanied by courage, which is the only true radical gesture. This is what Donna Haraway might call "the ushering in of the inappropriate/d." According to Haraway, the task of the inappropriate/d is "not to fit in the taxon, [but] to be dislocated from the available maps specifying kinds of actors and kinds of narratives."[3] Yet how can we cast off into the inappropriate/d without taking life preservers to buffer us against those uncertain waters? How do we do that without writing our own end?

The Metaphor of Water

As radical as swimming in the deep waters is, when our feet are undershadowed by the abyss that lies beneath, is it not, perhaps, also *too much* of a radical gesture? What is found there are the ends of experience, where our ancestors may never have gone or gone only in dreams and death and desire. What is also found there is a very real and intimate dread. Our mortality demands that we be concerned with our own undoing, so when we tread water over an abyss and our insecurities well up, of course we are going to head back to shore; back to more certain terrain.

Spending time in the deep is not an option unless we are willing to risk our own lives in order to know those waters. The price of becoming inappropriate means putting ourselves actively in harm's way and questioning our own limits. Therefore, reaching out into the void has become a paradox, and a deeply unnerving one.

As activists and artists, we strive to reject life-by-proxy, at every turn. Yet such reaching out, towards an immediacy of being, risks dissolving what already exists, threatening what we love, value and hold closest to us. To paraphrase Terry Eagleton, we cannot shine light on our monsters or else they will cease to be monsters. Indeed, monsters are deviant and menacing presences and they cannot be written in or out at our convenience and existences, they do not conform to our rules.[4]

People need monsters: we need the unknown, unfixed and uncharitable — not that we might inhabit or tame them, but so that we might breach them in search of difference and change. Therefore, "to monster" our lives, to allow the monsters in, we put ourselves at great risk. Yet if we do *not* "monster" our lives, we also put ourselves at great risk. We cannot hope for change without engagement, as that would be like a non-swimmer receiving a series of written instructions on swimming while standing at the shoreline, hoping to plunge in: "interesting ... but unable to express the wetness of water."[5] Processes of change and resistance can only occur through one's constant and persistent plunging in: this is the auto-antagonistic, self-agitating, active, open-ended pursuit of being.

TAKING THE PLUNGE

On the news, hundreds of sharks off of Australia's Gold Coast have converged on a massive school of baitfish and are feeding there. The sharks are motionless, they seem to be paralyzed, until some indeterminable moment when they leap forward; they know instinctively that if they do not catch their prey off guard, there will be no catch at all. The crystalline water is so mesmerizing and the camerawork so lucid and vibrant, almost hyper-real, that it is easy to get caught up, to become deeply enthralled and consumed by the scene. Spiralling around, beneath the reverent gaze, thoughts about the technology that made the shot possible begin to surface. Most assuredly they were taken from a helicopter, the photographer perhaps hanging out, perhaps holding on by one toe or being held on to by a production assistant with a deathgrip on the photographer's belt, perhaps being lowered on a rope, fastened to it with carabiners and harness, all for the sake of getting those extreme close-ups, the "catch of the day." The method of shark-frenzy photography adds to the element of danger already ushered in by the special, sinister place reserved for sharks in our imaginaries.

A friend tells me that he was required to hang out of a helicopter over Hollywood to get "that shot" — Hollywood Hills, Sunset Boulevard, Universal Studios and Mulholland Drive — for the reality show he is co-producing about the paparazzi. The paparazzi are the vultures of Hollywood, they are scavengers, bottom feeders, often preying on the rich and the famous, on sound bytes and photo ops, earning them such adjectives as "menacing" and "merciless." Yet they are also central to pop culture, the keepers of the treasure trove of the modern sacred. They extract the "who-dunits" and "whodunwhos" from the silver screen and release them on the pavement. They blend fiction and fantasy on the palette — and whoever applies them to canvas is secondary. They light up the outer reaches of infamy and are often tossed about brutally in the public imaginary like the very carrion they are said to feed on. They have the power to launch stars into the sky or to bring them crashing down, acting in full complicity with the reckless entertainment leviathan from which they scavenge.

I enjoy thinking of my friend, hanging out over Hollywood, the spiral propulsion of the chopper keeping him afloat among red-ceramic rooftops and palm trees as he shoots the lair of the predator-become-prey. There is something deviant, radical and inappropriate about turning the lens on those who help to craft the vacuum of pop culture. I realize my friend is little different from them, but from my vantage point, holding a camera becomes something other than polarizing another through a lens: it becomes a process of complexification. Fantasy, fact, art, evidence all mutate into one.

Hollywood. I'm stepping out into the bright lobby, leaving the credits and musical end notes of *Hotel Rwanda* behind. I'm blinking, I'm looking piqued as usual from the two-hour sit-in-the-dark and I'm suppressing a yawn. Already I'm feeling hatred for the movie in my gut. My hatred charts a parsimonious route that starts with the end of the movie and ends at its beginning. That is to say, hatred for the closing song floods in first and drowns out the rest of the film. The music, which mimics an upbeat south-central-African rhythm, borders on absurdity and obscenity when juxtaposed with the unutterable horror that has just been unimaginatively evoked over the past two hours. But not just the music. The words, as well. "If 'America' is the 'United States of America' and 'Britain' is the 'United Kingdom,' why can't 'Africa' be the 'United States of Africa'?"

The lively and sanguine windings of the song are unwelcome. They invite me to understand how the rebel-led slaughter of 800,000 civilians in three months may have transpired. On the screen it is reasoned out for me, explained in a language I am supposed to understand. The rhetorical questioning suggests that the international system might still save Africa, as the movie made it clear that the opportunity to save Rwanda in 1994 was horribly passed by. The song asks its audience to "please, finally, let Africa into your world view," a benevolent plea, it seems. But perhaps a different question would chart a different Africa still.

Why is it that the Hutu rebel slaughter-machine is so effortlessly portrayed as an unyielding and frenzied mob? The movie narrates a reality where the perpetrators are not people but a highly rational and efficient killing machine bewitched by hundreds of years of European colonial domination. They are the tool of hatred, so please, take pity on Rwanda, instructs the movie, it knows not what it does: they are not wrongdoers, but rather know-nothings or invalids, sick with the effects of colonization. In-valid: not responsible; indeed, it is the First World that is responsible, from colonization to non-intervention.

Why is it appropriate to chart the Hutus as having had a momentary lapse of humanity while it is inappropriate to delve into the fact that there is more underlying this crime than First World negligence? Why is it inappropriate to dive into the fact that it is a collective disaster, belonging neither to them nor us, but to everyone? Why is it inappropriate to embrace the possibility that all of humanity is a victim of this crime while also the perpetrator of it ... to understand that in the Rwandan violation against the laws of humanity there *is* no one to blame? The roots of atrocity seem to run so deep that we cannot hope to pull them out, no matter how strong the arm of Hollywood, without pulling the foundation up as well. So do we pull the rug out from under ourselves? Can we? Or do we try, instead, to understand that Rwanda of 1994 happened to all of us villainous victims, to internalize it not just as something we let happen, but as something that *does* happen, constantly? And to understand Rwanda as such, can the atrocities ever stop?

These are unanswerable questions, but such necessary ones if we are going to truly discuss human nature. Hollywood has managed to erect a security wall around these questions, and so I instinctively begin to scale that wall. I am awash with a desire for Africa, complete with its misery and mystery, its hope and whatever else might be found there. Please keep your Africa which has been security checked and modified for ease of consumption. The words at the end of the film — "Why can't Africa be the 'United States of Africa?" — coerce me to crawl down off the security wall and cease my questioning. I fight harder to hoist myself up … and over. This is my own personal activism.

On the Other Side of the Wall

On the other side of the wall, I no longer have to listen to Westernized propaganda about the desires of developing democracies. Instead, I welcome the barren scene. I am far from my Canadian home, ungrateful and pleased to be removed from the home that defines me and burdens me all at the same time. I am thankful for what I find here. On the other side of the wall, I have left behind the high-gloss, glossed-over exposé of the plight of Hutu and Tutsi civilians in the first days and weeks following the violence perpetrated by Rwanda's military and rebel leaders during the spring of 1994. I have left behind the veneer through which Hollywood would have us view reality. I reflect momentarily on a comment a friend once made about how art galleries are, in fact, art prisons and I superimpose the sentiment onto Hollywood: the reality prison. I smirk. I usher in the other story: that disaster is not always contingent on the international community's responsiveness. And I can't help but ask myself, What, then, is disaster contingent on? Suddenly, it is very cold and still in this new, unassuming milieu.

The inalienable fact about becoming prey is that it is frightening and transformative. Dread can lead to compulsion, enticement, self-deprecation, self-emulation, any number of powerful responses. Invariably, however, dread transforms. In analyzing Plumwood's description of becoming crocodile-prey (cited at the beginning of the chapter), Simone Fullgar writes: "We see in Plumwood's writing a lightness which … [enables] another feel for the world; a lightness shadowed by the heavy precariousness of life."[6] This "other feel for the world" comes from embracing the dreadful and the real properties of fear which are found in breaching and simultaneously creating the unknown. The dread is real and persistent, often rendering the fearful subject inarticulate.

ϟ

Something is not right. I'm standing against the wall and a wasteland stretches out in front of me. Not a sound, not a whisper betrays any sign of life. Out from under me, from deep inside me, a sense of terror wells up. Although the world around me is calm, there is a trembling somewhere beyond my periphery of vision or too far inside me to locate. There is nothing here, I think to myself, it is absolutely empty — no colour, no horizon, just endless grey on grey. If there are people here, I do not recognize them and they do not recognize me, or maybe they're just not approaching me, maybe they're staying away. I wouldn't blame them.

My fear seems to be charted by the fact that the other side of the security wall does not actually exist. In this space, I am not artist nor activist, not inappropriated nor even prey, only fool. Escaping the Hollywood story, I have not landed in the better, more real story but in much, much worse un-navigable, paralytic terrain. I get a sense of where real activity lies — not in running from walls and limits, but in trying to understand them. The ground underfoot rumbles and surges up and I scale back over the wall, narrowly avoiding being swallowed whole.

ϟ

I'm back where I'd started, the tailwinds of my adventure still ripe. In the back of my mind a new tune rises up, "Beat it, Hollywood, artless, soulless, static vacuum that you are …" I am now cozying up to the wall. I no longer see it as a mechanism of coercion but rather as a tool, as an artefact of disaster, yet also a barrier to it. I am resolved, for the moment, to guard it, not against trespassers or vandals but just to be near it, to gaze on it a little while, to accompany it and to understand what it is made of, its limits and possibilities, asking whether I am also a part of it.

Being at Risk

Between news briefs, anchor people grin through pointed, pearly anchor-people teeth and exclaim, "Those sharks are really having a feeding frenzy!" It is safe to laugh, the beach is patrolled, no human life is at risk, nature has set its course in a relatively safe and controlled manner. The image of the clean, sleek whisking tails pop up every half hour, on the half hour, and I gaze alongside the helicopter-mounted photography at the glide of long phantom-like bodies. Although I am being told that they are sharks, there is a foreign, extraneous temptation that beseeches me to believe that they are, in fact, catfish scouring the bottom of a riverbed for leeches. To my eyes, they appear no different. But I choose to believe the tale that my mind relays: these are, indeed, deadly, blood-letting sharks. Now the story gives me a thrill.

Thinking about what I should do with this knowledge, I wonder whether I shouldn't plunge my own body into the water with them. Perhaps from above, perhaps from helicopter-on-high — what a glorious performance it would be! Now here and now there, presto change-o! A real magician's spectacle: I would fit seamlessly into that glossy image. Albeit anachronistic, almost an anathema to the image's sleekness, I would be part of it nevertheless, feeling that I belong there, among the hunger of the beasts. D-A-N-G-E-R: the letters are thumped out by quickening heartbeats. Suddenly I have placed myself in imminent danger as I reach out to pet the smooth, sleek, circling bodies. My compulsion to "be there" undershadows all other realities and the water grows murkier underneath.

NOTES

1. Val Plumwood in Simone Fullggar, "Desiring Nature: Identity and Becoming in Narratives of Travel," *Cultural Values* 4, no.1 (October 2000), 66.
2. Edmond Jabes, "To Enlarge the Horizons of the World," in Mary Ann Caws, ed., *Manifesto: A Century of Isms* (Lincoln: University of Nebraska Press, 2001), 359.
3. Donna Haraway, "The Promises of Monsters: A Regenerative Politics for Inapproprate/d Others," in Lawrence Grossberg, Cary Nelson and Paula A. Treichler, eds., *Cultural Studies* (New York: Routledge, 1992).
4. Terry Eagleton, *The Ideology of the Aesthetic* (Oxford: Blackwell, 1990).
5. Sadie Plant, Preface to *The Most Radical Gesture* (Lodon: Routledge, 1992).
6. Fullggar, "Desiring Nature," 67.

PART III

Eco Art

CHAPTER 10

Garden the City:

ACTIVISM THROUGH INTERVENTIONIST ART

Melanie Kramer

It began with a muddled idea of integrating my interests in cities, gardens, art, inspiration, food, beauty and people. How could these ideas coalesce to create some kind of movement to promote growing food in the city? Beginning with a colourful, idealistic vision of strawberries on balconies and herbs in flowerbeds, I eventually transformed these vague ideas into the "Garden the City" project: an interventionist art project encouraging anonymous Toronto urbanites to grow food in urban spaces. Five years earlier I had never heard of interventionist art, of urban agriculture, of food security. I was more familiar with gardening, composting, public art and activism. But these interests expanded as I read about growing food in cities, on rooftops and community gardens, and as I saw murals and graffiti proliferate in the city and giant puppets appear at protests. Yet the question remained as to how to bring these interests together.

Whether it is through murals, graffiti, puppetry, storytelling, landscape design, popular theatre, guerrilla gardening, radical cheerleading, environmental art, critical comic strips or architecture, people are constantly designing creative ways to address struggles. Art and creativity have a place in effecting change, in creating dynamic places and in shaping the exchange of knowledge, stories and information. Defined as a chance encounter, interventionist art is "art that takes place outside an expected place and time,"[1] that melds easily with activism to take on the role of communicating a message in a unique, noticeable way. Artist Kim Pruesse describes interventionist art as almost magical — something that "come[s] into our lives by circumstance, accidentally encountered without brackets."[2] As I searched for a method to communicate my ideas about gardening in the city, interventionist art seemed to provide the means.

BUILDING ON THE PAST

Art has long been used as a form of activism to raise awareness around a variety of issues. One of the first artists to use the photomontage techniques as a popular form of communication was the German artist John Heartfield (1891–1968), a member of the Berlin Dada group and a producer of satirical collages. In the 1940s, he was "cross matching photographs to produce new meanings from familiar icons of Nazi Germany."[3] Heartfield imbued images with new messages through their juxtaposition with one another. He parodied Nazi messages and actions, often creating tongue-in-cheek posters, flyers and films. Although much less politically laden, Garden the City also used photocollage with text in the form of postcards. It was an attempt to give people a new perspective on their urban landscape and challenge them to reconceptualize the city, food growing in the urban context and notions of public versus private space.

The Situationist International movement that began in September 1957 helped to popularize creative approaches of intervening into people's daily lives. Loosely led by activist and intellectual Guy DeBord,[4] the movement used play, creativity and spontaneity to create situations and construct moments that challenged the everyday routine, rather than passively accepting the world around us. Situationist moments were attempts to change urban spaces as well as people's ideas about those spaces, about interactions with others and about the dominant capitalist system in which we are immersed. Situationists hoped to experience and to help others to experience *authenticity* in life. This would lead to a "detournement" — a diverting or turning of the system that usually keeps us bound to our everyday lives. As with many forms of activism, Situationists used a diversity of tactics to achieve their goals, including writing, drawing, graffiti and spontaneous street theatre, many of them interventionist in form.

In the mid-1980s a group calling themselves the Guerrilla Girls formed in New York City to counter the dominance of white male artists in the art world. They used posters, billboards, postcards and banners, as well as more traditional art installations and shows, to raise awareness about this domination and to agitate for change. Seeking to transform ideas and bring people to action, the Guerrilla Girls used city space and the people travelling through it as their canvas and audience. That the audience came upon these works unexpectedly was part of the strategy to provoke thought and ideally catalyze action.[5]

These strategies evolved into the Culture Jamming and Reclaim the Streets movements which became popularized in the 1990s. Both approaches use art and creativity to challenge public spaces and to communicate alternative messages with the public. From transforming billboards to holding street parties with giant puppets, from sidewalk chalk drawing to guerrilla gardening, these movements have used art as an intervention in urban spaces, as a form of activist communication, often with great success. Culture jamming changes people's environments by "jamming" (diverting, changing, exposing, disrupting or "messing up") dominant cultural forms such as advertising.[6] Reclaim the Streets uses spontaneity, fun and art to physically transform spaces (for example by planting a tree in the middle of a street or hanging art from an overpass) as well as to hopefully change people's ideas about those spaces, their possibilities and potential uses.[7]

Similar to Reclaim the Streets parties, interventionist art does not necessarily take on political, social or environmental issues; however, it can be a natural vehicle for such messages. Unlike advertising that reflects wealth, power and hegemony in our society, interventionist art does not require the resources of a wealthy corporation or organization to effectively communicate a message. Indeed, almost anyone can create an interventionist art project, yet issues around power and control still exist in interventionist art: Who is creating the work? How are their messages portrayed? To what media do they have access? How do they communicate with their audience? Do people need to be literate or speak a certain language to understand the message? The design process must ensure that the message is widely accessible through plain language, through the relationship between image and text and through the portrayal of people or activities.

GARDEN THE CITY

The Garden the City project took place in the City of Toronto between 2002 and 2003. Its main goals were both environmental (greening the city) and socio-political (encouraging greater food security). Yet it needed a creative means to achieve these goals. I had been entertaining a variety of ideas, including documenting reactions to local rooftop gardens, chronicling the experience of guerrilla gardening and making posters about urban food gathering. As I was taking a mixed-media art course at the time, my interest in collage began to grow and I wanted to explore it as a tool for individual and community expression. It is an art form that tends to be more vernacular and less intimidating than picking up a pencil or paintbrush; an art form accessible to a variety of ages and abilities.

Thus, in a cultural production course that I took at York before I developed my Garden the City project, I designed a collage exercise and questionnaire for two festivals in which people could explore their ideas about urban gardening. Young and old, all could take part. I supplied old magazines, paper, glue and markers and over thirty people participated. Following this visual community input, I eventually settled on a postcard format for my own collage because of the familiarity of the format. Not only are postcards instantly recognizable, but people often move in for a closer view, particularly if something in the image or text piques their curiosity or interest. Additionally, may people place postcards on their refrigerators or give them to friends; if posted or passed on, the cards could repeatedly represent their message. The community collages became voices contributing to my own design. Guidance from my project supervisor Deborah Barndt, my advisor Liette Gilbert and individuals with local organizations such as FoodShare and the Toronto Food Policy Council also helped to shape the project. An offer from a friend to build a website brought the project full circle by providing a source for more information, feedback on the project and contact between myself and the "audience."

Two designs emerged and 1,000 of each design were printed. The postcards were "drop lifted" (dropped or left for others to come across) in random places throughout the city, including libraries, subways, free newspaper boxes and coffee shops. The postcards were intended to intervene in people's daily lives, encouraging those who found them to grow food in the

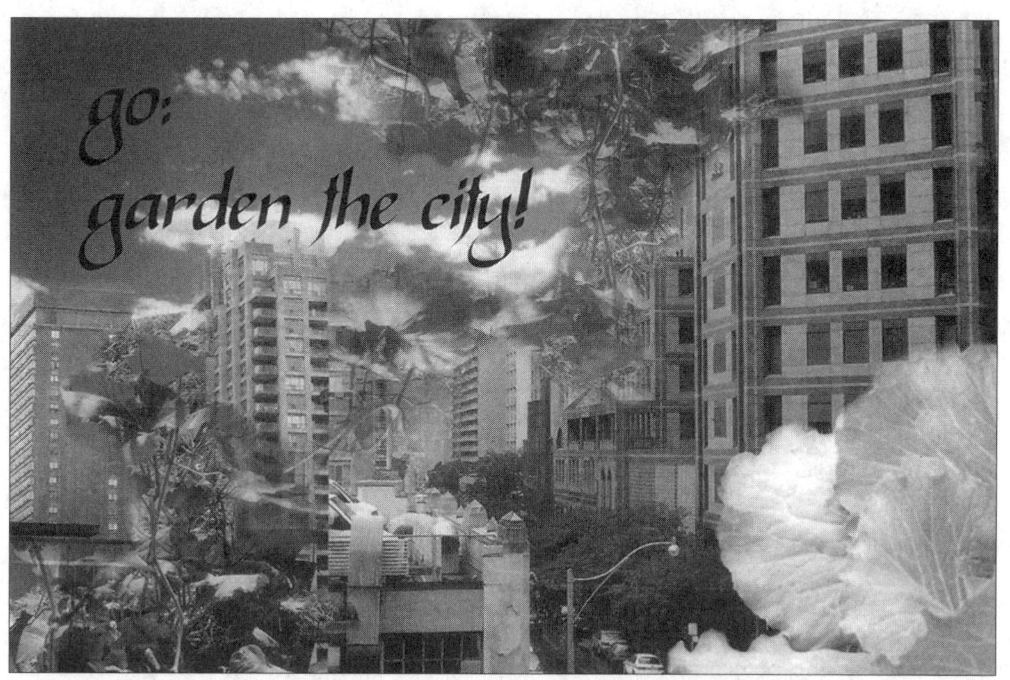
go:
garden the city!

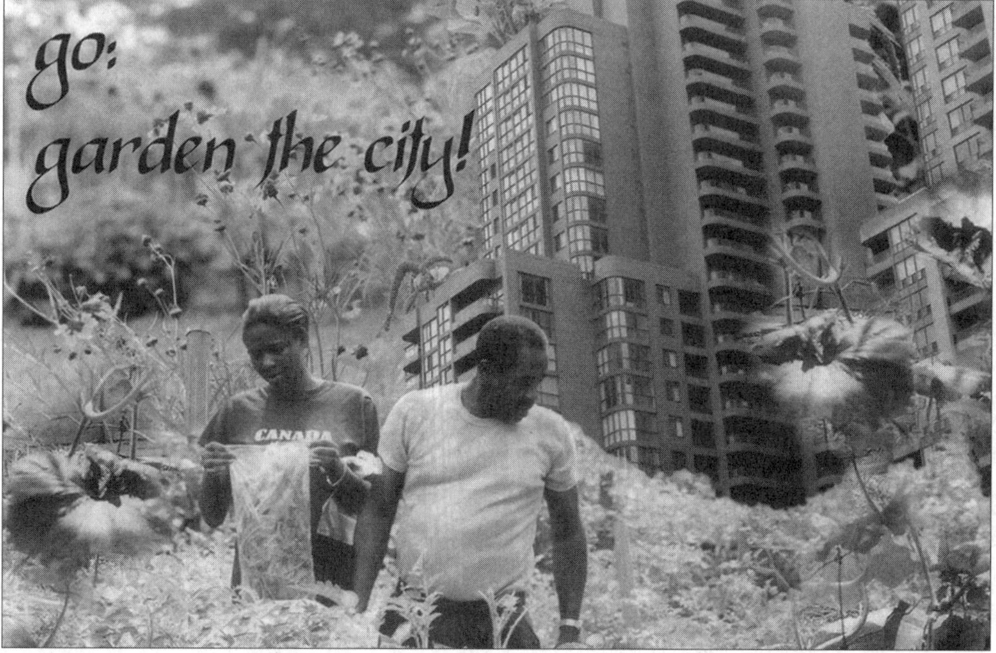
go:
garden the city!
CANADA

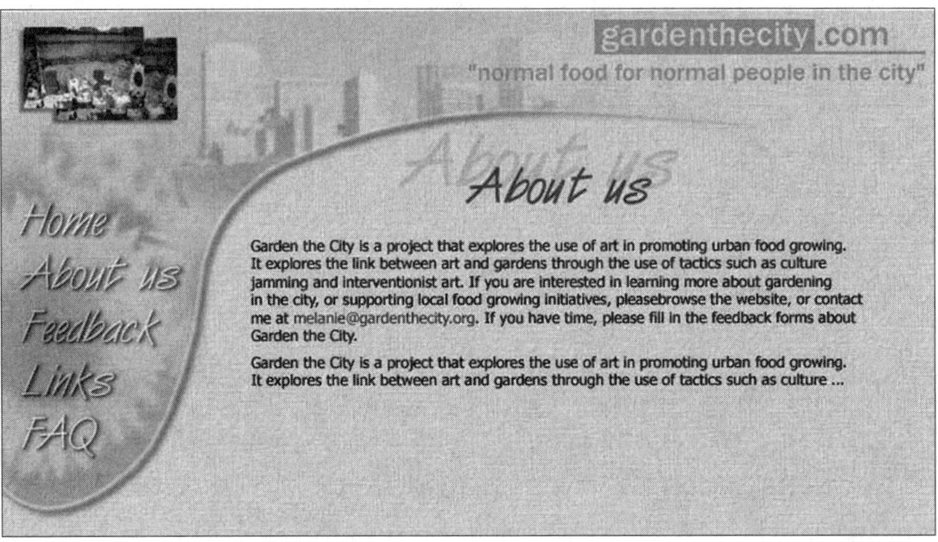

city or at least to visit the Garden the City website where they could learn more about gardening in the city, ask questions and offer their feedback on the project. This two-pronged approach had the advantage of potentially reaching more people and of communicating more information than I could fit onto a postcard. Yet it was also limiting because some people don't have Internet access and are not Internet literate and therefore might dismiss the entire message of the cards.

The cards themselves described gardening in the city using collage and text. The words encouraged people to "Garden the City" and to grow their own food, emphasizing that this could take place alongside or intermingled with flowers. Food growing does not have to be limited to a patch in the backyard. The images were attempting to demonstrate that gardening, particularly in unexpected places and unusual plant combinations, can beautify our urban environments at the same time that they provide food, stimulate shared interests, start conversations and become part of an urban ecology. I wanted the discovery of the Garden the City postcards to be a spontaneous, serendipitous moment in which seeds of vision, and hopefully action, were planted in the viewers' minds. Through these "moments" and through the postcard message that vibrant and creative urban spaces are possible, the Garden the City project attempted to help people imagine other possibilities for city life, for urban sustainability and self-reliance. I wanted to inspire them towards action to make those possibilities a reality.

As with all interventionist art projects, the unique distribution process became part of the message, in addition to the more explicit message(s) contained in the artwork itself. Indeed, the distribution process raised many questions about public and private space, their uses and questions about freedom of expression. What constitutes public space? How public is public space? How free are we as members of the public to express ourselves in those public spaces, within what limits and in what forms of expression? I found myself reflecting on these critical questions as I distributed the postcards. It seems that even where there are public spaces to which most, if not all, citizens have access, there are still restrictions on how that space is used and from which we are expected not to stray. These restrictions come in a variety of forms, from social norms and courtesies to rules and regulations, from policies to laws.

Examples range from Toronto's ban on "squeegee kids" who can no longer approach cars to wash windows for a few quarters, to restrictions around graffiti and sidewalk chalking, to laws which ban public nudity. Some restrictions are in the interest of public safety and most would agree they are beneficial. Others are hotly debated topics among citizens and politicians. In Toronto, the issue of a bylaw to restrict postering on public spaces such a public utility poles has been debated by city council. Proponents of restricting postering and enforcing fines have claimed that it makes the city look dirty and messy when old posters are not removed. Those opposing a restrictive bylaw claim that it is an issue of freedom of expression and exchange in public spaces that should be accessible and free of charge to all in society. When so much of the visible urban surface is taken up with advertising, should there not also be surfaces on which individuals can express themselves?

While some of these restrictions may be matters of common courtesy or decency, others can limit our freedom of expression. They may be simultaneously welcome and unwelcome, as one person's expression may be another's affront, insult or annoyance. Are these limits always reasonable? How could I explore my freedom to express myself artistically and my freedom to exchange ideas? How far could I push the boundaries?

RECLAIMING PUBLIC SPACE

In my search for deeper understanding of pushing boundaries, I became involved with the Toronto Public Space Committee (TPSC),[8] which held its first Art Attack in downtown Toronto on October 17, 2002. The event explored some similar questions I had about who has access to public space. As a prelude to Media Democracy Day, eager participants were provided with a plethora of crayons, chalk and markers to design and create their own messages on giant sheets of construction paper that would be posted around the city. Conveniently, the paper came in two sizes — one size fit nicely over ads in bus shelters, the second size fit over the ad space on public garbage bins. As Dave Meslin, founder of the TPSC stated, the "Art Attack" was about taking back public space: "What we have right now is a price tag on freedom of expression. So if you can afford $20,000 to put up a billboard, then you can express yourself."[9]

Art Attack was specifically held in opposition to the proposed anti-postering bylaw in Toronto that would limit posters in public spaces, particularly on utility poles, which are commonly used by citizens in many cities to post flyers, posters and notices. However, Art Attack transcended simple opposition to limits on postering. By claiming space in public places for displaying art, Art Attack questioned public access to freedom of expression, the corporate power to control what we see and read in public spaces and the edict of consumerism (want/need/buy) put forth by those corporate powers. According to Dale Duncan in *NOW* Magazine's coverage of the event, "whatever is being created here isn't being put up for the purpose of selling a product. It won't be an image that's been designed through extensive studies of the consumption practices and preferences of a target audience. It will be made to create dialogue."[10] Thinking about it, I realized that outside of utility poles and community information boards there are very few public spaces where I can engage in a visual dialogue with others ... for free.

TRANSFORMATION THROUGH DIALOGUE

While taking part in creative interventions such as Art Attack can inspire visual dialogues and bring about a sense of empowerment, issues of power and control are not eliminated simply by "taking back" the production process and expressing oneself. There are still deeper questions to be asked: Who has the resources and ability to start or continue such a dialogue? Who is it aimed at? Who is left out in the process?

Indeed, as with many forms of activism, it is often more effective when more than one approach is used. Interventionist art becomes one of many approaches towards activism, part of a "tool kit" that activists can use in combination with other approaches to awareness-raising and communication. During my project, after drop lifting postcards across the city and dealing with my own discomfort over the quasi-legal status of leaving things in spaces not meant for active expression and communication, I still had many postcards left. So I chose to broaden my original intentions and leave my postcards on information boards, window ledges and countertops — those public and private spaces that are designed to facilitate this type of public "conversation." Limiting oneself to only one approach also limits the scope of one's audience. Thus, the project expanded. But a question remained: Was this really a conversation or was it more of a one-way monologue, similar to that of advertising?

The Garden the City images and text that I created evolved from a process in which members of the public created their own collages and answered a questionnaire. The products of these sessions shaped the final postcards and their message. While I was the creator of the cards, and the message was entirely filtered through me, the postcards were thus already part of a conversation begun with those earlier collages and questionnaires. I saw this dialogue as being continued through the Garden the City website, which featured a feedback page, an explanation of the project and an email address encouraging people to share opinions and ask questions.

Not all interventionist art projects include opportunities for audience feedback, and in a sense, a feedback mechanism can take away from the ephemeral, spontaneous moment of interaction with the project. But feedback can take a number of forms, being as explicit or remaining as mysterious as the artist or activist desires. Interestingly, however, interventionist art projects are usually considered complete only upon the discovery of or audience interaction with the project. With no monitor or feedback mechanism, the creator is unaware of all interaction with the project. Sometimes this is part of the beauty of the project. Other times monitoring and feedback become an integral part of the project. Using video cameras, contact information (email, website), spaces for comment (on a wall, in a book, etc.) or perhaps a concurrent art show in a more formal space are common means of encouraging feedback and making the audience part of a dialogue rather than simply receivers of a message. Whether or not this is desirable depends on the message, its context and the author's intent or vision.

Interventionist art does integrate well with activism, but as with all types of activism it presents challenges and raises important questions. The practice is messy, experimental and non-conforming. But this slipperiness is part of the beauty of art and part of the marriage between art and activism. Pushing boundaries is what allows new ideas to flourish and inspire others to take their own action and to communicate in unique ways.

While the tensions remain between public and private space, between freedom of expression and societal laws and norms, between the expected and the unexpected in distribution methods, and in seeking "results" in an ephemeral practice, these are issues to be further explored, rather than problems to be "solved." It is also valuable to realise that public space for expression may not be as limitless as we think it is. Blending art and activism to reach people in new and innovative ways can create interesting contradictions, such as "result-oriented interventionist art," and with this comes new potential for inspiring thought and effecting change.

Transformation, whether in people's minds or their actions, is never easy nor straightforward, and it is usually generated by more than one approach. Interventionist art can bring together art and activism moving people toward dialogue and action. As artist Lisa Mark notes, not only do "these encounters urge us to give pause but, beyond that, they suggest a fantastical sub-strata of reflection and possibility beneath the quotidian crust of city life."[11] Writer Milenko Matanovic echoes the hope of creative projects when he states, "artists try things out, fail, pick themselves up, work fiercely, and in the end, the work may still fall short. There are no guarantees. Still, the idiosyncratic gifts of the artist, with all their uncertainties, may be exactly what we need to create a more humane, sustainable and beautiful world."[12]

It is not known if those individuals who encountered a Garden the City postcard began to grow food in their yard or on their balcony or joined a community garden, although several email messages sent to the website (no longer operational) indicated that this was likely. Additionally, it did facilitate discussion and exploration of these ideas and how to turn them into action, particularly within the City of Toronto. Most significantly, it demonstrated that individuals or organizations can find creative ways to reach people and attempt to effect change, to move beyond what is usual. It is these attempts, however messy or slippery they may be, that allow glimpses of that fantastical sub-strata beneath everyday, conventional city existence.

NOTES

I would like to dedicate this chapter to my mom who has inspired me in the arts since I was a child, and to my dad who has engendered in me a commitment to social justice, gardening and critical thinking.

1. Suzanne Lacy, "Seeing Mud Houses," in Kim Pruesse, ed., *Accidental Audience: Urban Interventions by Artists* (Toronto: Offsite Collective, 1999), 70.
2. Kim Pruesse, "Introduction," in Pruesse, ed., *Accidental Audience*, 9.
3. Gavin Hodge, *Zygosis Montage: John Heartfield and the Political Image* (New York: First Run/Icarus Films, 1991), video-recording. His original name was Helmut Heizfelde.
4. Debord's most popular work which inspired the Situationist movement and many others after is *The Society of the Spectacle.*
5. Guerrilla Girls, *Confessions of the Guerrilla Girls: How a Bunch of Masked Avengers Fight Sexism and Racism in the Art World with Facts, Humor and Fake Fur* (New York: HarperCollins Press, 1995).
6. Kalle Lasn, *Culture Jam: How to Reverse America's Suicidal Consumer Binge — And Why We Must* (New York: Quill, 1999); Naomi Klein, *No Logo: Taking Aim at the Brand Bullies* (Toronto: Vintage Canada, 2000), 279–310.
7. Klein, *No Logo*, 311–324.
8. See Toronto Public Space Committee at www.publicspace.ca for current Art Attack projects.

9. Catherine Porter, "Activists Take on Poster Bylaw," *Toronto Star*, 21 October 2002. Retrieved 13 May 20003 from www.publicspace.ca/artattackstar.htm.

10. Dale Duncan, "Ads for Art's sake, Lousy Promo Wastes Yellow," in *NOW* Magazine, 24 November 2002. Retrieved 13 May 2003 from www. nowtoronto.com/issues/ 2002-10-24/news_story6.php.

11. Lisa Gabrielle Mark, "The Secret Life of the City," in Pruesse, ed., *Accidental Audience*, 15.

12. Milenko Matanovic, "Turning the Sword," *Yes! A Journal of Positive Futures* 22 (Summer 2002), 15.

CHAPTER 11

Salmon Tales:

ECO-ART ACTIVISM

Aileen Penner, Jacinda Mack & Lee Bensted

"Telling Salmon Tales" is a collaborative and participatory arts-informed research project that explores the intersections of salmon and human lives. Each of us has strong roots in British Columbia,[1] and we came together in a graduate course to co-create an installation of silk-screened, salmon-themed banners for York University's annual Eco-Art and Media Festival. We were primarily motivated by a shared history of growing up near wild salmon rivers and our increasing concerns over the destructive practice of salmon farming on BC's coasts. Through our exhibit we hoped to provoke critical and creative dialogue about salmon–human relationships and to challenge dominant and reductionist understandings of salmon as mere sources of protein or profit. What began as an arts-informed research project, however, has now shifted towards community art, activism and education in a community context. In this chapter we explore visual art as an important element in counter-hegemonic struggle. Although other forms of signification like academic prose or journalistic reporting are crucial in disrupting dominant discourses, we argue that visual art allows us to see and experience the world in a radically different way. It also allows us to focus on why salmon matter.

Salmon are a keystone species. That is to say, many ecosystems and animals (forests, bears, eagles) and humans depend on them. In BC, wild salmon are under threat from overfishing, habitat destruction and the effects of climate change. In recent years another threat has emerged: farming Atlantic salmon in Pacific waters. Industrial salmon farming involves raising salmon in floating net-cage pens in the ocean. This practice has been linked to ecological damage through the spread of parasites to wild fish, fish escapees competing with wild salmon and fish excrement and antibiotic accumulation under net pens that smother other sea life. Farmed salmon also pose a risk to human health; studies have found high levels of PCBs and other chemicals in the farmed fish. In addition, many of these fish farms are located in traditional territory never ceded by First Nations. Finally, there is the ethical question of turning wild creatures into what are, in effect, protein machines.

TRANSFORMING RELATIONSHIPS TO SALMON

Thomas King argues that stories are all we are; we can't understand the world or ourselves without telling a story.[2] Every day we tell ourselves, or are told, stories about how the world works. Thus, as King notes, we need to be careful of the stories we tell. We understand telling stories as a political act that is integral to educating for social and environmental justice. Drawing on feminist and Aboriginal research methodologies, as well as popular education and community arts practices, we share stories through our art and invite the audience to become co-participants by sharing their own experiences and ideas.

Our arts-based activism is an effort to challenge hegemony. Hegemony is the process by which discourse (or a political exchange of ideas) solidifies and is seen as "natural" or as "common sense." Hegemony is always an active process where meaning is fixed in particular ways and for particular interests. Often, this struggle reinforces unequal relations of power. For example, while there are many ways of understanding salmon, it is commonly understood as a foodstuff, a commodity or a natural resource. In the case of BC salmon farming, the industry has worked to naturalize a number of narratives: farmed salmon as the economic saviour of small, coastal communities; as the food to prevent world hunger; as a reliable source of protein and other healthy nutrients; and as the solution to overfishing of wild salmon stocks.

Resisting hegemony is also an active process.[3] Through textile art we have attempted to challenge some of these "common-sensical" ways of understanding both wild and farmed salmon and to open up spaces for the creation and understanding of new and less destructive meanings.

In recalling how our relationships with salmon were formed (or transformed), we recognized moments of embodied and experiential learning. We agreed that a traditional academic research project could not capture this affective dimension. Arts-informed methods offered greater possibilities to engage ourselves and the audience in a multi-sensory and cross-cultural way. We chose a visual arts experiment that combined silk-screening and textile art with creative storytelling. The result was research transformed into collaborative art-making, text into stories and readers/viewers into participants and active witnesses of history. As Butler-Kisber argues, "form mediates understanding,"[4] and by using arts-based methods we hoped to evoke emotions that tend to be excluded from "objective" studies; we wanted to provoke the imagination to conjure up new possibilities. What follows is a detailed description of the four banners that make up this installation, each of us speaks to our own visual representations of and personal connections to salmon.

Jacinda's Banner: Colonization of the Salmon People

The "Colonization of the Salmon People" speaks to the ongoing struggles that Aboriginal people face, in particular those of the Nuxalk Nation on the Northwest Coast. Self-described as Salmon People, we, the Nuxalkmc, maintain that our connection to salmon is beyond sustenance; it carries significant cultural, spiritual and social importance in understanding the world and our place in it. The Salmon People are also the storied beings of the rivers and oceans who now face similar experiences with imposed sickness and devastation, displacement and colonization. The banner speaks to the interconnectedness and equal value of the worlds above and below water.

The banner is in the form of a totem pole, our witness to the burden of history and associated responsibilities of knowledge bestowed. The backdrop of the banner is the grey "blanket of colonization," similar to those used in residential schools and by early traders. It is covered in splattered red paint, the blood of past and present Salmon People and signifies the

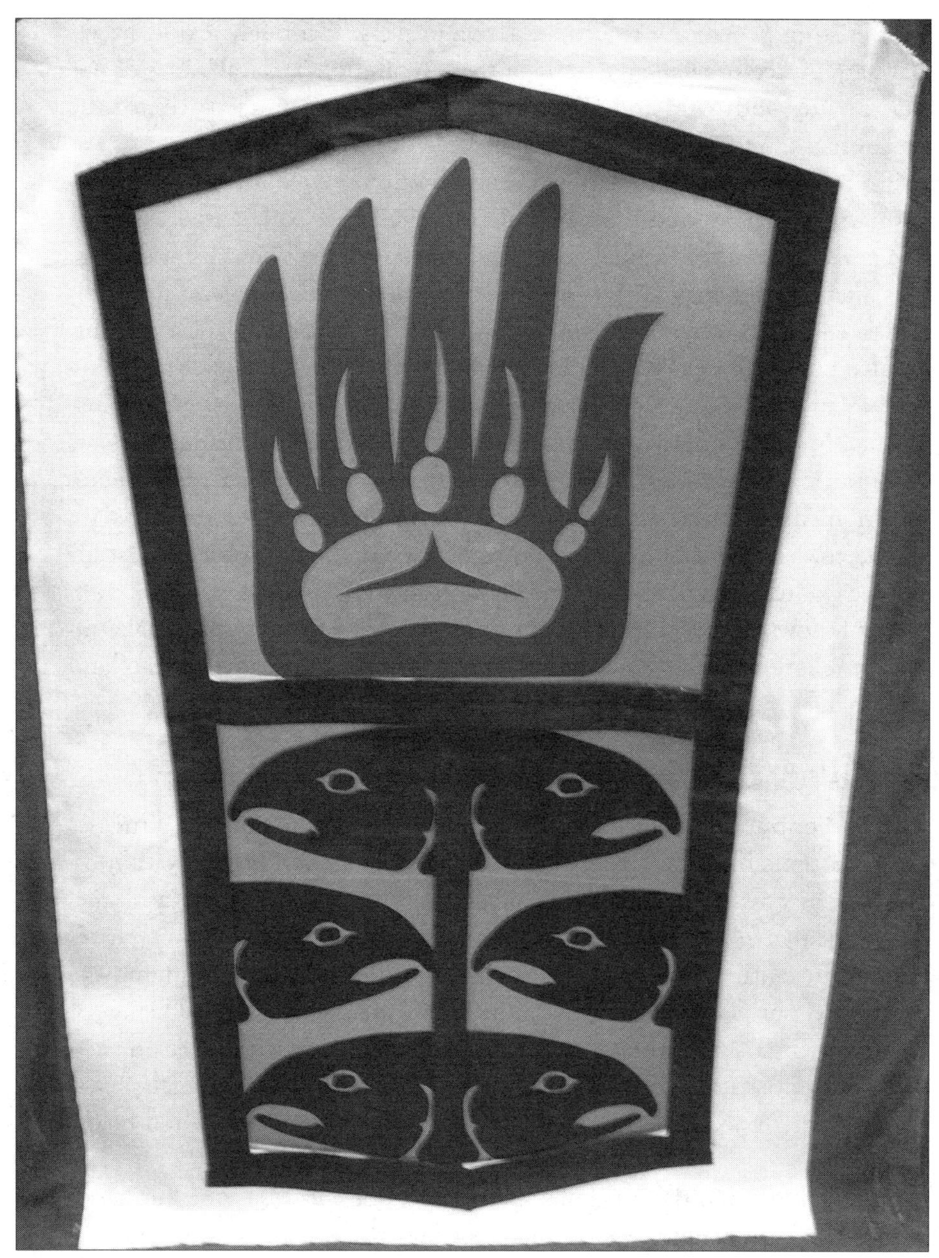

Jacinda's Banner/Bear Clan and Salmon

harsh realities of sickness, grief and loss that continue to plague us. At the top of the pole is the sun, on whose eyelashes the first Nuxalkmc slid to Earth under the cloaks of animals. The sun symbolizes life and our spiritual connections within the natural world. Within the life-giving sun is the cedar tree, whose roots nestle fragile salmon eggs, nourishing creatures of land and sea, forests above and waters below. Beneath the sun is the Grizzly Bear with a salmon in its stomach, representing my family and the symbiotic relationship of salmon with many other beings and intersecting life systems. Interrupting the story is a salmon pen, hostile and toxic, warning us of the dangers of breeding a sick and soulless being; with no connection to the world in which it lives. The final image of a potlatch copper signifies wealth and regeneration.[5] Salmon is the foundation, upholding a people, culture and relationship to the Earth, contradicting the commodity value of salmon in capitalist societies. The final image of the human hand mingled with the bear paw signifies my personal struggle and commitment to protecting what it means to be one of the Salmon People. Although much of the banner tells a raw truth, it remains hopeful, shining its copper light on issues that affect us all, and for which we are all responsible.

Aileen's Banner: Crossing (Disciplinary) Boundaries

As a child growing up in BC's interior, I had the fortune of living near some of the most productive salmon rivers in the province, and the misfortune of witnessing the large-scale damming of those rivers. This contradictory experience only emphasized the disconnect between industrialized society and the natural world, and I see these same processes at work in industrial salmon farming today.

"Crossing (Disciplinary) Boundaries" looks at the relationship between humans, nature and technoscience in the salmon farming debate. My banner highlights the notion that in order for humans to treat salmon as machines, there is a profound disconnection that must take place in discourse that encourages us to see these storied beings only as commodities. I wanted to emphasize themes such as the role of science in salmon research as well as the multiple disciplines involved in any salmon research. I chose two central images: the machine salmon and the handmade ladders connecting a fragmented, spawning sockeye salmon.

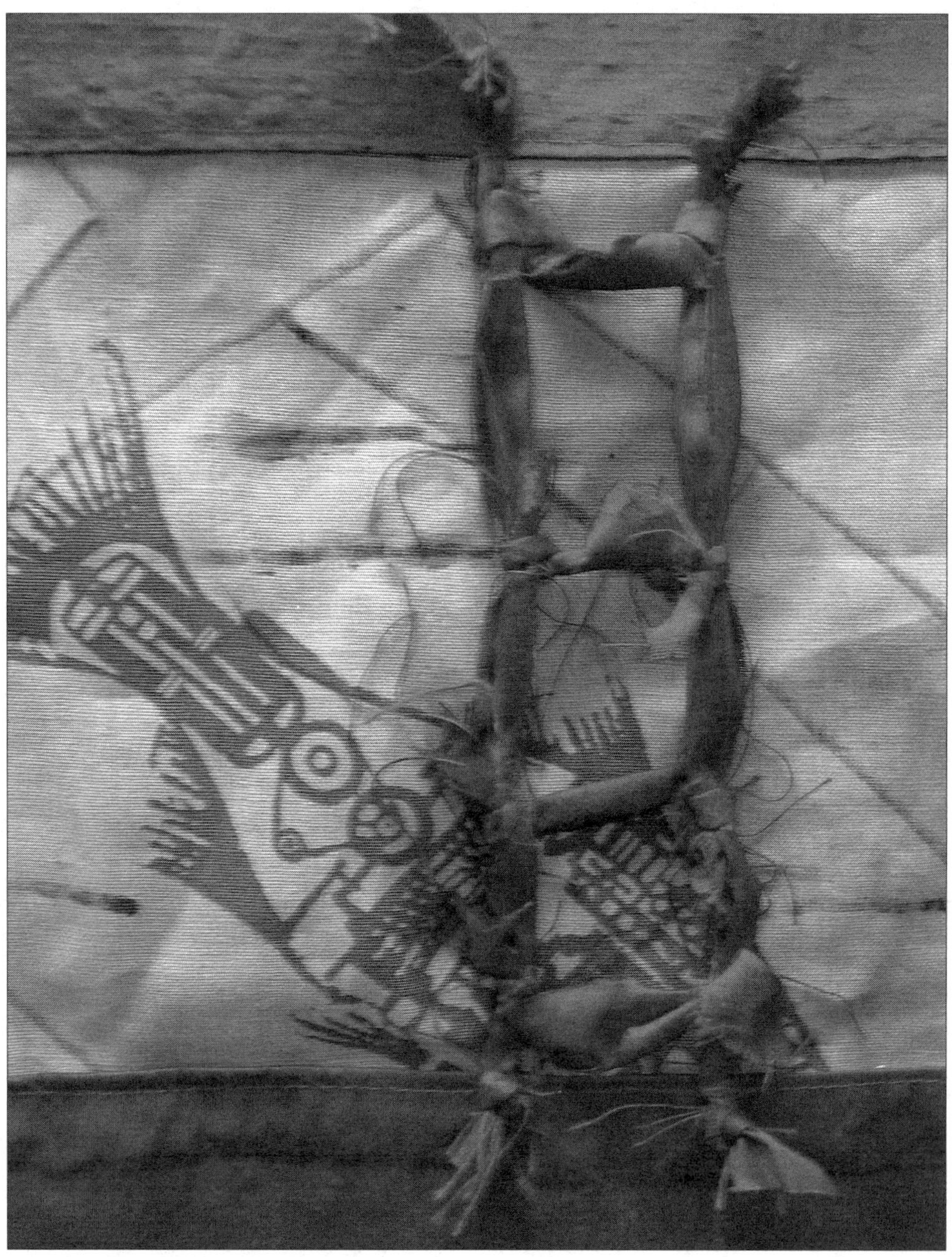

Aileen's Banner/Fragmented and commodified salmon.

The mechanical salmon image represents a dangerous story that, once let loose in the world, will claim the mantle of Truth. This reductionist science salmon story, absent of responsibility, takes knowledge of the part and extends and universalizes it to the whole. These totalizing stories pretend to be disconnected from power and politics. The green machine salmon draws our attention to the process that brings the farmed salmon to the supermarket shelf.

The ladder image has two aspects. First, for decades, humans have constructed fish ladders to help spawning salmon bypass dams and other barriers on the river. Second, the ladder metaphor encourages us to think about salmon across disciplines. Salmon conservation tends to be discipline-specific. Scientists and resource managers talk to one another but rarely speak about the social, that is, the concerns of social science, political science, philosophy and ethics. I was also conscious of the fact that the language I chose to speak in (i.e., visual art) often has to struggle for recognition in the "hard sciences" (e.g., biology). Thus, our project concerns the ladders we have to build to speak across differences, just as the future of wild salmon depends on conversations across disciplines and world views. But, like the twisted and knotted raw red silk of the ladders in my banner, these intercultural, interdisciplinary ladders are handmade, flimsy, experimental and contingent.

Lee's Banner: Regeneration Stories

"Regeneration Stories" tells a story that revalues processes of regeneration in and among humans and others. In the course of my graduate research, I discovered that salmon have shaped my family's history on the BC coast for four generations. My resistance to industrial salmon farming practices deepened as I explored this history through conversations with my grandmother about her childhood at the Harrison Lake salmon hatchery and recalled my own childhood experiences of wild salmon conservation. It was, however, a story from my father's struggle with cancer in 1998 that moved me to consider this resistance within the biological, political and spiritual framework of regeneration.

During the last few months of his life, my dad had chosen wild salmon to accompany him, metaphorically, in his upstream journey against cancer.

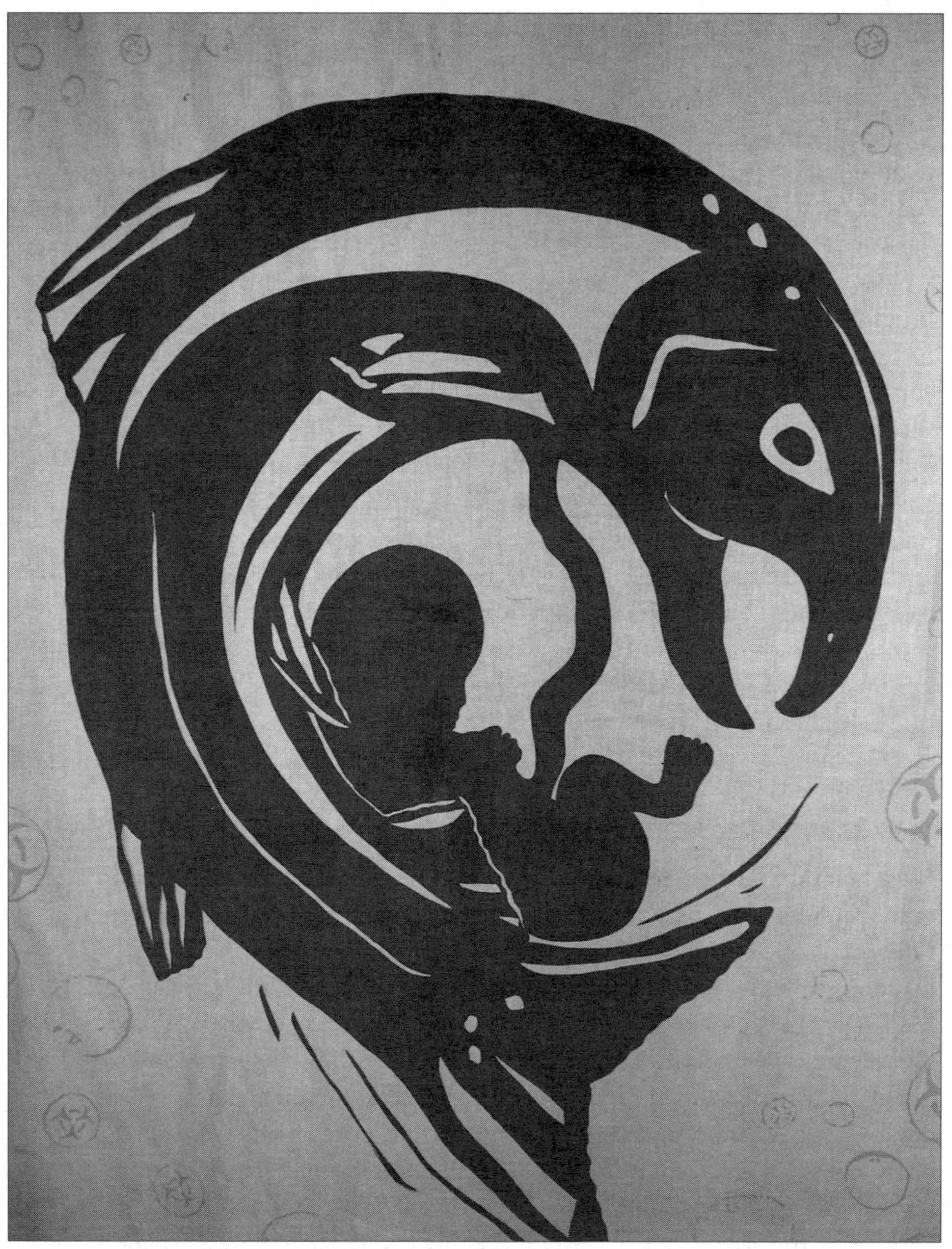

Lee's Banner/Human Fetus in Salmon

He visualized wild salmon swimming through his body, devouring every cancerous cell in sight. And like the salmon, his body returned in death to replenish the river and ocean waters off the BC coast. Several years later I came to understand this transformation as a profoundly spiritual and political act, a counter story to the Western reductionist or machine-view of the world (and salmon) that prioritizes the independence of human beings from the natural world.

The banner has soft-sculpture tree roots that transform into human arteries and veins, depicting the intimate interconnections between humans and the environment. Water is the life-blood that nurtures us at birth, flows through our bodies, the forests, air, rivers, oceans and salmon. Air bubbles silk-screened with the biohazard symbol inside suggest all is not well in this ecosystem. Toxins, cancers and other chemicals threaten the health of our internal and surrounding environment. The central image, an adult salmon curled protectively around a human fetus suggests that salmon — bearers of embodied, regenerative wisdom — are also *our* protectors.

Retelling: Weaving Many Truths

Recognizing the partiality of all stories, we wanted to piece together the salmon stories, always recognizing that there is never one grand narrative. The fourth banner is a woven tapestry of cloth, ideas, stories and words, a radical retelling of common-sense ideas about salmon. For the weave, we chose pieces of fabric (used in making our individual banners); we wanted the retelling to act as a collage of material, ideas and stories. The cedar mat weave was inspired by Jacinda's story of the Nuxalk tradition of placing the first salmon that comes up the river on woven cedar, prepared by the women in the community and offered as a gift. The salmon offer themselves as gift to humans, with the understanding that people must return the offering with a ceremony to ensure the return of salmon year after year.

Many stories emerged (and continue to emerge) as part of the interactive nature of the fourth banner. We invited participants to add their own salmon stories to the collaborative banner with fish hooks and safety pins. Notable stories included: "How I became an anti-capitalist: my one-man strike against the salmon processing industry," a photo story of a First Nations salmon BBQ and a retelling of a chiropractor who accepted salmon (the only currency available) in exchange for his services.

Another important goal of our project is to spark personal and political activism to boycott farmed salmon. At each event, we make available information about destructive practices of industrial fish farming. We also print a series of T-shirts and canvas tote bags with explicit anti-farmed salmon/pro-wild salmon messages in order to provoke discussion and critical engagement with the issues and ideas of our project and its political stance.

A Unique Experiment in Art Activism

The unique collaboration behind "Telling Salmon Tales" was a form of research as pedagogy and political action. We became textile artists/activists by exploring how to silkscreen, sew and weave. We also shared our diverse perspectives on salmon with each other as we co-created the installation. Together we explored how to graphically capture diverse messages about salmon and then watch the images speak in ways we had not considered. Finally, we taught and learned from each other through an ongoing dialectic of action and reflection. Our commitment to engage not only the benefits but also the inevitable tensions of collaborative work — such as questions around representation, leadership and expectations regarding process and the final product — has produced a close friendship among all of us.

We chose to incorporate stories because they engage us in an active dialogue, one where the readers, writers and artists make meaning together. The banners are also in conversation with each other and with the stories pinned to them. Each time we install our exhibit in a new space, we host an artists' talk. The interactive aspect of our project contributes to its uncertain, surprising and open-ended evolution. Stories added to the fourth woven banner move the textual and visual discussion into new areas, which in turn provoke an evolving dialogue among co-participants and readers. Like the totem pole, we become witnesses of these (hi)stories, and the stories we choose to tell about them are our inheritance and responsibility.

"Telling Salmon Tales" is also an ongoing experiment in eco-art activism. Although the project was initiated in an academic setting, it now continues to move into diverse community spaces. It transcends the often-strict boundaries of academia, which often promotes competitive individuality and abstract thought at the expense of concrete practice. Alternatively, the project is a regeneration and reclamation of community through its

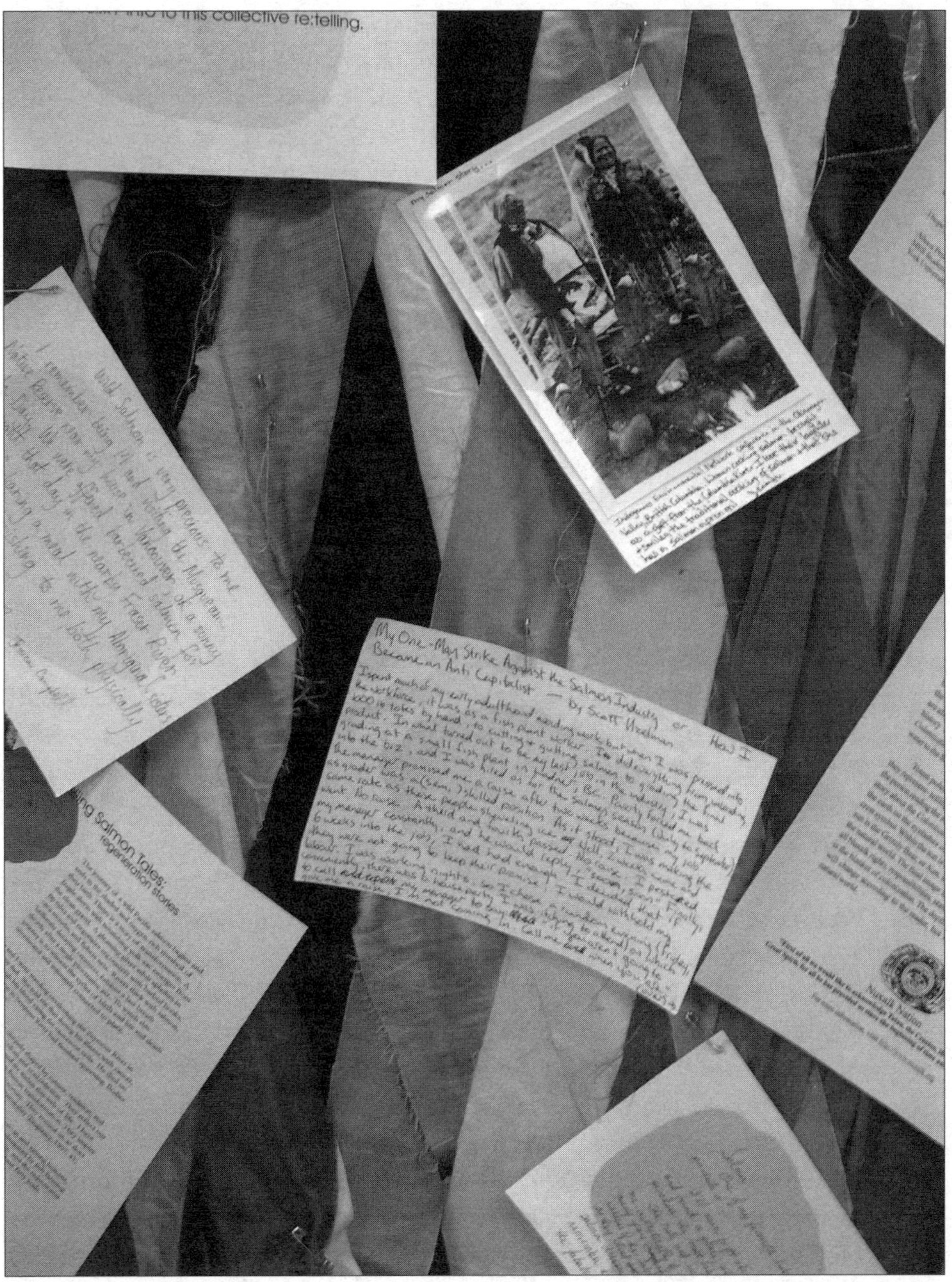

Fourth Banner/Weaving New Tales

inclusiveness of shared ideas and personal experiences. Participation by local communities is, in effect, direct action because participation provokes awareness and acknowledges individual and collective responsibilities and relationships.

Our challenge is to encourage the understanding that salmon–human relationships are personal *and* political. The controversy over salmon farming is but one example of a global trend towards the commodification and de-spiritualization of the natural world and our relationship to it. We chose salmon because they connect us to a place and home, and to each other. Salmon are a part of who we are, as British Columbians of European descent and as a Nuxalk woman. The collaboration of our efforts highlights the understanding that although we may have different histories and experiences, we are all connected and share in the responsibilities for the stories we tell.

"Telling Salmon Tales" grows and changes every time we install it in a new space. One of its greatest strengths is the layered understanding that occurs through people's interaction with the project. Discussions, ideas, interpretations and stories continue to emerge, encouraging people to think differently about salmon. The woven banner, in particular, speaks to the power of collaboration and collective voice so necessary in activism.

Since its inception in February 2004, "Telling Salmon Tales" has been exhibited several times. It has appeared at the Eco-Art and Media Festival at York University; the Ontario Institute for Studies in Education Festival at York University; the Ontario Institute for Studies in Education (OISE)/University of Toronto student research conference; the Spirit Matters: Wisdom Traditions and the "Great Work" Conference at OISE's Transformative Learning Centre; and at From Agriculture to Culture: The Social Transformation of Food Conference in New York City.

"Telling Salmon Tales" continues to have a presence in the community. In the summer of 2005, it was the centrepiece of a two-month long exhibit at CityScape Community Art Space in North Vancouver, a gallery dedicated to local community arts and education. We collaborated with storytellers, elementary students and the local community through artists' talks and shadow puppet workshops about the wild salmon lifecycle. As researchers/artists/activists/educators, we consider this shifting terrain with optimism and ongoing inquiry. It is our hope that the project can serve as pedagogy of example, and that it can inspire others to take up arts-based practices and other non-traditional forms of activism, research and education.

NOTES

Aileen, Jacinda and Lee dedicate this chapter "to the wild salmon."

1. Although "British Columbia" is a colonial label contested by sovereign First Nations of the Northwest Coast and beyond, it is used here for simplicity in describing a geographical and political area that is home to Pacific salmon species and those who depend on them.
2. Thomas King, *The Truth about Stories* (Toronto: Anansi Press, 2003), 32.
3. dian marino, *Wild Garden* (Toronto: Between the Lines, 1997), 103–112.
4. L. Butler-Kisber, "Artful Portrayals in Qualitative Inquiry: The Road to Found Poetry and Beyond," *The Alberta Journal of Educational Research* 48, no. 3 (Fall 2002), 230.
5. A potlatch copper is a sheet of copper formed into a plaque with carved figures etched into its surface. These figures are taken from the chief's *smayusta*, or creation story, depicting familial wealth and responsibilities. It is used at potlatches, the huge community gatherings hosted by a chief to commemorate and celebrate name-giving, memorials and other important family events.

CHAPTER 12

Confessions of a Community Artist:

A LETTER TO MY FELLOW EARTHWORKERS

Sau Wai Tai

For three months in 2002, I facilitated a group of eight York University students in the making of earthballs. They were rounded objects of various sizes made of earth and straw. We created them by fingering through piles of soil, tramping on and shaping them into spheres both large and small. Then, we packed these earthballs with wildflower and wild grass seeds and placed them at select locations around campus. Close to these earthballs were installations that unmasked stories about nature, women and people of colour in this place. The work was named Earthballs and Murmurs of a Place, and the group was known as the Earthworkers. This chapter is a letter that I have written to the group members, sharing with them my reflections on the experience we shared when we were together. The letter is also my special thanks to Mina Au, Tonya Graham, Kristine Kemmel, Kari Kokko, Giovanna Luisi, Melissa Valja and Tzah Yavin for their partnership and ardent work, as well as to many others who helped to make this earthly dream possible.

Dear Fellow Earthworkers:

Traces of the earthballs we made together at York University are probably now hard to find. The large ones tumbled and left scar-like markings behind. The small ones simply dissolved and returned to the soil. The wildflower seeds that we embedded in them might have bloomed once or twice and perhaps have established themselves for those that were placed at remote or less visible locations, covering the scars like a healing process. The wildflower seeds that arrived with the earthballs at more central locations and took root had a lesser fate. Their growth was forbidden and they were mowed down by the maintenance workers to keep the university's prominent green spaces manicured and monocultural. The installations that were set up close to these earthballs were removed by the maintenance people; others disintegrated on their own. I heard disappointment in some of your voices, when it seemed our earthballs had not altered the main landscape of the campus. It took us a while to come to terms with this reality, even though we knew that wildness was not permitted in this highly charged symbolic place. I managed to find comfort in knowing that we had helped stage an untamed performance for the university.

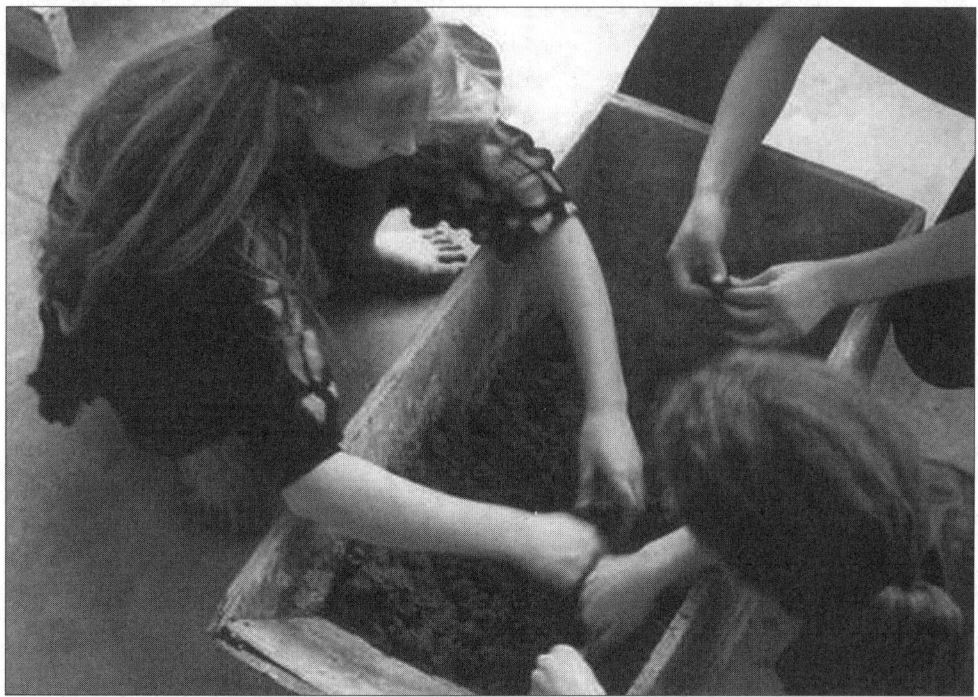

Kari and others working wildflower and wild grass seeds into the top soil.

It might have been easier for me to deal with this disappointment than for most of you, because part of my drive behind this place-based endeavour was to unmask the power, images and hidden stories embedded in this campus. This project addressed a deep need within me. I had felt alienated and out of place here, and I knew I was not the only one who felt that way. Over 75 per cent of the people I interviewed on campus for an earlier study had indicated that they were also unhappy here and they tried to spend as little time on campus as possible.[1] They were also feeling alienated by the layout of this campus and had very little sense of belonging. Like you and me, they desired change. I felt a need to look at the roots of this alienation and to share this process with other members of the university community.

As I researched the causes of this alienation, I found that many places are created to serve authorities and to maintain a certain order in a society. These placess are often produced by professionals trained under Cartesian principles who tend to embrace a fragmented and hierarchical world view and regard humans as autonomous individuals. These professionals are not trained to create a space that fosters community and connectivity, but rather geographical ambience. A city, for example, often reflects the spirit of the nation and the dominant mentalities of its dwellers.[2] Yet it is often designed to lead people into believing that life is a series of isolated events, as its design has no sense of context.[3] As Eleanor Hanley says, life cannot be isolated from eco-social location. Everything we do is set in ecological-historical-social contexts as part of the process of coming into being.[4] In other words, no space is merely geographical. A place is often a product of heightened rhetoric, and the images that are created and consumed as signs that control our psyche, bodies and mind by producing desires and fears.[5] A university campus is not exempted from this complicity. David Orr points out that a typical university campus is designed and built like a modern city, with a hidden agenda to teach individuality and to prevent the development of a sense of place, love for nature and community. It does so by hiding certain histories and by teaching a fragmented world view that fosters ignorance and defiance.[6]

At York, the most important or heavily used green space is the Common. It is surrounded by a shopping mall, Vari Hall — the main campus building known for its dome-shaped representation of this particular ivory tower

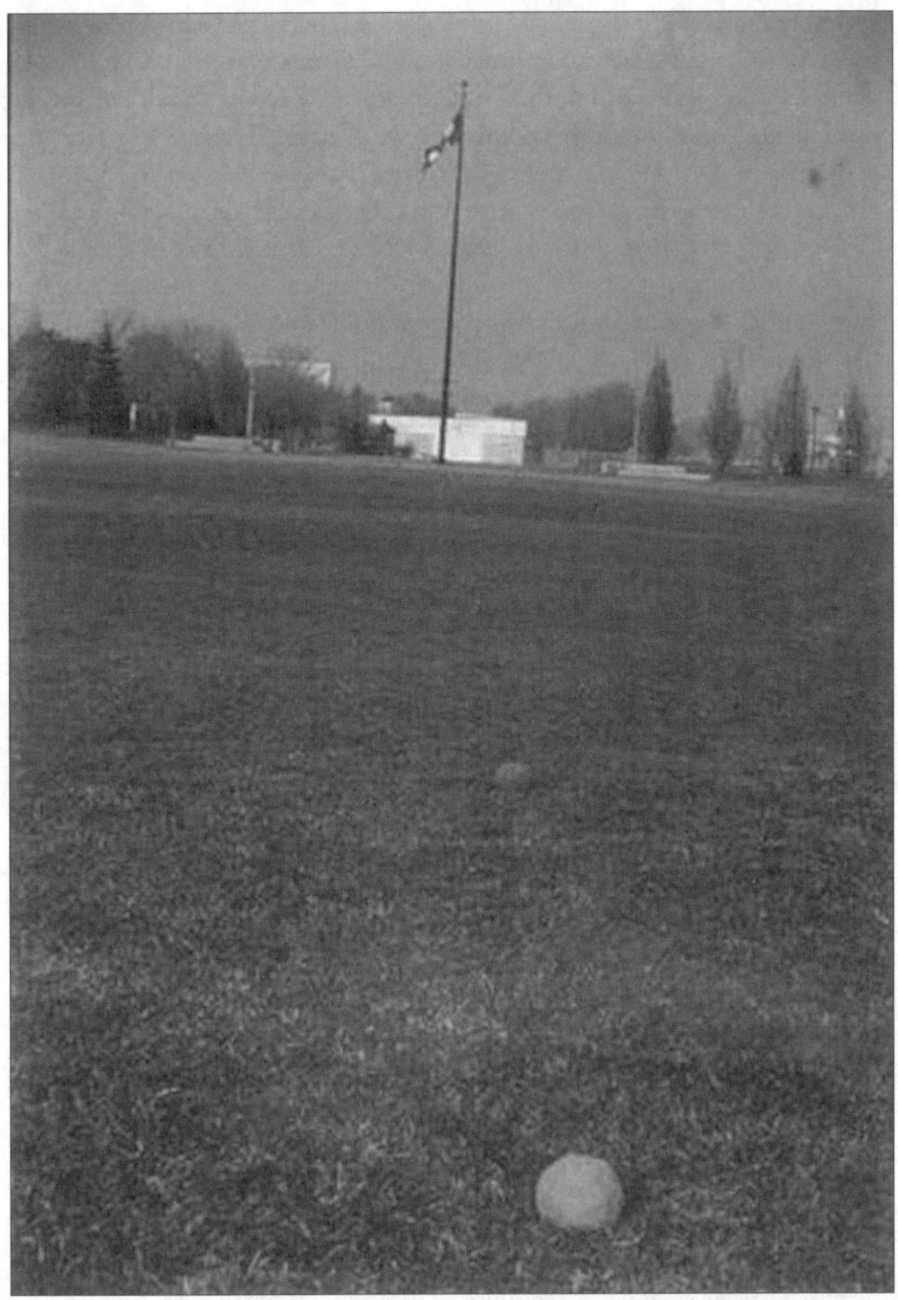

The mini earthballs connect to the national flagpole at Varsi Hall.

— and a national flag pole. These major landmarks are signs produced by a web of power, namely, consumerism, knowledge power and state power, and they are there to reinforce one another. When I was doing my research regarding the past and the present of this university, I was further confronted by other connected sources of power ingrained in this place, including naturism, racism, sexism and other forces that dichotomized the world in hierarchical orders as described by ecofeminists.[7] As I looked at the planning and archives documents of this university and its adjacent area, and as I walked around the place and talked to the local community, I encountered hidden histories and forgotten stories that tell tales of the obscured power that affected the environment, women, people of colour and other disadvantaged groups. I became a witness with an obligation to draw attention to this place and to make space to bring these stories above ground. I did not mention this when I first invited you to the project, I only described the processes and what I intended to co-create. It's not that I wanted to mislead anyone, I just didn't want my agenda to prevent you from using the project for your needs or from making your own discoveries.

Creating Earthworkers

None of us Earthworkers were from Toronto. We were either from overseas or from smaller towns in Ontario. Most of us were women, and the most dedicated to the project were the women among us. All of us seemed to need something beyond what York's environment offered. We were also not happy that the campus was not addressing nature's needs. We started with a desire for alternative ecology and aesthetics in the place of York's universal design that gave rise to the sense of placelessness. We dreamed of earthballs and wildflowers, of wanting to be in touch with earth. We joined the project for fun, for comfort, to regress or to progress, depending on who we were. Kari relished the warmth and soft touch of the soil, and her quiet intimate moments with it. Tonya enjoyed being in the heart of a life-giving miracle that would continue to grow. Mina was making up for her lost opportunities to know nature. She had never been allowed to swim in Macau's murky estuary water. Tzahi, a pro-peace Jewish nuclear scientist from Israel, was there to play like a little boy. The mud pool was a play space with no nuclear weapon, no hometown politics and no grown-ups.

He wrote after one session, "I felt like a little boy. I wanted to throw clay on everyone. I wanted to sit naked in the clay."

We converged and created a space for the group in a corner of the Sculpture Studio, where we brought soil in from an on-campus construction site. We were like foreign objects in the fine arts community, creating tension as well as curiosity as we engaged in the Earthball project in unconventional ways. Our work was collaborative, in contrast to the usually individualistic practice of the conventional fine arts world. A number of the students there could not quite believe that you were in the studio with me as volunteers, wondering what the payoff was for becoming involved in this messy work. Yet most of the fine arts students that came to chat with us were intrigued by this collaborative work. We added even more oddity to the scene when we sang, danced and even drummed as we worked with the soil. Sometimes silence fell among us, as we chose to interact with the soil in solitude and in meditative ways.

Actually this Earthwork project was already a more structured and understandable version of my original proposal. I enrolled in a visual arts course to guarantee myself access to studio facilities. When it was my turn to present my project idea to the class, I sensed tension and heard ringing silence after I announced that my project would be about place and people, and that it would be totally dependent on what I worked out with the on-campus resident community, of which I once was a part, so that the project would meet the needs of this community. However, an artist giving up autonomy for mutuality was not something familiar to the class. I had to alter my plan to make it more conventional. Besides, the university's administrators needed structural details before permission could be given for any installation work on campus.

Fine arts students were not the only group that found us different. Coming out of the studio with soil on our clothes invited looks and questions. I was glad that you returned words and gazes to those that questioned our "soiled" appearance. Tonya and Kari, as well as others, used Earthworks as a defence against the dominant Cartesian world on campus that values order over chaos, cleanliness over fuzziness, rationality over emotions, culture over nature. I was no different from you and had used my graduate work to explain my "unsightly" appearance, but I had also asked myself, Why do we need to justify having earth on our clothes, or our being different? Wouldn't that be reinforcing the power and culture that we are resisting? According to our reasons, our "deviant" behaviour warranted a place in the centre only because it was labelled "academic," which gave us a "rational" shelter. Only later did I realize that what was more important was that, at that moment, we felt empowered. After all, life bends and turns. All resolutions are only temporary resolutions. There will be more situations for us to learn or to unlearn again as long as we remain sensuous and open. Maybe what Giovanna shared with us during our finale dinner represented our change in position: "Getting dirty was something we were denied, but I am not worrying about it anymore, for I know now getting dirty is okay."

SOWING NEW SEEDS OF LEARNING

At a recent community arts conference in Toronto, I was struck by the use of the word *education* in connection with phrases like *teaching skills, skill development,* the *culturally rich* and the *culturally deprived.* This suggested a conscious or subconscious dichotomized hierarchy between artists and grassroots communities. I was critical of this perspective, yet I wasn't immune from repeating or reinforcing it. I could think critically, but to critically act I needed another kind of transformation. Your involvement in the Earthworks project brought me the critical self-awareness and experience that gave rise to emotions for motivating actions.

None of us had expertise in sculpting earth and keeping it a living medium, we were all the same in this aspect of the project. The problem was not with my hands but with my speech. Loaded with "knowledge" from my studies and the research on the campus, I unknowingly considered myself above the rest and assigned myself the task of teaching my fellow partners. Worse still, I had a tendency to teach through speech and logic. I knew most of you had been involved in social and environmental movements, but when I encountered something *problematic*, my immediate desire was to correct it with what I deemed *appropriate*. I would then regard you as *empty vessels* only to be filled by my *knowledge*.[8] Mainstream schools and churches I attended, the media and other institutions I worked and lived with, had taught me to value words more than interconnection, and speaking more important than listening. When I felt a sense of "urgency," fearing that I might miss a teachable moment, I took over your space for discovering and creating your own knowledge.[9] I imposed my own view.

I love doing theory. Existing theories are tools for me to understand how the world is organized according to the theorists, and I can build on them or do my own part of theorizing when necessary. To me, this is healing and liberating as the process helps keep my head above water and takes me to the sources of turbulence, by connecting my personal situation to the pubic domain.[10] However, I should not have assumed that you all wanted to do the same. My obsession with *teaching* prevented me from getting to know you more. When I realized that I was imposing myself on the group, I began to pull back and say less.

Holding back and speaking less did not mean I was passive. I was actively listening and learning, but now I was more selective about when I would speak or act, since we all could teach and learn a lot from each other. With our fingers and/or feet in the mud, we shared many of our hometown and travel stories. Through these exchanges we together *visited* beauty pageants in a small town; an estuary city where its citizens were afraid of blackish water; families struggling to understand their young vegan members; permaculture farms in Australia with young Canadian volunteers; a country where armed conflicts were not news anymore. From these visits, complex and even difficult knowledge emerged to let us see beyond the obvious and how we were intertwined in the power games. Ecofeminism emphasizes that there is no single vector of power, but rather multidimensional interconnected forces.[11] These *visits* and the dialogues they generated among us helped us to pull out threads from different locations and see their complex connections.

It was also your contributions that powered up the installation *There Was a Serial Sexual Assault that Happened on Campus in the Summer of 2000*. Most of you were living on campus when these attacks happened. You told me that during those days the resident community was weary and angry. The unfortunate incidences also brought Tonya and me to a self-defence class for women, where we met for the first time as we learned to yell and kick together. Mina and Giovanna were living in one of the high-density buildings whose residents frequently used the pathway through the naturalized farmland where the first and the last assaults took place. They were also working with Campus Security then, and thus were my major inside informants on what had happened. They witnessed how the department swung from denial to hysteria when it tried hard to deter women from using obscure paths by associating fear with nature. Some students resisted such rhetoric by organizing Take Back the Night vigils to frequent those places instead of succumbing to the rhetoric of victimhood and fear. As the tactics to deter failed, the university resorted to transforming the naturalized farmland into a car park and setting up surveillance cameras to monitor it 24/7. The university attempted to have both nature and women under control and framed the perpetrator as only a sick individual who had no connection to a larger political fabric. As part of the installation, seven small red jackets with the image of the lost wilderness printed on top were hung on the trees lining the new car park. I put short notes inside these jackets to murmur controversies to passersby who cared to stop and read what was in there.

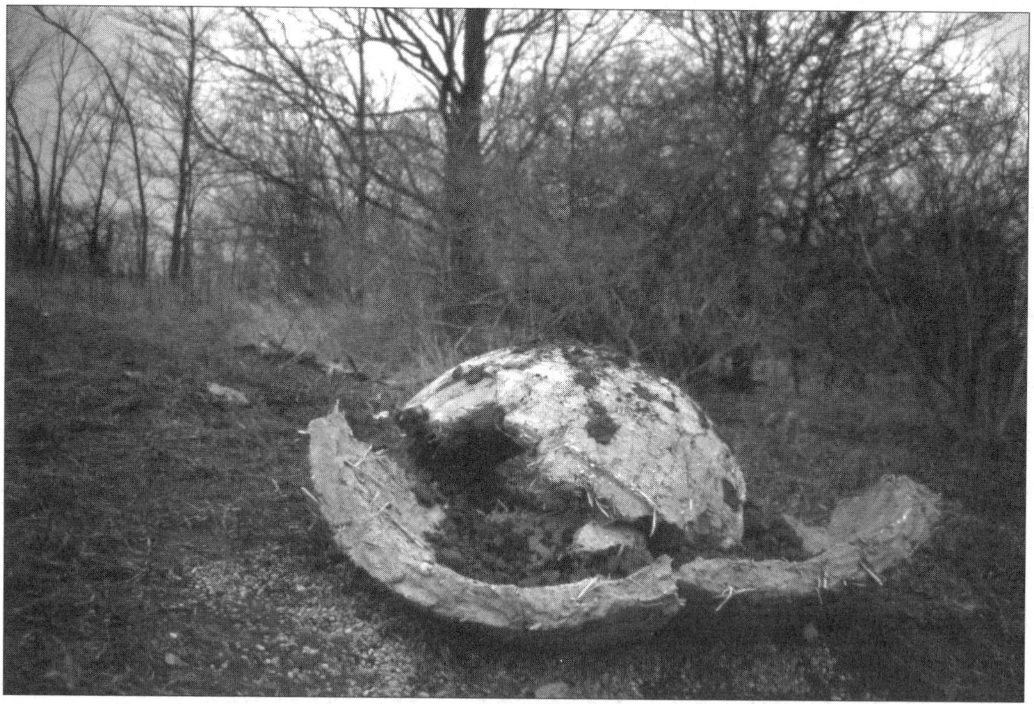

The broken earthball standing at the edge of the historic farm and the newly paved car park.

Installation, Connection and Disintegration

Kari and I retraced the locations of the assaults and found a remnant of the historical farm where one broken earthball should be installed. Moving the earthballs was the climax of the project. The 3-feet-in-diameter semi-spheres of soil and seeds were extremely heavy. Tackling this task and accomplishing it together strengthened the bond among us and enhanced our Earthworkers' identity on campus, because moving these earthballs around commanded the attention of everyone. Installing the earthballs also marked the end of our partnership. At the dinner celebrating our finale, we chatted about what this project meant to us. Tonya said: "I want to get involved in building earthen houses ... It is because this communal process makes me crave more." For Melissa, the project made her appreciate her mother who has been gardening all her life. The project also helped her survive Toronto. "It is so built up that to physically touch earth is so rejuvenating, especially during those days that I was really depressed. The whole act also gave me connection to people, nature and everything," she said. Giovanna enjoyed a unique experience she had never had before, and the project helped her to understand a more traditional way of living.

At the dinner, I gave you back the pictures you drew about your relationships with the environment before the project started, and asked you to describe the changes you would like to make to your drawings if you were to draw these pictures again. Melissa took the lead, responding that while she would keep the composition of her drawing, she would add people on the trail that she was hiking. A number of you echoed her response as you also felt that you were no longer alone. Mina's brick cocoon that confined her would be opened up so she could be in touch with a much larger world of friends and nature. Kari still wanted to be under a tree, looking at the shadows of a city from afar.

To me, your responses confirmed that this project managed to help us build a dynamic community where there was a balance between subjectivity and collectivity. The dialectic between the individual and the collective made room for difference, openness and connectedness. The relationship was like a dotted line[12] between *I* ···· *We*, in contrast to the *I* ≡ *We* relationship, in which the solid bond may breed one dimensionality and insensitivity, as it prescribes that the individual is the same as the collective or vice versa. The dynamic community we formed opened my eyes to how essential both elements are to an intentional community.

This project might have ended for you when summer holidays began and many of you left campus for home. But for me, an important chapter of unlearning was still awaiting. I believed I was not anthropocentric, until the earthballs defied my will. The large earthballs tumbled and fell apart prematurely, despite measures we had put in place to help them stay upright. There was one earthball on the fringe of the campus, whose silhouette I would see when I rode home in the evening. Then the sky broke open. After four days of downpour, the silhouette disappeared. I knew this was only nature taking its course, but it made me restless. The image of the silhouette kept coming back to me along with low rumbling sounds associated with its fall. This created a dissonance within me as I could not come to terms with the reality.

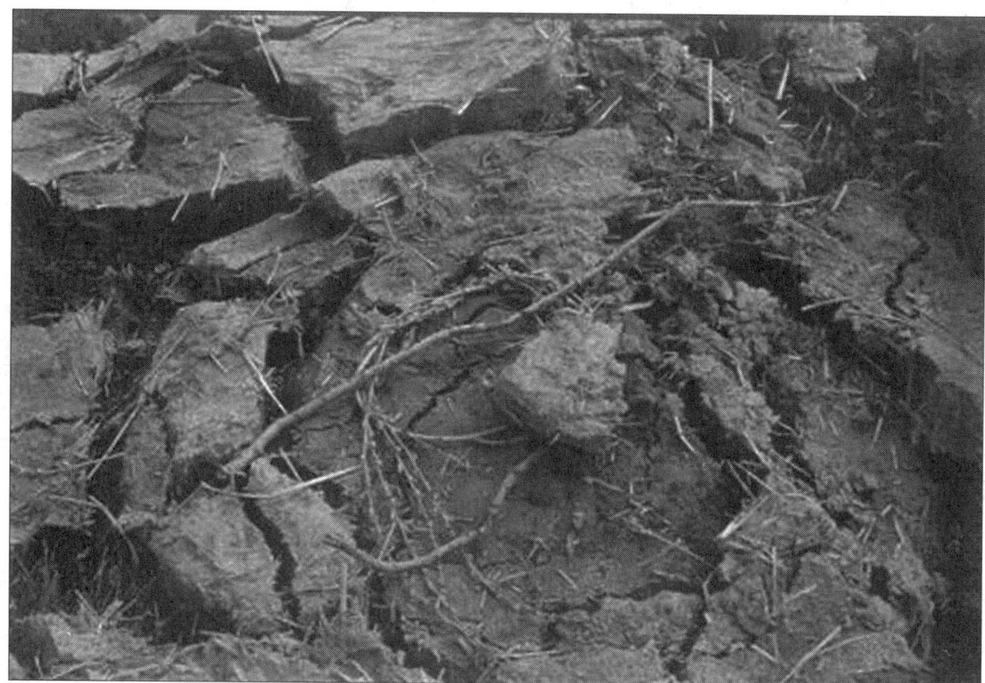

A large earthball tumbled to the ground and created this interesting pattern.

This struggle with the disintegration of our earthballs was my wake up call. I was non-anthropocentric intellectually, but deep down, I desired to control it all. The soil I worked with was only instrumental to me as I denied my utilitarian mentality. My willingness to know the soil was subconsciously driven by my desire to master it, so that it could be used to challenge the modernistic regime on campus. The elements, however, including the inclement weather, despised my plan. These earthballs tumbled to the ground and shattered by their own weight. As they gradually disintegrated, they looked like open wounds and were actually more powerful in their fallen state because they were "juxtaposed" against all things planned, defined and managed on campus — the manicured lawns, the huge car parks and air-conditioned big-box buildings. They seemed to be inviting passersby to question all the projected harmony, wellness and certainty. They were there challenging humans' naïveté and autonomy. An early summer that was hot and dry slowed down the *healing process* by making it hard for the wildflower and wild grass seeds to grow, leaving the scar-like patterns visible till the first snow.

I avoided talking about this with anyone, even when some of you asked. I lost the opportunity to know and to understand more deeply the impact of these tumbled earthballs. I only talked to people about the installations associated with the earthballs, as the effects they produced were of great encouragement to me. The questions chalked on the pathway where a fox had been seen trotting to the Law School brought people to share with me their fox-related stories whether on or off campus. I also overheard people asking their friends *Have you seen that fox?* which initiated conversations that otherwise would not have emerged. The installation brought attention to the relationship between the disappearing wildlife habitats and the way we develop a place. These installations bracketed off other noisier images during their short presence and created space for the rise of different emotions, voices and eco/communities.

Both the earthballs and the installations are now gone, and the group has dissolved. At one point, I wished that this was a totally open-ended project with a community on campus, instead of a temporary project. Nonetheless, we made our presence felt by the campus community at large. We generated interest and dialogues among passersby; we created spaces for silence and stillness so that small voices within and outside us could be heard. Not everybody reacted positively to this presence. Those aligned with the prevailing power and order resented us, as we were unfamiliar, and to some, even dangerous. Yet, by and large, most were curious; some contemplated our creations and wanted to be part of this space.

This project was transient, just like the student population on campus. We may never know how much stillness, resonance and dissonance we generated in that place, yet we do know that they are mobile, visceral experiences that people carried within them. Besides, such experiences may be more powerful in their absence, like the tumbled earthballs and your presence.

NOTES

1. Elise Houghton and Sau Wai Tai, unpublished study on the relation between students and York University's main campus (2000).
2. Bernard Rudofsky in Michael Hough, *Out of Place* (New Haven: Yale University, 1990), 19.
3. Hough, *Out of Place*, 5.
4. Eleanor Haney, *Transforming Life in the World: The Great Commandment* (Cleveland, OH: Pilgrim Press, 1998), 107–108.
5. Jean Baudrillard, *Simulations* (New York: Semiotext, 1983), 42–43.
6. David Orr, "Reassembling the Pieces: Ecological Design and the Liberal Arts," in Gregory Smith and Delafruz Williams, eds., *Ecological Education in Action: On Weaving Education Culture and the Environment* (Albany: State University of New York Press, 1999), 229–230.
7. Val Plumwood, *Feminism and the Mastery Over* (London: Routledge, 1993), 43–59; Karen Warren, "Taking Empirical Data Seriously: An Ecofeminist Philosophical Perspective," in Karen Warren, ed., *Ecofeminism: Women, Culture, Nature* (Bloomington: Indiana University Press, 1997), 3.
8. Paulo Freire, *Pedagogy of the Oppressed* (New York: Continuum, 1970), 57.

9. Ibid., 58.

10. bell hooks, *Teaching to Transgress* (New York: Routledge, 1994), 60.

11. Warren, "Taking Empirical Data Seriously," 3.

12. The idea of a dotted relationship is borrowed from Michelle Fine's concept on working the hyphens, which highlighted the dismissed connections between self and others and their co-evolution. Michelle Fine, "Working the Hyphens: Reinventing Self and Other in Qualitative Research," in N.K. Denzin and Y.S. Lincoln, eds., *Handbook of Qualitative Research* (Newbury Park, CA: Sage Publications, 1994), 70–79.

CHAPTER 13

Tellingsmiths:

THE WORK OF PLANTING TREES AND THE POLITICS OF MEMORY

Pariss Garramone

> The truth about stories is that that's all we are.
>
> — Thomas King, *The Truth about Stories*[1]

I plant trees, lots of trees. I plant them in clear-cuts. I walk, eat, work and sleep in or right beside these clear-cut northern Canadian forests for four months of each year. They say this is a sustainable forest. They say its Crown land. It is colonized land — but they don't say that.

I have worked in forestry labour since 1989. Through discussing my work with others, I have realized that many people do not link my forestry work to deforestation practices or issues of sustainability. Many people refer to my work in the forestry industry as simply "tree planting" — a "good" environmental summer job without questioning the real reasons behind tree planting. My work in clear-cuts has left me with many questions. One of these has to do with the way Canada's natural environment is presented — that is, as "natural," the "romantic forest" and as a "Canadian wilderness" where no one lives. This, in turn, has made me think critically about forestry labour itself, the many contradictions negotiated as a tree planter and my role in maintaining what is a colonized landscape. It has made me want to write critically about it.

For the rest of the year, I write papers, lots of papers. I am a graduate student. I live and work in/with other colonized environments, colonized landscapes of knowledge — other clear-cuts.

I want to think about the politics of tellings and the "social and human interest in the act of telling a story as political intervention."[2] Are academic writing practices political? In this essay, I explore how I use zines in my academic work as a way of exploring the political within the writing practices of the university. In particular, my work with zines is autobiographical and I am interested in how memory work is written. What stories does one tell? What does one remember and how is the act of writing not only political but also an act of memory?

I am interested in not just any stories but in the stories of the every day. I think that it's through the telling of ordinary lives that oppressive power relations can be revealed and fictions, such as those presented as "woman," destabilized.[3] As Joan Solomon said, "In a world where an oral tradition has been almost lost, where agendas and stories have been constructed through the institution of the 'mass media,' how do we know who we are?"[4] I question who this "we" is.

I have been making zines with friends for the last seven years. I decided to bring together zine-making and forestry work after I realized that not only were zines a great way for forestry workers to talk to each other but also that zines could facilitate mutual learning — both within the forestry labour community and beyond. For my master's research I created *Her Hand Made Forest*, an autobiographical zine that linked narratives and images as a way to explore writing an environmental autobiography in new ways. Zines are one type of alternative media, and most often they take the form of a self-produced magazine.[5] The self-production or Do-It-Yourself (DIY) aspect of zines allows me to self-publish and to publish my words in my way. Like many alternative forms of media, zines can be a form of subversive communication, which can take up difficult subjects in unique ways; zines are a way of talking back. My research with zines and my zine-making have focused my struggle with the "un-get-roundable"[6] issues

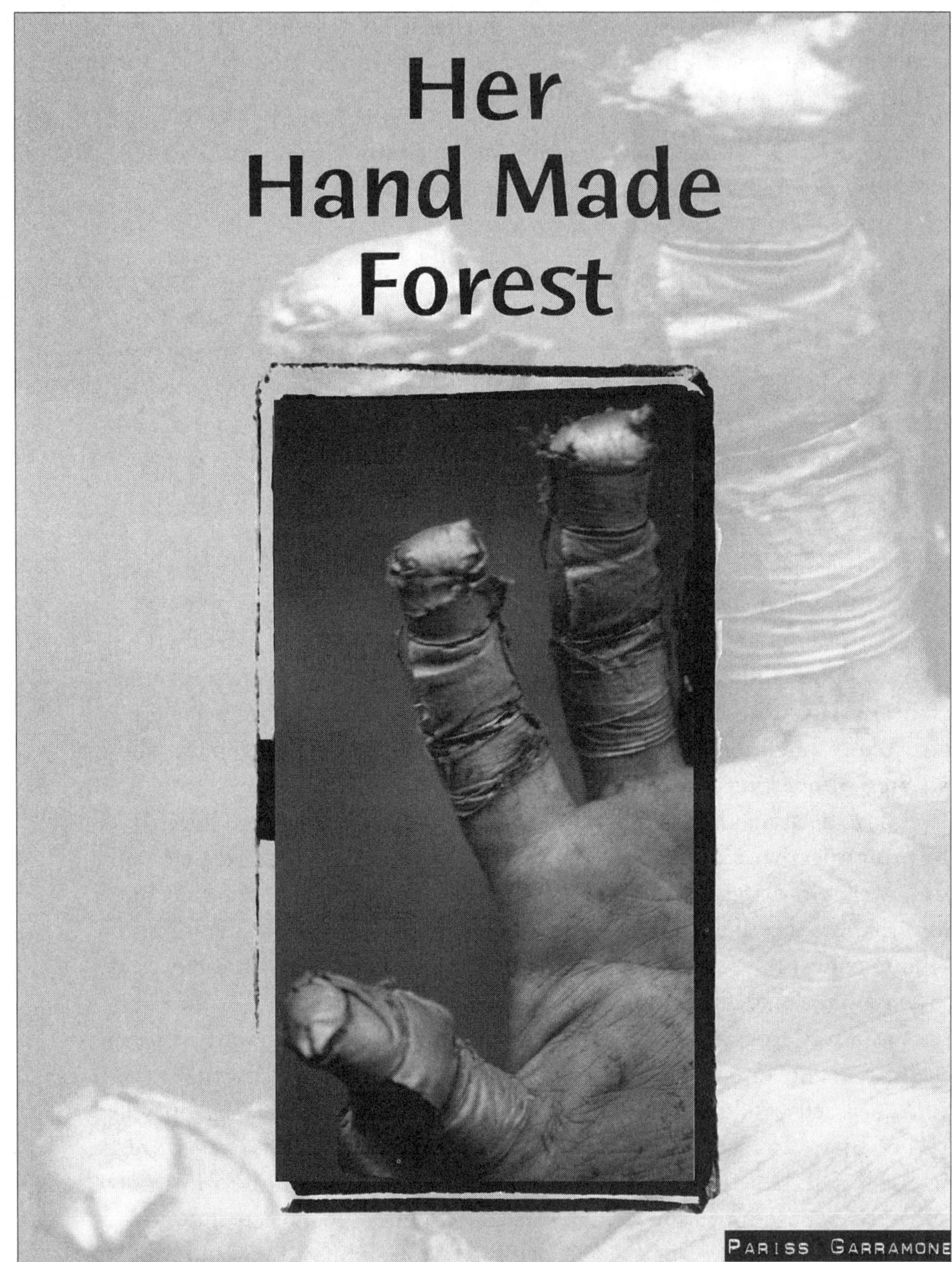

Zine Cover for Her Hand Made Forest.

of representation and interpretation.

First, I should tell you a bit about why I am writing this …

Clear-Cuts

I reach into the ground over 3,000 times each day — each time I plant a tree my hand feels the earth and feels the roots of each tree I plant.

Excavation process — a different kind of digging: I have discovered that the roots of the term anecdote mean "secret, private, or hitherto unpublished narratives or details of history."[7] Linked to the history of this word is both gossip and sham — shameful tellings. Anecdote and theory are both tellings, yet they are created as binaries, fiction versus truth. What might publishing do to an anecdote, what might publishing really mean to stories? Does publishing make tellings into the truth, a truth?

The zines I make are homemade publishing, and I work with creating public art that incorporates narratives and images. I often think of my work as being personal writings that are moved into published space, which problematizes the binaries of public and private. My work with zines is an ongoing practice of creating autobiographical tellings that struggle with the theoretical aspects of life-history. In my use of zines as part of my research practice, I consider how published space influences the language I use, the stories I tell and the images I create. It is by "doing" life-history research that I meet again, and differently, the theory involved with writing the self. In fact, I see my work as creating a theoretical understanding through critical practice.

Autobiography has also been termed confession.[8] I do not see stories or storytelling as innocent. I see my autobiographical writing as a form of feminist confession, yet not an essentialist claim to identity. I see my work as confessing to my actions, my writings and to what I think are the motives behind the writings. This is a confession — a confession about confessing and also a response to the question, How do I write these memories into public spaces?

My work with zines attempts to embody the writing of autobiography. Zines are a mixing of genres, images and autobiography, unique pieces woven together. The writing of autobiography is also a piecing together through exploring the fragmentary practice of memory, the incommensurability of experience and, with this, the partialness of confessions. Autobiographies are joint tellings created by listener and teller.[9] Zines, like the autobiographical tellings they often hold, are also co-created by writer and reader.

I am interested in using images, even in my writing. The metaphor of the clear-cut has many layers of meaning and is an image that continually reappears throughout my work. I see "clear-cutting" as a practice of colonization, as scars carved into the environment. I understand environment as Ronald Nepreud[10] does — as not only the natural and built landscapes but also as the cultural landscapes that map spaces into places and relationally create meanings. I use the metaphor of the clear-cut to engage with what it might mean to think about what is cut out, "clear-cut" away, excluded and colonized. The use of images, imaginings and imagery through metaphors, has often been cut out of academic discussion. Patricia Williams questions how the everydayness of metaphors "mask[s] the hierarchies that make racial domination frequently seem so 'natural,' so invisible, indeed so attractive?"[11]

How do images/imagery, imaginary and imaginings link throughout my work? I want to begin with the imaginary; in particular, Michèle Le Doeuff's "collective imaginary."[12] As Lorraine Code points out, knowledge has "expunged" or clear-cut away "imagination and interpretation" from "cognitive projects."[13] By working with stories, as Le Doeuff states, academic "discourse is inscribed and declares its status through a break with myth, fable, the poetic, the domain of the image."[14] Genevieve Lloyd illustrates that it is the language of images, metaphors or "sensitive points" within academic writing that when taken up can "open out the reading of texts to the cultural contexts in ways that are often dismissed."[15] I have been struggling to find ways to include memories within my academic papers. To do so, I work with both my own autobiography and with the memories of other women working in forestry labour. Moving memory into language and then into scholarly work takes me through many layers of interpretation. How do I transcribe the taped interviews, translate pauses and fractured thoughts and represent in some authentic way the stories entrusted to me?

It is important to consider the action involved in the practice of creating knowledge claims. Knowledge claims are not an innocent action, nor simply a representation. To "imagine the strange" and not make the strange familiar is a difficult task, which involves "listening closely."[16] Yet many have imagined "into" others' lives without listening. My initial idea for my master's autobiographical research project was to collect stories of women forestry workers. However, my research really began by questioning the purpose of pursuing the knowledge of others. As Sarah Lucia Hoagland argues, "observation is value-laden" and epistemology or coming to know is "enacting something rather than representing something else."[17] From here, I considered turning the focus of my work on myself, to enact or come to know my own story before representing others' stories.

The zine project that I produced for my Master of Environmental Studies played with images, imaginary and imaginings as it linked together autobiography and a process of reinventing the family album,[18] a double exposure of sorts. Through *Her Hand Made Forest*, I represented my her/story in a public, self-published alternative magazine. I decided to look at my own stories of forestry labour instead of representing other women's stories in order to begin thinking about how personal stories of the self can be written into academic research and how these stories can be treated as knowledge and theory. In creating this zine of my own stories, I struggled with the personal process of writing the self. What self would I disclose? How was this a political project of understanding how one creates herself in relation to others?

Witness to a Clear-Cut

> When you stop to think about it, you soon realize that our imagination is what our whole social life is really based on.
>
> — Northrop Frye, *The Educated Imagination*[19]

I decided to focus on my work on forestry labour because my work as a tree planter has made me a witness to what is often termed "sustainable forest practices," but what is actually enormous clear-cuts and excessive timber waste. I have worked extensively in the forests of Ontario, Alberta and BC. For me, witnessing involves being called to listen. However, autobiographies or confessions are joint tellings created by listener and teller. They can create witnesses, responsible "close" listeners who perform stories of the self. These in turn may create other witnesses, responsible "close" listeners of these stories/tellings/confessions. This "being called" is not innocent; there are implications. I am implicated in the practice of clear-cutting through my work with multinational forestry companies. I want to suggest that "close" listening allows the contradictions within autobiographies to be explored and not ignored.

The witness, as Donna Haraway describes it, not only sees and hears but also testifies.[20] This testimonial, the scientific/academic paper, uses and creates a language that is crafted by those deemed "able" to bear witness and "able" to testify "credibly." Trinh T. Minh-ha describes an anthropologist's/academic's task as that of a *bricoleur* and not that of an engineer; she describes the difference as being one who uses the tools at hand. The tools she is referring to are our voice and our language, and in particular the crafting of tellings through a mastering of language.[21] I think of my work as that of a tellingsmith, a term I use instead of wordsmith. As Minh-ha points out, academics are handy with the language tools they already have and are less interested in creating new words. Yet I do think that as tellingsmiths, as "close" listeners who are interested in talking back, we might be building new ways of telling new stories.

Minh-ha also relates academic testifying to the concept of gossip, which she describes as talking together about others (from the Old English godsibb). Gossip, like witnessing, also implicates us. Minh-ha states, "[She] who lends an ear to gossip already accepts either sympathizing with or being an accomplice to the gossiper."[22] For me, the use of gossip, or knowledge as rumour, highlights the discursive nature of knowledge and relates to how the stories of the everyday are knowledge. However, I take heed in Code's cautionary words that in using the term gossip, we continue to position certain types of knowledge at the margins, mainly the stories of women.[23] I do, however, want to think of the work of academics as gossip, in order to align the knowledge found in certain cannons with "the words on the street" — that is, the stories found in zines.

When I write zines, to whom am I speaking? Minh-ha describes the writing practice of naming and quoting, the typical communication within the academy, as the "paying off of old scores between white men."[24] In the zines I make, I mix genres and academic language with how I talk with friends and how I talk "on the block" while tree planting. By combining different discourses in one zine, a dialogue across differences begins. A zine can play with how and what one writes, and offer a way of talking back.

Scars/Public Secrets

> The words you use are like the clothes you wear. Situations, like bodies, are supposed to be decently covered.
>
> — Northrop Frye, *The Educated Imagination*[25]

I drive for hours. I am still in the clear-cut, on muddy logging roads. They say that a thin border of trees should be between the road and a clear-cut. They say it's to help the animals, that it is to relieve the edge effect, that it is a sustainable practice. They don't say it's to keep people from seeing the clear-cut.

The stories in the zine are about my dis-ease with everyday situations I experienced working in forestry labour. By discussing my dis-ease I am exposing some of my vulnerabilities. Yet stories of discomfort are most often discussed privately, whispered to friends, seen as gossip. I am also interested in the double exposure of engaging in both a theory-making practice that blurs the academically policed boundaries of theory and practice and working with stories that are about rethinking engagement with theory and theory-making. I love the words of Lorrie Neilsen, who writes:

> We suffer from hardening of the categories in the research enterprise. Science is not art. A story is not knowledge … We are still caught in binaries, oppositional thinking, and we still spend a considerable time defending borders, being gatekeepers … the regimes of thought we create through language are, after all, stories we tell ourselves about how our enterprise works.[26]

Creating autobiographical narratives is memory work, and it is about remembering and forgetting. In developing my autobiographical narratives for my zine, I revisited my personal journal writings. From these ordinary writings, I crafted short stories that discussed the gender, class and racial issues I experienced while working in forestry. I also began to excavate my photo album, not for illustrations to the stories but for images that could be read as another text.

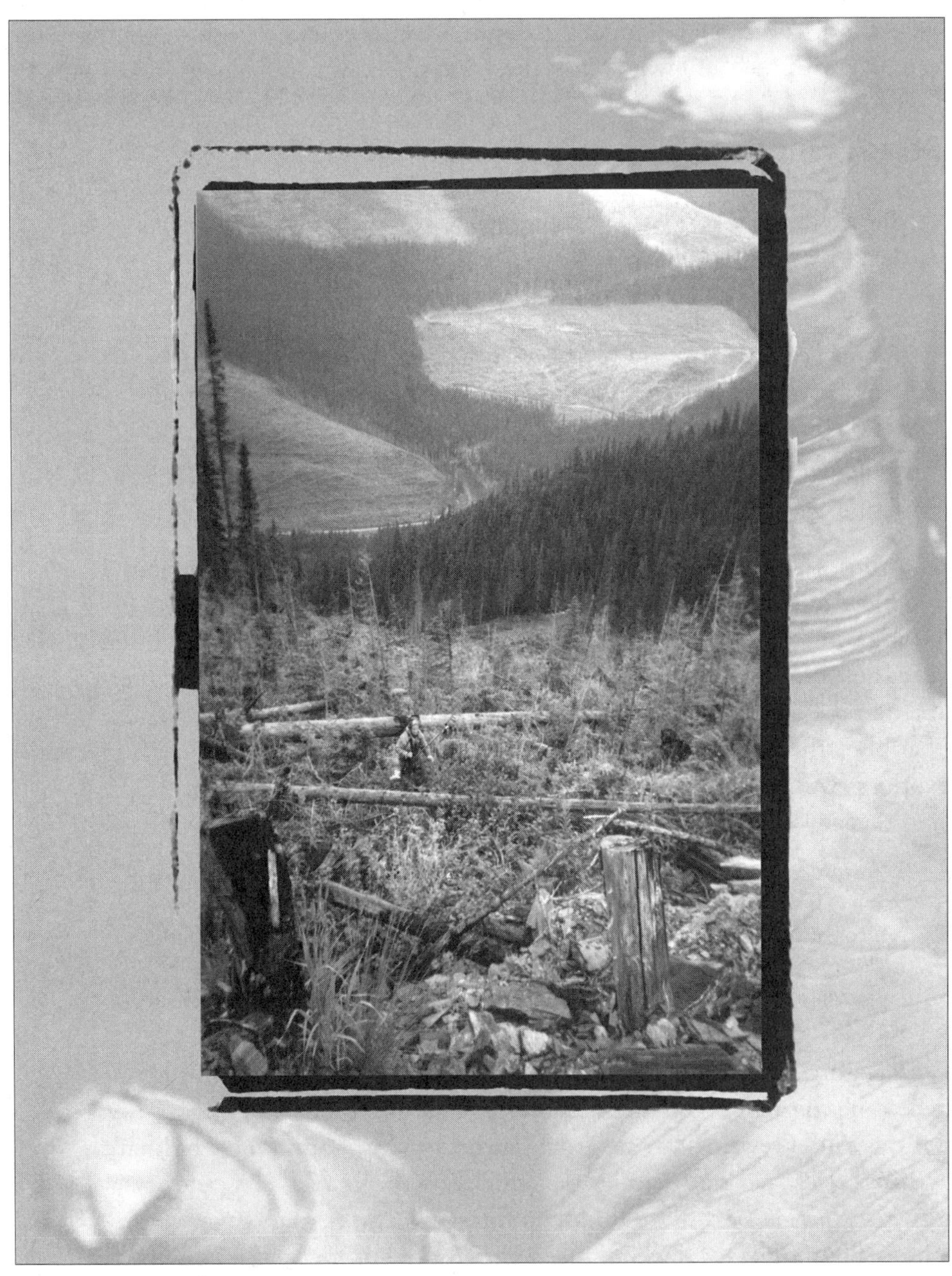

Clear-cut/Fallen Trees.

What do I remember? My role as author privileges my interpretation as well as my selection of what is remembered and how it is remembered; once it is written, and an image is made, my attending to this experience makes only certain phenomena meaningful. I made choices and framed my experience by choosing to record and reflect on what, at the time of writing, I found engaging. I like how Kathleen Weiler discusses the constructed nature of experience and limits of language needed to represent these experiences,[27] and how Joan Stanley eloquently weaves these ideas together:

> In diaries, letters and photographs we present a version of ourselves which is partial. It leaves out bits of us that we think the reader or viewer might not want to know about, or that we might want to keep a secret. The account has a specific frame. There may be no such simple unproblematic thing as the "real truth about me" in a journal, letter or picture, just endless interesting versions of ourselves, different not only each moment but in each letter, journal page, poem or photograph.[28]

Similar to the fragmentary nature of memory work presented by bell hooks,[29] I have come to understand how past events and memories of the past can be a non-linear way of shaping/imagining the present/future. A haunting question for me is, What might memory reveal in what it attempts to conceal?

Are my stories fictions? Sidonie Smith says, "Autobiographical narration begins with amnesia,"[30] and explains that amnesia is necessary in the formation of self-identity because of the fragmentary nature of memory narration. Michael Lambek and Paul Antze echo this as they comment that "memory begins when experience itself is definitively past. The ground between the spectator and the object of her gaze begins to lengthen; the connections between the two grow uncertain."[31] Memories are fluid, and each time they are recalled, they are remembered differently. If I were to write this zine again, would I choose the same stories, write them in the same ways? What would I forget? What *did* I forget?

Forgetting is both active and important with regard to identity. Lambek and Antze argue that "identity is not composed of a fixed set of memories but lies in the dialectical, careless activity of remembering and forgetting, assimilating and discarding."[32] bell hooks, in her autobiographical book *Bone Black*, suggests that forgetting is continually learning what is valued as sameness and what is deemed different is in need of forgetting. hooks also explores, through her use of form and content, how the fragmented nature of understanding, of partial truths and the messiness of experience create a knowing subject.[33] I align my autobiographical narration with how hooks explores ideas of continually revisiting, revisioning and renegotiating the past as part of knowing the present, and as part of creating a process of making sense of one's self. I also reflect on Ann Kuhn's understanding of building connections between the public and the personal: "Memory work makes it possible to explore connections between 'public' historical events, structures of feeling, family dramas, relations of class, national identity and gender, and 'personal' memory."[34]

I have come to see my research as a process of writing autobiography through the making of zines. I see it as a messy type of piecework with a political purpose, where unique and sometimes risky fragments are linked and woven together through my own story.

BEYOND CLEAR-CUTS

> The fundamental job of the imagination in ordinary life, then, is to produce, out of the society we have to live in, a vision of the society we want to live in. Obviously that can't be a separate society, so we have to understand how to relate the two.
>
> — Northrop Frye, *The Educated Imagination*[35]

It is the role authors play in the rewriting of social narratives, which inadvertently teaches us how to be in/between identities, that is critical for social change. To think of a handler of dominant-language practice as a magician, an enchanter of words and meanings is to think about the role an academic plays as a crafter, a trickster of language/meanings/metaphors. As a writer and researcher, I am a tellingsmith; I am both a trickster and hopefully a "close" listener interested in talking back. I use my work on zines as an attempt to wedge open a space in academic writing practices where new ways of writing and creating knowledge cannot only be imagined but also can be engaged, linking images with the imaginings of stories. As a tellingsmith, I am interested in building new ways for telling subversive stories.

Throughout this essay I have suggested that imagery, imaginary and imaginings can be the "sensitive points"[36] taken up in academic work in creative ways, such as through the practice of making zines. Through attending to the "collective imaginary"[37] — which generates metaphors that mask colonial practices — and by developing an imaginary that produces new images, we can "root" new metaphors to live by. Engaging with the political practice of telling stories — through an attentive and critical writing practice that challenges how theory and knowledge are written and by whom — will allow me to continue zine-making as a form of direct action against the colonized spaces of the academy and the forest industry.

NOTES

I'd like to dedicate this chapter to Tiina for telling it like it is, and to Steve and Frances for love and support always.

1. Thomas King, *The Truth about Stories: A Native Narrative* (Toronto: House of Anansi Press, 2003), 153.

2. Walter D. Mignolo, *The Darker Side of the Renaissance* (Ann Arbor: University of Michigan Press, 1998), 24–25 as cited in Sarah Lucia Hoagland, "Resisting Rationalities," in Nancy Tuana and Sandra Morgen, eds., *Engendering Rationalities* (New York: State University of New York Press 2001), 134.

3. M. Theobald, "Teachers, Memory and Oral History," in Kathleen Weiler and Sue Middleton, eds., *Telling Women's Lives: Narrative Inquiries in the History of Women's Education* (Philadelphia: Open University Press 1999), 9–24.

4. Joan Solomon, "Introduction," in J. Spence and J. Solomon, eds., *What Can a Woman Do With a Camera? Photography for Women* (London: Scarlet Press, 1995), 9.

5. Chris Atton, *Alternative Media* (London: Sage Publications, 2003).

6. Clifford Geertz, "Being Here: Whose Life Is It Anyway?" in Clifford Geertz, ed., *Works and Lives: The Anthropologist as Author* (Stanford: Stanford University Press, 1988), 145.

7. *Oxford Dictionary Online* (2004). Retreived 20 April 2004 from http://dictionary.oed/com.

8. Ruth Felski, "On Confession," in S. B. Gluck and D. Patai, eds., *Women's Words: The Feminist Practice of Oral History* (New York: Routledge, 1998), 83.

9. See for example, Katherine Borland, "'That's Not What I Said': Interpretive Conflict in Oral Narrative Research," in Robert Perks and Alistair Thomson, eds., *The Oral History Reader* (London: Routledge, 1998); Michael Lambek and Paul Antze, "Introduction: Forecasting Memory," in Paul Antze and Michael Lambek, eds., *Tense Past: Cultural Essays in Trauma and Memory* (New York: Routledge, 1996); V. Skultans, *A Testimony of Lives: Narrative and Memory in Post-Soviet Latvia* (New York: Routledge, 1998).

10. Ronald W. Neperud, *Context Content and Community Art Education: Beyond Postmodernism* (New York: Teachers College Press, 1995).

11. Patricia J. Williams, "The Emperor's New Clothes," in *Seeing a Color-Blind Future: The Paradox of Race* (London: Virago, 1997), 15.

12. Michèle Le Doeuff, *The Philosophical Imaginary*, trans. Colin Gordon (London: The Athlone Press, 1989).

13. Lorraine Code, "Rational Imaginings, Responsible Knowings: How Far Can You See From Here?" in Tuana and Morgen, eds., *Engendering Rationalities*, 261.

14. Le Doeuff, *The Philosophical Imaginary*, 1.

15. Genevieve Lloyd, "No One's Land: Australia and the Philosophical Imagination," *Hypatia: A Journal of Feminist Philosophy* 15, no. 2 (2000), 27.

16. Code, "Rational Imaginings, Responsible Knowings," 269.

17. Hoagland, "Resisting Rationalities," 134.

18. Joan Stanley, "Accounting for Our Days," in Spence and Solomon, eds., *What Can a Woman Do With a Camera?* 17–28.

19. Northrop Frye, *The Educated Imagination* (Toronto: CBC Enterprises, 1983), 57.

20. Donna Haraway, *Female_Man©_Meets_OncoMouse* (New York: Routledge, 1996), 24.

21. Trinh. T. Minh-ha, *Women, Native, Other: Writing Postcoloniality and Feminism* (Bloomington: Indiana University Press, 1998), 62.

22. Ibid., 68.

23. Code, "Rational Imaginings, Responsible Knowings," 231.

24. Minh-ha, *Women, Native, Other*, 57.

25. Frye, *The Educated Imagination*, 57.

26. Lorrie Neilsen, "Scribbler: Notes on Writing and Learning Inquiry," in Lorri Neilsen, Ardra L. Cole and J. Gary Knowles, eds., *The Art of Writing Inquiry* (Halifax: Backalong Books, 2001), 263–264.

27. Kathleen Weiler, "Reflections on Writing a History of Women Teachers," in Weiler and Middleton, eds., *Telling Women's Lives*, 40.

28. Stanley, "Accounting for Our Days," 25.

29. bell hooks, *Bone Black: Memories of Girlhood* (New York: Henry Holt, 1996).

30. Sidonie Smith, "Performativity, Autobiographical Practice, Resistance," in S. B. Gluck and D. Patai, eds., *Women's Words: The Feminist Practice of Oral History* (New York: Routledge, 1998), 109.

31. Lambek and Antze, "Introduction," xiii.

32. Ibid., xxix.

33. hooks, *Bone Black.*

34. Ann Kuhn, *Family Secrets: Acts of Memory and Imagination* (London: Verso, 1995), 4.

35. Frye, *The Educated Imagination*, 60.

36. Lloyd, "No One's Land," 27.

37. Ibid.

PART IV

Art Heals

CHAPTER 14

Arts in Detention:

CREATING CONNECTIONS WITH IMMIGRANT WOMEN DETAINEES

Oona Padgham

It is estimated that 20,000 to 200,000 immigrants live in Canada without full legal immigration status. Most became non-status because their visitor or student visas lapsed or their refugee applications were denied. Non-status immigrants live, work and attend schools in our communities. They pay taxes, raise their families and participate in Canadian society. But people without official immigration status live with the constant fear and uncertainty of their lack of status being discovered and ending up in jail or detained at a detention centre, like the Heritage Inn. Approximately 8,000 people are deported from Canada every year.

Looking inconspicuous along a strip of suburban highway, the Toronto Immigrant Holding Centre, or the Heritage Inn, borders a mall, a car rental and a Tim Hortons. But the Heritage Inn serves a more sinister purpose than its name implies. Located at 385 Rexdale Boulevard and formerly a hotel, the Heritage Inn has been converted into an immigration jail that can hold up to 300 people. Montreal, Quebec City and Vancouver also have immigration detention centres, and there are people held on immigration violations in jails across Canada. At the Heritage Inn, each converted hotel room holds up to four occupants. The men and women are segregated, separating families and loved ones. Children held in detention are usually with their mothers. Detainees are incarcerated until their documentation and citizenship are confirmed or until they are deported back to their country of origin. This can take anywhere from a few days to several months.

The group No One Is Illegal (Toronto)[1] works on developing and supporting campaigns for immigrants' rights through education, mobilization and networking. Its primary focus is on people who do not have full legal immigration status. No One Is Illegal organizes forums, rallies and days of action and is actively involved in the "Don't Ask, Don't Tell"[2] campaign in Toronto, a campaign which seeks to make city services available to all Toronto residents, not just those defined as "legal" by the state. In December 2003, No One Is Illegal began an arts group project with the women and children being held in detention. The story of this arts group is told through a conversation between Oona Padgham and three other members of No One Is Illegal (Toronto) — Jean McDonald, Farrah Miranda and Sima Zerehi — who are involved in the Arts in Detention Group project.

CREATING ART/CREATING CONNECTIONS

GETTING STARTED

Oona: Why did you start an arts group in the detention centre?

Sima: I was doing other work in the detention centre and it was clear that something was needed, some kind of positive activity. Someone suggested we do an art group and the idea fit. Art production is a good way for people who do not all speak English to relate to each other. It is also totally distracting and different from the everyday routine people in detention face. We thought that we could use the art produced to do outreach and education, to build awareness around detention. It is a way for participants to document and communicate their experiences to people outside the detention centre.

Oona: What opportunities does the art group provide for the women and children in detention at the Heritage Inn?

Farrah: It gives the women a social space that is free of guards where they can talk to each other. It gives them a chance to get out of their rooms and do something that is actually human.

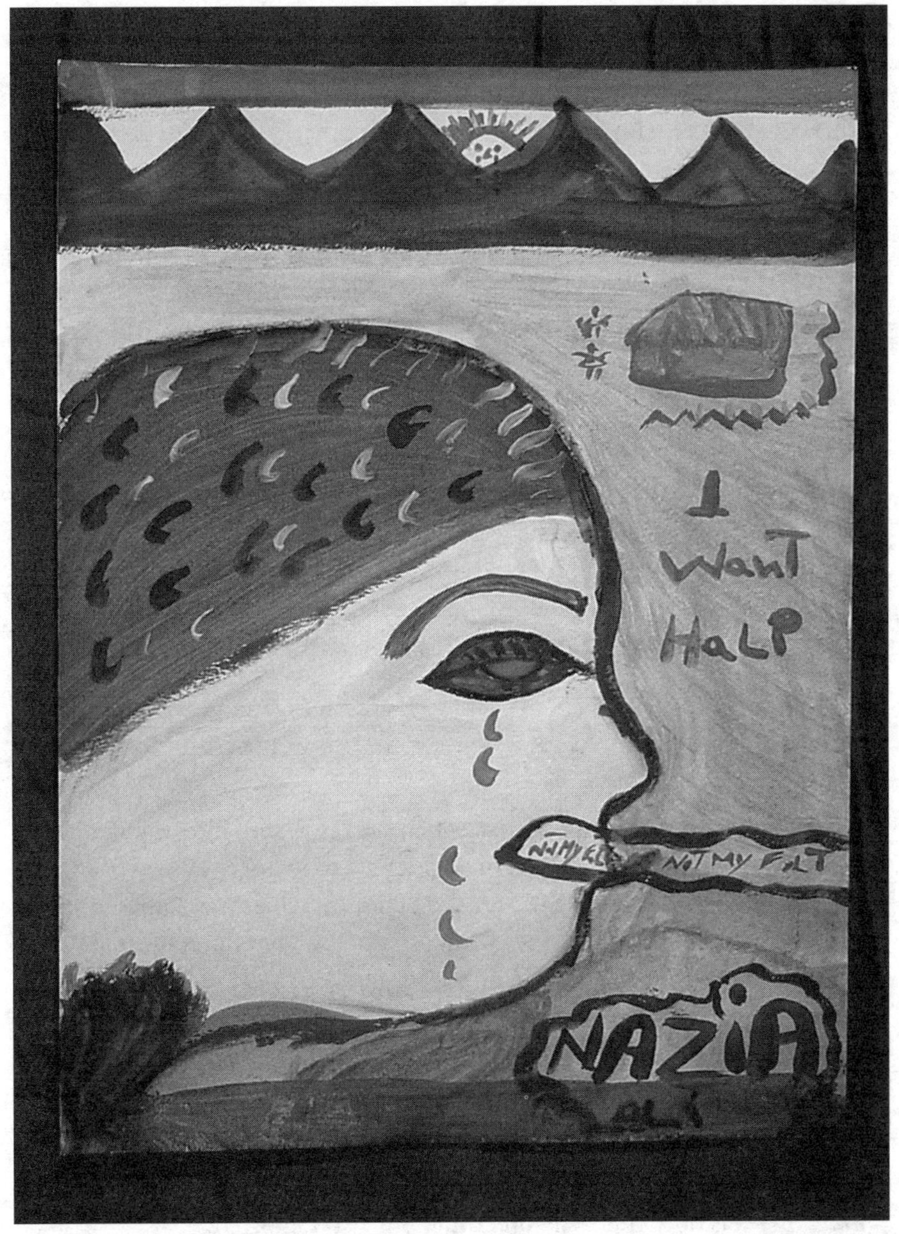

"I Want Help"

Jean: The only other thing they have to do is watch television. At the new detention centre at the Heritage Inn,[3] there are three different levels, so the art program gets women and children from different levels who wouldn't otherwise have any interaction to meet each other and talk to each other.

Sima: Through the work they produce and by interacting with us, the women get a chance to get the message across about their situation and what it feels like to be in detention. A lot of their work is quite political, whether it's images of their homes and children or families, or explicit political messages and phrases. Often their art talks about wanting to stay in Canada, wanting to be free, stating that they are not criminals and that they shouldn't be in detention. It gives them an outlet to tell their stories.

Jean: The art group is a really big deal, especially for the women and kids who have been in there for a long time. The more they come, the more they open up. People who at first weren't so interested came to look forward to the group and would come as soon as they would see us.

PROCESSING TRAUMA

Oona: Many of the women and children are very traumatized by their experience in detention. Do these issues come out in the art group? How do you deal with that?

Sima: There was this Iraqi woman who had just come into the detention centre. She was the only one in hijab and the only one who spoke Arabic. She was totally traumatized. She didn't know what was happening, or where she was. She came to the group after being pretty much lifted out of bed by some of the other women. She was under the covers and had been there for a day and wouldn't even stick her head out. She came down and drew a picture of a corpse bleeding. She communicated that the corpse was her husband and that Saddam Hussein had killed him. That was as much information as she could get across to us.

Oona: Did she keep coming to the group?

Sima: She was only there the one time. She was deported.

Farrah: There is so much pain in what these women and children have experienced. It's there in the isolation and in the loneliness. The group provides a space for women to talk about that pain and to talk about their experiences if they want to. It's really hard to be in that space and know that we get to go home and continue our lives, while they're bound to this horrible detention centre and most of them are going to be deported. It's a really grim reality to have to face.

Oona: How is the art group different than you imagined it would be?

Sima: I thought it would be a lot grimmer, and it is, but there is more, too. There were days when I was working as a volunteer with an NGO that provides basic services at the detention centre and I would see forty people and thirty of them would be in tears. But in the art group, you also see people supporting each other, you see how they survive and keep up their sense of humor and joy of life and optimism. There is almost a forgiveness of everything that was happening to them. I feel awed and humbled by the people inside, their courage and their perseverance. To see these women help each other survive is an affirmation that expressions of humanity and organizing can happen in the worst, most desperate contexts.

Farrah: Prisons are set up to separate people from each other, but no matter how the immigration and enforcement authorities try to keep people isolated from each other, they can't take away the support and connections these women share. The art group is the only thing at the detention centre that pulls all these women from different places to the same table, looking at each other, facing each other. It's really human.

Oona: How does the art group affect the lives of the women and children in detention?

Sima: Some of what happens in the group continues after our art session. I know there are connections made between some of the women because I see them outside hanging out after … there is spillover.

Jean: In some of the activities the women work on something together. One time we did profile drawings of shadows. One person stands while the other person does the profile, and then you color in your own profile. People were laughing. It was really fun and we always had music on. I specifically remember this one moment. The song "Lady in Red" was playing, and almost everyone in the room started singing. It was so funny.

Sima: Since we started the art group, a couple of the women who have been there for a long time started an origami project that took off through the whole detention centre. They began making little origami birds and moved on to huge, intricate pineapples. The women gave them out as gifts to each other and to us, and used them to decorate their rooms.

Oona: And this didn't come from you guys?

Jean & Farrah: No! They did it on their own.

Sima: I think the art group inspired them. One of the women knew how to do origami. She shared her knowledge with other women and it just took off. There were assembly lines of women working on this big-ass pineapple using newspaper, magazines, whatever they could get their hands on. The art thing has really taken on a life of its own outside of the group.

Oona: What images and themes are repeated in the art?

Sima: There are lots of pictures of home and family: the landscapes of Costa Rica, the beaches of St. Lucia, the fields and deserts of Iraq. There are many pictures depicting homeland and longing.

Farrah: Some of the women do pictures of the kind of prints you find on fabric from India.

Jean: And hearts with their boyfriend's names.

Sima: Things like "I love Canada, I want to stay." It's heartbreaking.

Farrah: Drawing on my own perspective, I wouldn't have expected that anybody in there would say "I love Canada." But where these women are coming from and the reality they have to go back to makes this country an incredible place where they just want to stay.

CHILDREN IN DETENTION

Oona: A lot of people don't realize that Canada regularly incarcerates the children of non-status immigrants. What did you learn from the art group about the impact of detention on children?

Jean: I remember this one little girl who was three years old. When she and her mom first came to the group, she had lots of energy. She was running around and excited to be painting and drawing. Two weeks after that, and then another two weeks later, she became a different child; she was quiet, passive and had so much less life in her. The consequences on a three-year-old being held in detention for one month, two, three months and more are physically and emotionally visible.

Farrah: There was a period of time in the winter at the Celebrity Inn when detainees were not allowed to go outside for months. There was a small fenced in area in the back and no one was even allowed out the door, even though there were very young children in there.

Sima: Almost all the women that we work with have a strong sense of family, and they are dealing with the tragedy of broken families. They don't know where their sons or husbands or fathers are. The heartbreak of terror and loss is overwhelming.

Farrah: Women with children have this terrible burden of trying to hold everything together so that their children aren't equally as terrified. They don't have anyone to talk to, they can't cry or yell, to show their anger and frustration. They try to hold it in. The strength of the women who do that is incredible.

Jean: I remember one woman whose daughter was with her. I think she was eleven or twelve. The mother had this terrible guilt about what was happening to her daughter. It wasn't her fault, and I am sure she knew that deep down, but at the same time she wanted so badly for this not to be happening to her daughter.

CONNECTIONS

Oona: Do you see the art group as being political?

Sima: Yes. At the beginning of each session, we announce that we are a political group and that part of our purpose is to get the message out to the world about the conditions and effects of detention centres. We also talk about our own personal experiences with immigration, which helps to break down the barriers and explain our motivation for being in the detention centre. I've talked about my personal experience with immigration to show that this is something I have a lived experience and connection with. We understand this because we have been through this in our personal lives with our communities and our families.

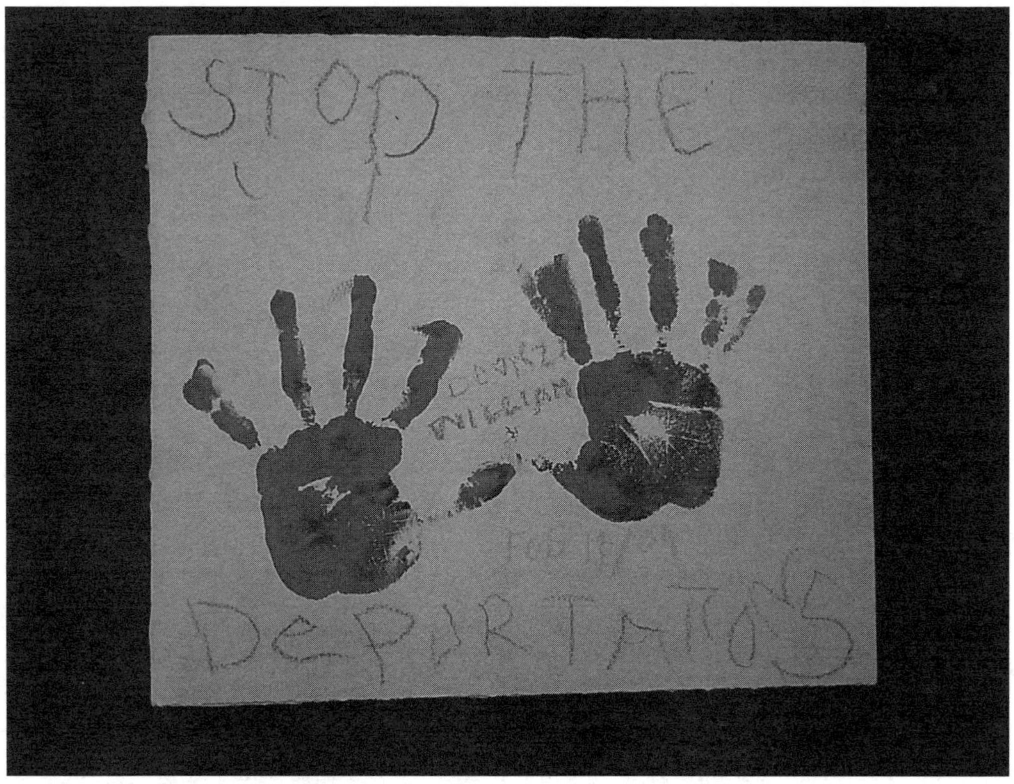

"Stop the Deportations"

Oona: How does the art group project fit into the overall work done by members of No One Is Illegal in Toronto?

Farrah: It gives us a sense of who is in the detention centre and what communities are being targeted in Toronto.

Sima: We also get a sense of how people are arrested. We see the connection between police, employers and landlords and being in detention. There are huge numbers of people, mostly men of colour, who are randomly stopped by police when driving a car. Women are often the targets of landlords who want to increase the rent or evict them, so they report the women to immigration. Employers often post bail for detainees and then withdraw the bail when people demand wages.

Farrah: There are also women who have called the police because they are being abused and then they get thrown into detention. This effectively tells abusers that it's acceptable for non-status women to be abused. As political organizers we know that we have an urgent responsibility to send a very loud message to our government that this lack of protection for women in abusive situations can't be tolerated.

Sima: It's really traumatic to see women doubly victimized: first at the hands of their abusers and second when they call the police for protection. Often the initial reason they walked into a police station or called 911 is totally ignored when their lack of status is discovered. I have had women in detention crying again and again, just wanting to have the police go to question the person they reported, to somehow make it all worth it. Some of these women still have scars and bruises on their body.

Jean: The work we do in detention makes it urgently clear how necessary a Don't Ask, Don't Tell policy is in Toronto. When women end up in detention because they've reported a sexual assault or laid charges of domestic abuse, there is obviously a huge problem. Similar cases arise for families who are living underground after a deportation order has been issued — if they try to put their child in school, it's likely that immigration officers will be waiting to arrest them. The vulnerability of people to exploitation is extreme.

Sima: I don't think any other kind of work would have taught us so much or made us as committed to this area of activism. And I don't think it could have been done with a different group of people. I think there are certain areas of work that have to be done by women. I don't know how to stress that enough.

The Arts in Detention Group provides the women detainees with an opportunity to connect socially and politically with each other and with the activists who organize the group. It serves as a distraction from the painful drudgery of life in detention and the looming possibility of deportation. For women with children, it is also a chance to share some of the responsibility of childcare and for the children to be with other people. For both

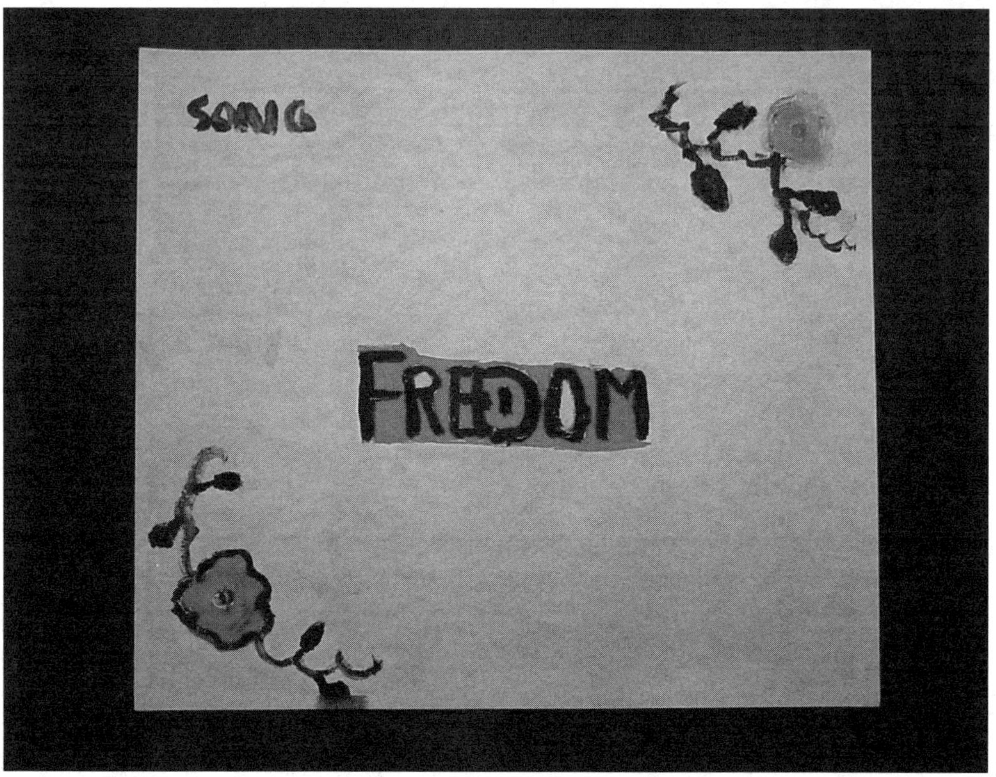

"Freedom"

the women and children, it is time away from the guards. The art itself is an outlet for frustration and pain, but also an opportunity to express hope for the future and joy in life.

In addition, the group is part of a larger anti-deportation, anti-detention movement, and the women who participate in the group know this. The women from No One Is Illegal are activists working to end deportations and detentions; this helps to establish trust with the women in detention. The art group provides a space for activists and people facing deportation to connect and share knowledge of who is in detention and how they got there, and to develop strategies to fight against deportations. As a continuation of that political work, No One Is Illegal is beginning to display the artwork produced in the detention centre at events and galleries as an educational and outreach tool for developing allies and building solidarity among immigrant and activist communities. The artwork produced is powerful and viewers cannot help but be touched by the expressions of fear and loss contrasted with images of home and family that the women and children convey in their artwork.

NOTES

An earlier version of this article appeared as "Drawing Detention: A Conversation with No One Is Illegal," *Fuse,* 2 May 2005.

1. The slogan No One Is Illegal has been taken up by groups around the globe. In Canada, there are No One Is Illegal groups in Toronto, Victoria, Vancouver, Montreal and Winnipeg. These autonomous organizations are loosely affiliated and sometimes work together on campaigns and strategizing.
2. The campaign calls for city services to be provided on a "don't ask" basis — that is, residents are not required to provide information on their citizenship in order to access services (such as emergency services, schools, social assistance, social housing), and city employees who do have access to such information "don't tell," meaning that such information is not passed on to other government bodies.
3. The Heritage Inn was opened in April 2004. Prior to that, the Toronto Immigrant Holding Centre was located at the Celebrity Inn, which was also a fully functioning hotel.

CHAPTER 15

Language as Landscape:

NAVIGATING POST-CONFLICT RECONSTRUCTION WITH BOSNIAN YOUTH

Heather Hermant

A FEW HOLES SHOT THROUGH A BOARDED UP WINDOW LET IN LIGHT, illuminating old toys, a photo on the wall of a once young couple. Two boys and a girl sit around. They came to visit their grandmother when the war started. The first week, they watched TV and played outside. But "the big bang" put an end to electricity. Light and TV became old candles and even older toys. Nothing but silence surrounds them now, their presence almost irrelevant to the world. They are afraid of the great authority of the dark silently floating around their fragile bodies. Five-year-old Vladimir is the childish cry behind the silenced voice of fear.

Vladimir (almost crying): I'm calling grandma if you don't give it baaaaaack!!!!!!!!

Marica (angry, pulling his hair): Oh, you're such a cry baby, here's your stupid toy!!

Vladimir: Why can't we go outside and play?

Marica: We can't go outside, dummy, something strange is happening … can't you hear?

— From *The Turtle* by Vladimir Tomić, 2003[1]

From 2001 to 2004 I worked as a facilitator for the Brčko Academic Scholarship Program. Brčko District is the only entity in Bosnia[2] where all public infrastructures, from government to policing to education, integrate the three predominant ethnic groups: Croats (Catholic), Serbs (Orthodox Christian) and Bosniaks (Muslim).[3] The Program coincided with the ethnic reintegration of the Brčko District school system, a gradual process that began in September 2001. The Scholarship Program was initiated and funded by the U.S. Department of State and administered by AYUSA International (Academic Year in the U.S.A), an international youth exchange organization based in San Francisco with a regional office in Belgrade.[4]

The Program brought together twenty-two high-achieving teenagers of all ethnic backgrounds for the purpose of "bolstering desegregation and school reform by introducing promising youth … to successful models for

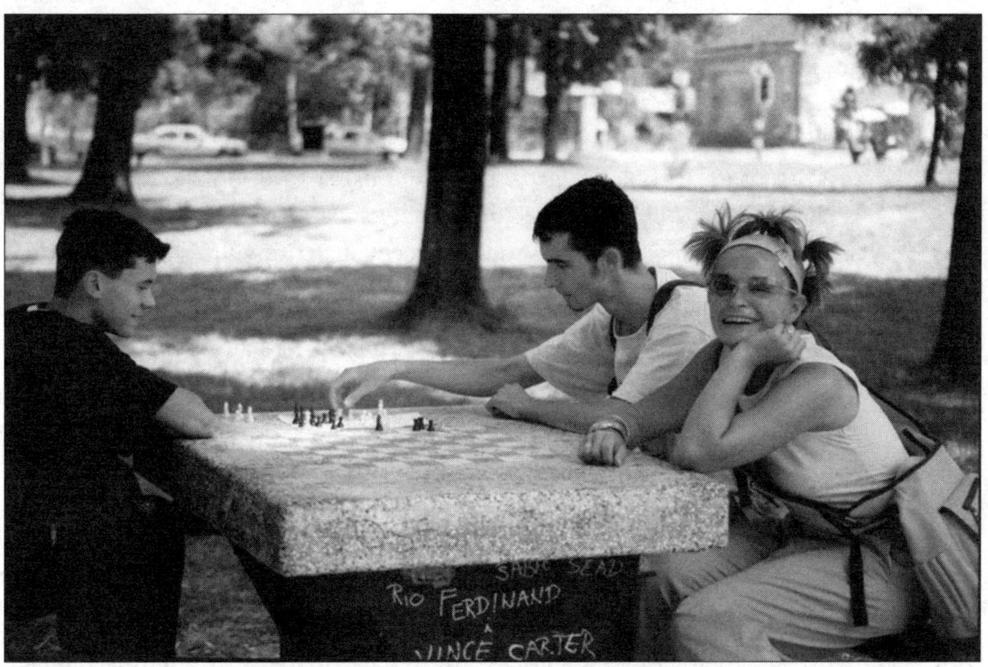

Students from 2001, self-titled 'Pioneers,' play chess in the central park. Note the name of an American sports figure etched onto the table.

pluralism in the U.S."[5] Participants attended a summer school in Brčko, where they developed projects to be carried out in their home communities in the fall. They then spent the winter in the U.S. living with volunteer host families and attending high school. Upon their return, they did follow-up community work. Four groups of students participated between 2001 and 2005. By June 2004, the last students to have spent high school in segregated classrooms graduated.

In this chapter I describe tensions I encountered with the youth in Brčko and discuss how I navigated these through narrative arts-based practices. I focus on how English, the operating language of the Program, emerged as an instructive site of refuge, collaboration and exclusion. Brčko students associated English with a successful future, and it made sense to improve their English in time for their trip to the U.S. English also served as an available space for sharing difficult memories, which might be politicized or silenced in their local languages. However, in a broader context, English holds geopolitical meaning, which I felt acutely while my students may not have, especially given that the Program began just prior to 9/11 and ran through the start and escalation of the war in Iraq.

Ethnic reintegration among Bosnian students has been intimately tied to a mandate to bolster integration of Bosnia into global capitalism. In Brčko, international peacekeeping soldiers, U.N. appointed administrators and funders, and post-conflict reconstruction NGO workers (like myself) have largely operated in English or German, the languages that are guiding market integration, and have worked with translators. Market expansion is led in Brčko largely by the United States in competition with European Union countries, to whom Bosnia can offer a potential source of resources, cheap labour and consumers. As was the case with post-communist Eastern Europe, privatization is likely to ensure that most formerly state-owned, state-run industries will be controlled by foreign multinational corporations. Bosnia is also of strategic interest geographically for both the European Union and the United States, located as it is between the Middle East and Europe. It was in this general context that my students were being offered scholarships to participate in an English-language based, U.S.-funded intitative. Given the mix of mandates at play, I came to view English as a problematic mediating bridge, a temporary tool to use carefully, and move away from as I worked with the youth.[6]

I illustrate this view through a discussion of newspaper (2001), theatre (2003) and peer mediation (2004) projects. I layer my reflections with excerpts from my own diaries and memories, and with student narratives and interview excerpts I gathered, in order to show how the process felt to me. Through these excerpts I point to conflicted metaphors of home, shelter and migration.

What did I bring and what was my position as part of the Program? I am a Canadian performer and journalist. I lived in Budapest and worked throughout the region from 1997 until 2003. In 2001, I was invited to be a workshop facilitator for the Scholarship Program summer school, intially to lead workshops in journalism. I took on greater responsibility in subsequent years, influencing the summer school program design, bringing in other facilitators to work with me and structuring the summer school around a broader vision of community building and the arts. I did most of the Bosnia work before I began to use "community arts language"[7] to name my collaborative, improvisational approach to "teaching." I operated from an assets-based model of community development, which, contrary to strategies that produce dependent communities, aims to identify and mobilize local strengths for building unexpected relationships and for maximizing contributors to projects.[8]

I do not speak the languages of Bosnia, once known as the single language of Serbo-Croat. Language is a focal point of conflicting ethnic nationalisms in Bosnia. In 2001 my colleagues and I, our students and the broader community safely referred to all local speech as "the local language." Today, local people more openly refer to their languages as Bosnian, Croatian and Serbian. These are mutually intelligible, just as dialects of English are, though Serbs use the Cyrillic alphabet, an alphabet often not intelligible to young Croats and Muslims for a host of reasons that range from segregated schooling to refugee experiences abroad. Not knowing any of these languages was central to my experience. However, my own multilingualism (English from birth, French from age five in a francophone school, Hungarian later in life) shaped my awareness of language issues in Bosnia.

WRITING BRČKO: THE NEWSPAPER PROJECT

> Jay (my American colleague) draws a sketch of Europe on the blackboard. He is preparing students for how much or how little their American hosts might know about Bosnia from the news. "Opposite Italy over here maybe, Croatia," he says. "Bosnia. Oh yeah, and Kosovo." He draws a circle. Just then a local teacher in the back of the class blurts out angrily, "Kosovo is NOT a country! You cannot draw it like that!" A group of students cheer. They must be Serbian, united behind Kosovo. I see the divide for the first time, from the outburst of some and the silence of the others.
>
> —*Journal excerpt, 2001*

The 2001 students came into the Program one month prior to reintegration, the first to sit in an officially sanctioned multi-ethnic classroom since before the war. Ten months earlier, protests against reintegration had shut down the schools. Walking home in mixed company was a bold act that summer. In a context where people *are named by* forces of ethnic nationalism, narrative is a potential site of agency in self-definition, a site of dialogue through listening to others' experiences, and a site of collaboration and community generation. I understand "narrative" as any telling based on real life history. Through gathering community narratives in and out of class, students generated the material for Brčko District's first multi-ethnic student newspaper. The shared production process was an enactment of a new multi-ethnic imaginary in a larger context of segregation (or rather, a re-enactment of a very old multi-ethnic imaginary damaged to the brink of erasure by war).

To get the newspaper laid out and printed, AYUSA hired Bora, head of the Brčko Press Centre, to give journalism workshops and see the paper to printing. I took notes during his workshops, where students flipped back and forth between local languages with Bora, and English with myself and Jay, the foreign facilitators, while Serbian colleagues sat with and sometimes translated for us:

> S and A say they will interview the mayor. S says 75% of youth want to leave Bosnia. What's he gonna do about that? J asks where the stat came from. Bora says the source should be quoted. E asks what alphabet the paper will be in. D asks whether there will be ads. Bora says we have to decide. O says we don't have space for ads. S says she can't read Cyrillic. E says everyone knows Latin. Jay says why not drop English, and do Cyrillic

> and Latin. S says why not do all three. There's widespread support for this. R says writers can just write in their own language. S says we have to show we're multi-ethnic. M says but we all study English and we all understand Latin, it's international. Bora says all alphabets are international. A says the editors should decide on the language. The main editor says no, that's not democratic. Bora says he has no problem with a trilingual layout.
>
> —*Journal excerpt, 2001*

The language issue would become most challenging at the layout phase, when space constraints forced compromises on content, which were necessary to accommodate the translations. In the meantime, I ran workshops that began with a self-interview, where students wrote their own autobiographical statements and presented these to the class. I then asked those listening to re-present each autobiography as a biography. This was part of a strategy to talk about listening, how to zero in on the main points presented and how to recognize where the listener might be interpreting incorrectly. This prepared them to go out and interview people of their own choice in the community. For example, one student who was herself interested in becoming a police officer, interviewed two Scottish community police officers from the international peacekeeping force. Two other students interviewed their mayor. Students then presented their interview experiences to the class. We worked on how to shape the interviews into articles. We analyzed sample articles for balance. We talked about how to identify and give voice to different stakeholders as part of the objective of fair reporting.

At the same time, students were working on their own creative non-fiction, writing stories about their own life experiences. We formed editorial teams according to their interests, and they were charged with tasks ranging from reporting news to reporting sports and fashion, handling photography and art and doing translations. By the time summer school was finished, there was a wealth of material. I left Brčko as they entered the layout phase with a fairly clear idea of the mix of material they wanted to see in the paper, representative of the activities they had engaged in throughout summer school. Bora was to then help them with layout for a target launch date in the fall.

The first issue was politically correct. It defered to authorities and was written in English, with translations in Latin or Cyrillic alphabets according to the chosen language of the author of each article. The American district supervisor's visit to the class with the mayor was on the cover. The mayor's interview took two pages. Creative writing about students' wartime experiences, funny or not, were not included. Bora had a lot to do with how this issue turned out, so the students asked to work autonomously on the second issue without adult intervention. In the next issue, the big headline read "HI! This Is Who We Are ..." Creative writing, funny and not, took up the most space, and all the writing was published in English. Several subsequent issues were also published in English.

Creating this one project together was a major accomplishment, but I was left asking how much the product — and its audience — mattered. Program participants, American hosts and local youth who understood English could access the content of the English-language issues, but many locals did not speak English. Did students choose English partly to avoid local judgement? The choice had primarily been about youth asserting their control of the paper, but I wondered if internal group unity had been forged at the expense of the community. I also worried about asking students to risk too much through writing assignments on real life experiences, challenges, memories and dreams. Was I a voyeur, encouraging stories that fit neatly into post-conflict aid metanarratives, or worse, risking students' retraumatisation?

Oral Stories: The Theatre Project

> Late one night, through a hole in the boards, the boy spots a turtle in the garden. He sneaks out and befriends this creature with its house on its back. He confides his fear of the dark, and invites the turtle to his birthday. His cousins ridicule him for his wild imagination. After a very long time, the boy's mother returns. She cries with relief that the children are unharmed. Vladimir asks hopefully, "Mom, can we bring the turtle home with us? Can I have a party?" He is more upset about leaving the turtle behind than he is happy to see his mother again. When the family is reunited in their flat that night, the war over, they hold hands and make a vow to forget.
>
> — From *The Turtle* by Vladimir Tomić, 2003

I structured the summer school of 2003 around an oral history project as an example of community building through the arts. The theme was "What is Home?" I had students collect stories from elders in their segregated neigh-

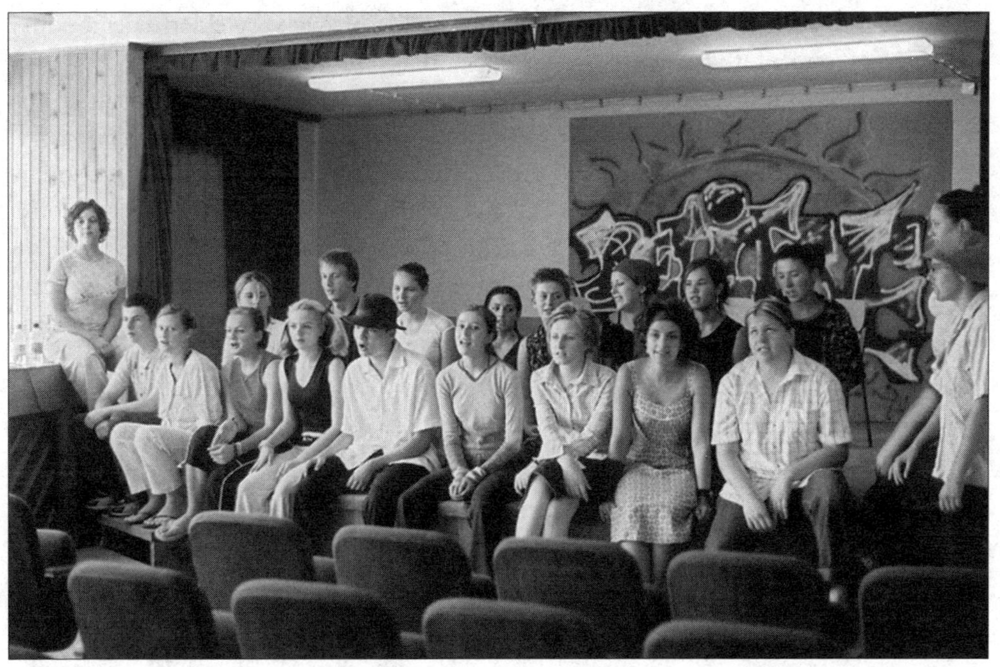

Rehearsal in the school theatre against a graffiti board back-drop.

bourhoods and bring them back to share with the class, while also sharing their own personal stories. I invited another facilitator to work with me to help the students adapt four of these stories to short plays.[9] I also had them write their own personal monologues about the meaning of home. The monologues and the plays formed the theatre night, in which all students from the summer school performed. Some of the students also made giant graffiti paintings to exhibit at theatre night, one of which served as a backdrop for the performance. All summer school students participated as actors in one of the plays, and some also recited their monologues on the meaning of home. Through this event, crafted from local experience, students and their audience "visited" across the ethnic and generational divides, in a shared space. The theatre night took place in a high-school theatre. Guests included parents, family, friends, teachers, local press, politicans and internationals.

The Turtle was one of four stories adapted to stage for the theatre night. Another play told the story of an interethnic marriage that had stood the test of time, and was adapted from the life of two very elderly neighbours of one of the students. Two other plays addressed anti-Roma (Gypsy) racism and teenagers coming of age. The latter, about a girl striving for independence, made controversial use of music, which accompanied TV announcements of the dead during the war. Students chose it for a choreographic sequence in which the girl breaks free from what holds her back. They saw this as giving a cue to their elders to move past the war.

During the theatre night, we were once again faced with the language issue. The students wanted to perform in English, but part of my motivation for doing the project was to build bridges within the community and to celebrate it through its own stories. To perform only in English would be to exclude a large part of that community. Ultimately, students wrote synopses of the plays in the local languages, which they printed and handed out to the audience. A student from each play also introduced his or her group's play with an overview in their own language.

Interspersed between these short plays, eight students recited their monologues on the meaning of home. I asked four of these students to recite their monologues in their own languages so that those in the audience who did not understand English would understand some of the monologues and have a sense of what the monologues in English might be about. This was a very difficult decision for me. I had suspected with the newspaper project that English had been a medium through which students could share difficult stories with one another, while partially protecting the tellers from broader local judgement. Thus, when theatre night came, I assumed it would be difficult to recite a monologue about home in a local language, because the war and its impacts were very much present in these monologues.

It came down to a judgement call on my part. The students I asked to recite in a local language were students I felt were confident about doing so and whose stories did not seem to me to be potentially contentious in a public multi-ethnic arena. Where before my students had used English themselves as a place of refuge and exclusion, on theatre night, I felt I was using the value of English as a simultaneous outlet and a refuge many of my students seemed to need. For those who did not understand English, I hoped that the body gestures would tell them what the words did not, and that the words that could be understood might speak to those words that were not understood. It was like a dance around and through a complex landscape. Still I wondered whether even having had just a few of them recite their monologues in the local languages might have been pushing them to risk too much.

The following summer (2004), I had a group interview with several of the students from that theatre night. Here is what two of them had to say about their experiences reciting the monologues:

> *B*: I had to do mine in the local language … If I had to do it in English, I would have just said, "Here's what I wrote," but in Bosnian everyone could understand. It's more personal in your own language.
>
> *Me*: Did it make you feel nervous?
>
> *B*: Yeah, a lot.
>
> *C*: It's safer in English.

In reflecting back on the theatre project, I realize that these students identified this contradiction: they felt their messages of reconciliation and the need to get past the war urgently needed to reach their elders. Yet most of these adults, including many of their parents, could not understand English.

Metaphors in Motion: The Peer Mediation Project

> I hear TRAINS, first time since the war! They've almost finished rebuilding the leveled mosque. The strip is packed at night. It definitely feels different than 2001 when there was no one out, so much tension. Maybe I can't tell if there's tension anymore.
>
> Our neighbour who has no roof on half her house is weeding in slippers and housecoat. More tile on her bombed roof each year. I'm watching a stork labouring a curve, wings outstretched, winding to landing behind her roof, its neck tucked in like plumbing as the feet reach for place.
>
> —*Journal and video diary excerpts, 2004*

In August of 2004, I trained students in Peer Mediation, an alternative dispute resolution system run by and for youth.[10] This strategy empowers young people to solve their own problems and uses theatre techniques and role-playing. Students learn how to use non-judgement and facilitation skills when they assist others in resolving conflicts, and at the same time learn to understand their own individual behaviour patterns. Peer mediation programs exist in schools across North America and Europe. One of Canada's oldest programs is found at Toronto's Westview Secondary School, where I first observed peer mediation training and talked to students about its effectiveness, before I left again for Bosnia.[11]

I felt peer mediation could answer a challenge I posed for myself. In the summer school program, I wanted to find a way to move beyond English towards a sustainable and ethical exit strategy for the Program in its final year. In 2004, I went to Brčko a week before summer school began and spent one week training eight former students of the Program so that they could shadow me and assist me as I trained the final group of twenty-two participants. I also worked with two local teachers to ensure that they could provide adult support for the students in the long term.

My aim was to have students from across the generations of the Program work together in running their own peer mediation project as a collective and seek their own funding if they so desired. I viewed mediation as a project that could enhance the strengths of Brčko, reinforce non-violence strategies and empower youth. I wanted to train the students in English and then have them act out mock mediations in their own languages to see how it felt, what kinds of adjustments and changes they might make to adapt the system to their context and then to lay out a plan from what they had learned for initiating a broader community project in their own languages.

Over the four weeks of training, students brought real conflicts from their own lives to the workshops, and we turned these into role plays. One such role play emerged from one participant's conflict with his father over wanting to get his eyebrow pierced. We converted this into a conflict between a boy and his girlfriend who didn't want him to go ahead with the piercing. In one improvisation, without discussing what the outcome might be, two students played the part of disputants and two played mediators. Through much back and forth, the disputants told their sides of the story and listened as the mediators summarized each time a disputant spoke. From the sidelines, I reminded them of the steps they needed to keep in mind: it was the the mediators' roles

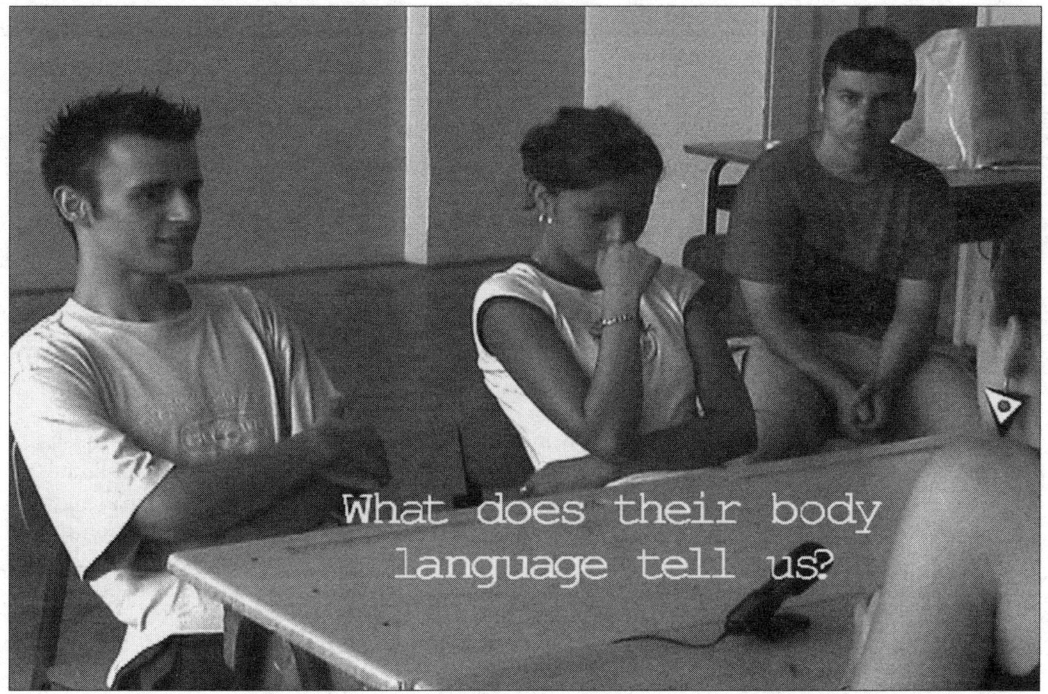

A mediation over a contested eyebrow piercing. From Peace Starts With Me.

to encourage the disputants to say how they felt each time they heard the other disputant talk.

Ultimately, the four students arrived at a solution that had been jointly proposed and negotiated by the two disputants. As a class we then talked about how it felt for the four actors to do the mediation. The mediators talked about the frustration of maintaining a stance of non-judgement. The class offered their feedback on how the mediators had performed. We analyzed the feasibility of the solution, which was more about communication within the relationship of the young couple than it was about the piercing. We could have done this same mediation with different students, ten different times, and we might very well have seen ten different solutions. The solutions the students came up with were often quite different from what I as an adult might have proposed or foreseen. The point, however, is that over and over again the students acted as if they really were disputants, or mediators, and they worked hard to maintain their calm, their commitment and their willingness to listen and arrive at a solution. We filmed some of the mock mediations for a peer mediation training video entitled *Peace Starts With Me.*[12]

By enacting many such mediation scenarios throughout the training, the students expanded their repertoire of behaviour, challenging themselves to think about how they act socially on a daily basis and how they might transform their approach to disagreement in their daily lives. They also saw what they could accomplish as mediators and, as disputants, how great a feeling it was to facilitate a workable solution. I watched as their initial skepticism about the feasibility of a peer mediation program in Brčko gave way to enthusiasm.

> We did mock mediations in the local language today. I asked How did it feel? "It sounds really funny." What sounds funny? "There are just some things that sound strange in our language. 'Make eye contact' doesn't really have a translation." I'm so glad these issues came out because they became aware of what work they have to do to think about whether this could work here. They were really excited. It was fantastic.
>
> — *Video diary excerpt, August 2004*

Throughout the mediation training, we also undertook a parallel project aimed at underscoring the importance of community interaction in projects. To this end, we ran a homemade card project. Students brought in trash paper from which to make homemade note cards. They distributed these to friends and family, who inscribed onto them mottos for young people to live by. Mottos are mini-narratives that affirm local knowledge. They resonated inspiration as we explored conflicts through mock mediations. "If you want to love and respect others, first you should love and respect yourself," reads one, in English. "You will never know the rose if you don't also know the thorns," read another in Cyrillic. Through mottos, the community contributed to this youth empowerment and non-violence project.

This final group of the Scholarship Program also held a theatre night at the end of summer school. Amid dance sequences, music and plays, they incorporated mock mediations in order to present the mediation idea to the public. This time they performed in the town's largest public venue, in all local languages, plus English. At the end of the performance, they floated like birds across the stage, embracing each other as they crossed

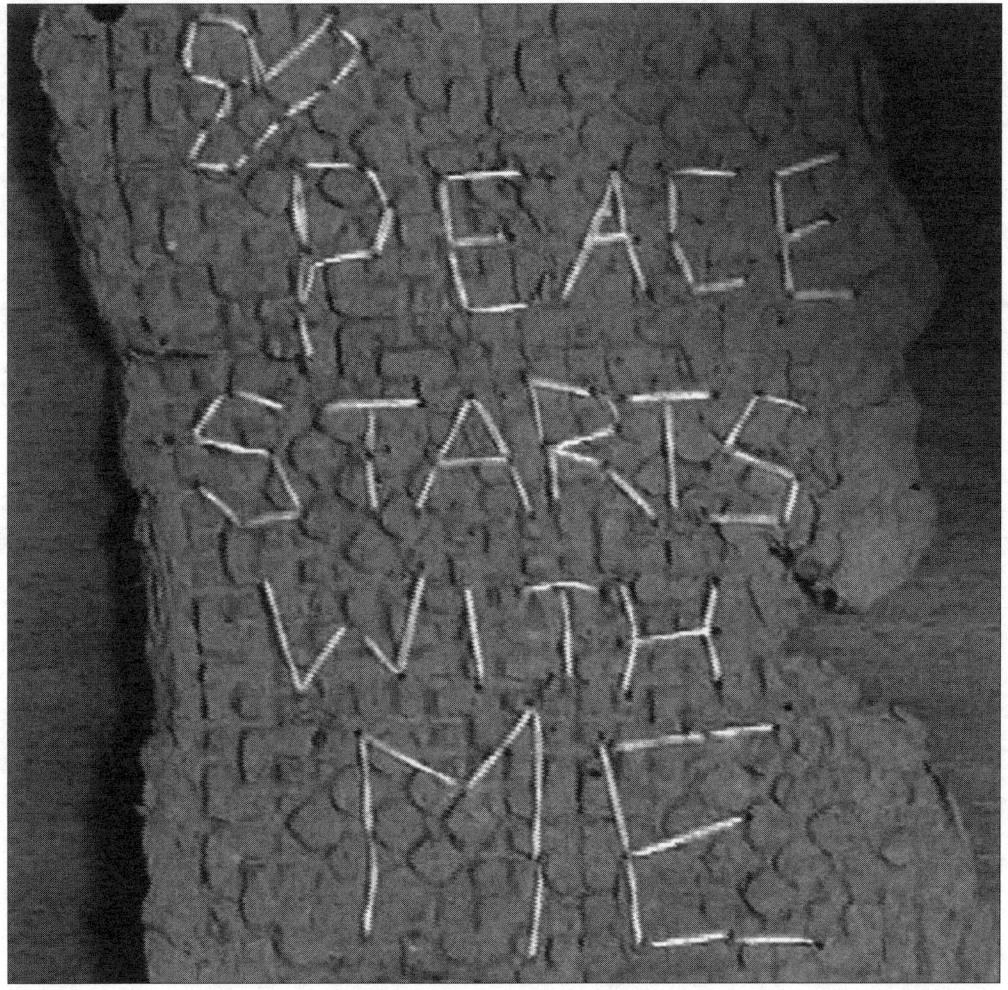

The author's contribution to the postcard collection, 2004.

paths, then wandered off stage and through their audience, handing out the motto-inscribed note cards, disseminating local knowledge across the ethnic divide.

From the peer mediation training, students have now also created a local language peer mediation training manual and with the co-operation of local principals, they are running peer mediation workshops in their own languages with elementary school students. They don't need English to do so. In class and out, this last group of students, who entered the first fully reintegrated schools in Bosnia in September 2004, all comfortably refer to the "local language" as "Bosnian," "Serbian," "Croatian" or "our language."

In Bosnia, group arts processes built space in which trust could be cultivated (though not necessarily realized) among students and between myself and my students. The resulting productions — a newspaper, plays, mediation — are like quilted canopies that I continue to look at, as ways to remember and to process the meaning of unresolved contradictions. I carry these contradictions around like loose threads tied around my index finger, reminding myself of their rich value. Among the many questions these arts practices undertaken with youth in Bosnia unveiled was the question of finding the right language with which to navigate. Through not knowing, and at the charged and often uncomfortable intersection of the local and the global, what I came to realize is a more complex understanding of what language *is*. Language is a context, culturally and experientially crafted and deployed. Sometimes it is the texture of a well-known home. Sometimes it is a state of departure, of arriving, of moving towards, within or away. Sometimes on the trajectory between languages we can find a place for hovering around what is so difficult to express.

NOTES

A Martin Cohnstaedt Graduate Research Award for studies in non-violence from York University's Centre for International and Security Studies supported this research. Photos and film stills by myself and student comments from interviews conducted by myself in 2001 and 2004. Names withheld to respect privacy.

I dedicate this chapter to the young people of Brčko and to Orunamamu, storyteller, mentor, friend and grandmother-in-residence at the YellowLegs Storytelling Museum, Oakland, California.

1. Tomić was a Scholarship Program participant and was seventeen when he wrote this play, which is based on his own life. He lives in Brčko. The excerpts are assembled from my own Program archives from 2004 and from an unpublished script-in-progress given to me by Tomić in 2005. Used with permission.

2. I use Bosnia for Bosnia and Hercegovina.

3. "Bosniak" accommodates those for whom religion is not the only identifier, given that Bosnian Serbs and Bosnian Croats each have religious and cultural terms through which to self-identify. Bosniak also avails the term Bosnian to all regardless of ethnic identity. However, I never heard anyone use Bosniak in Brčko, neither locals nor internationals. I use Muslim, Serb(ian) and Croat(ian) according to local practice.

4. At the suggestion of American educator Jay Miller, the Program's first facilitator, Milena Krstić of AYUSA Belgrade hired me.

5. "Brčko Program: Program Goals." *AYUSA Online*. Retrieved 10 March 2005 from www.ayusa.org/about/grants?grant=Brčko.

6. On how participants interrupted metanarratives of aid and globalization, see Heather Hermant, "Narrative and Arts-Based Strategies for Conflict Resolution: A Case Study from Brčko District, Bosnia," in Ryerson Christie and Elizabeth Dauphinée, eds., *The Ethics of Building Peace in International Relations: Selected Proceedings of the Twelfth Annual Conference of the Centre for International and Security Studies* (Toronto: York University, 2005), 233–258.

7. Deborah Barndt, "By Whom and For Whom? Intersections of Participatory Research and Community Art," in Ardra L. Cole, L. Neilsen, J.G. Knowles and T. Luciani, eds., *Provoked by Art: Theorizing Arts-Informed Research* (Halifax: Backalong Books and Centre for Arts-Informed Research, 2004), 221–234.

8. John P. Kretzmann and John L.McKnight, *Building Communities from the Inside Out: A Path Toward Finding and Mobilizing a Community's Assets* (Chicago: Institute for Policy Research, Northwestern University, 1993); John P. Kretzmann and John L.McKnight, "Assets-Based Community Development (The Role of Nonprofit Organizations in Renewing Community)," *National Civic Review* 85, no 4 (1996), 23–27. Am Johal, whom I invited in 2002, introduced the model. We emphasized that goals need not be weighed in economic terms.

9. I invited actor-educator Ben O'Brien in 2003 to help transform stories into theatre. Jelena Gasić of youth NGO One World Our World Belgrade fulfilled this role in 2004. O'Brien introduced me to the work of Michael Rohd, *Theatre for Community, Conflict and Dialogue: The Hope Is Vital Training Manual* (Portsmouth, UK: Heinemann, 1998). Rohd uses methods of Augusto Boal, American improvisational theatre guru Viola Spolin and others with the aim of empowering communities through theatre.

10. See D. W. Johnson and Roger Johnson, "Conflict Resolution and Peer Mediation Programs in Elementary and Secondary Schools: A Review of the Research," *Review of Educational Research* 66, no. 4 (1996), 459–506; D. W. Johnson and Roger Johnson, *Teaching Students to be Peacemakers* (Edina, MN: Interaction Book Company, 1995).

11. The Westview mediation program was set up by Claude Grimmond as part of his master's thesis work at York University's Faculty of Environmental Studies many years ago. I observed peer mediation classes at Westview taught by Theresa Smith (herself trained by Grimmond and no longer with Westview) who provided me with resources I used in Brčko. Irena Radić of AYUSA Belgrade organized the logistics of contacting and bringing together a group of eight past Program participants for voluntary peer mediation training in August of 2004.

12. Heather Hermant and Brčko Peacemakers, *Peace Starts With Me: A Peer Mediation Training Video* (unpublished). Filmed by Marko Jočić .

CHAPTER 16

Acts of Embodiment:

EXPLORATIONS IN COLLABORATIVE PHOTOTHERAPY

Stephanie Conway and Julia Winckler

IN A CULTURE WHERE WE GIVE MORE AND MORE POWER TO EXPERTS, WE need to learn to make sense for ourselves. The practice of phototherapy is about engaging in creative acts that make meaning through connection and that render the unconscious more visible. Working together, we create a performative space, embodying our experience on film. "Statements in pictures … embrace a wider range of bodily experience than intellectual verbal statements can … they give the sense of a deeper-rooted kind of knowing."[1] Photography has long been used as a tool of self-knowledge and a means of expression. Phototherapy puts an emphasis on the collaborative process of creating images that bring key moments of our lives to light.

In this chapter we discuss some of the insights we have gained while practising phototherapy. In 1996, we met in Toronto at Rosy Martin's workshop "Re-enactment Phototherapy: Memory and Identity" and began an ongoing collaboration. At the time, Julia was a social worker in Toronto with an interest in using photography in the therapeutic process. Stephanie was completing a Master in Environmental Studies and ran an experimental photography course at an alternative high school in Toronto.

Over several more sessions, we were able to create spaces of varying depths in which we shared fears, fantasies and pain. This formed the basis of a strong and lasting friendship.

We want to share our explorations with phototherapy in the hopes of inspiring others to try this powerful method for themselves. In the first section, we define phototherapy as a working method. We situate the practice by presenting the pioneering work of British photographers Jo Spence and Rosy Martin. In the second section, we discuss our own experiences with phototherapy, including step-by-step guidelines, which are followed by individual analyses of two recent sessions.

PHOTOTHERAPY AS A WORKING METHOD

In the work we do, we explore the intersections between photography, the politics of representation and therapeutic uses of the camera.[2] Phototherapy is a technique that aims to challenge and unfix established practices of seeing and knowing. "Clearly, if psychoanalysis is the 'talking cure,' then phototherapy could conceivably be the 'seeing cure.' It should become a priority to work to find ways to produce new photographs which can begin to address the silences, absences and disavowals that are continually being dealt with in therapy."[3] The most original aspect of phototherapy, as compared with traditional therapeutic and photographer–sitter relationships, is its collaborative process: we are both subjects *and* objects of the gaze. Phototherapy blurs the boundaries between the public/private sphere, the personal/political and therapist/client. It offers a non-hierarchical form of therapeutic intervention based on a trusting relationship.

Phototherapy was practised by British photographer Jo Spence as early as the 1980s, often in collaboration with Rosy Martin. Spence (1934–92) laid the groundwork for phototherapy by exploring her own life experiences and "putting herself in the picture." She took her discoveries into the public domain, "'making strange' the everyday, normalized, institutional practice and codes [of photography] … so that their commonsense, unquestioned notions become disrupted."[4] When Spence was diagnosed with breast cancer she made self-portraits that challenged cultural expectations of illness. "Will I be a heroine or a victim? … I had no desire to be either; I merely wanted to be 'seen' as a person in the daily struggle to restore equilibrium and health to myself."[5] (See Image 1.) As Terry Dennett,

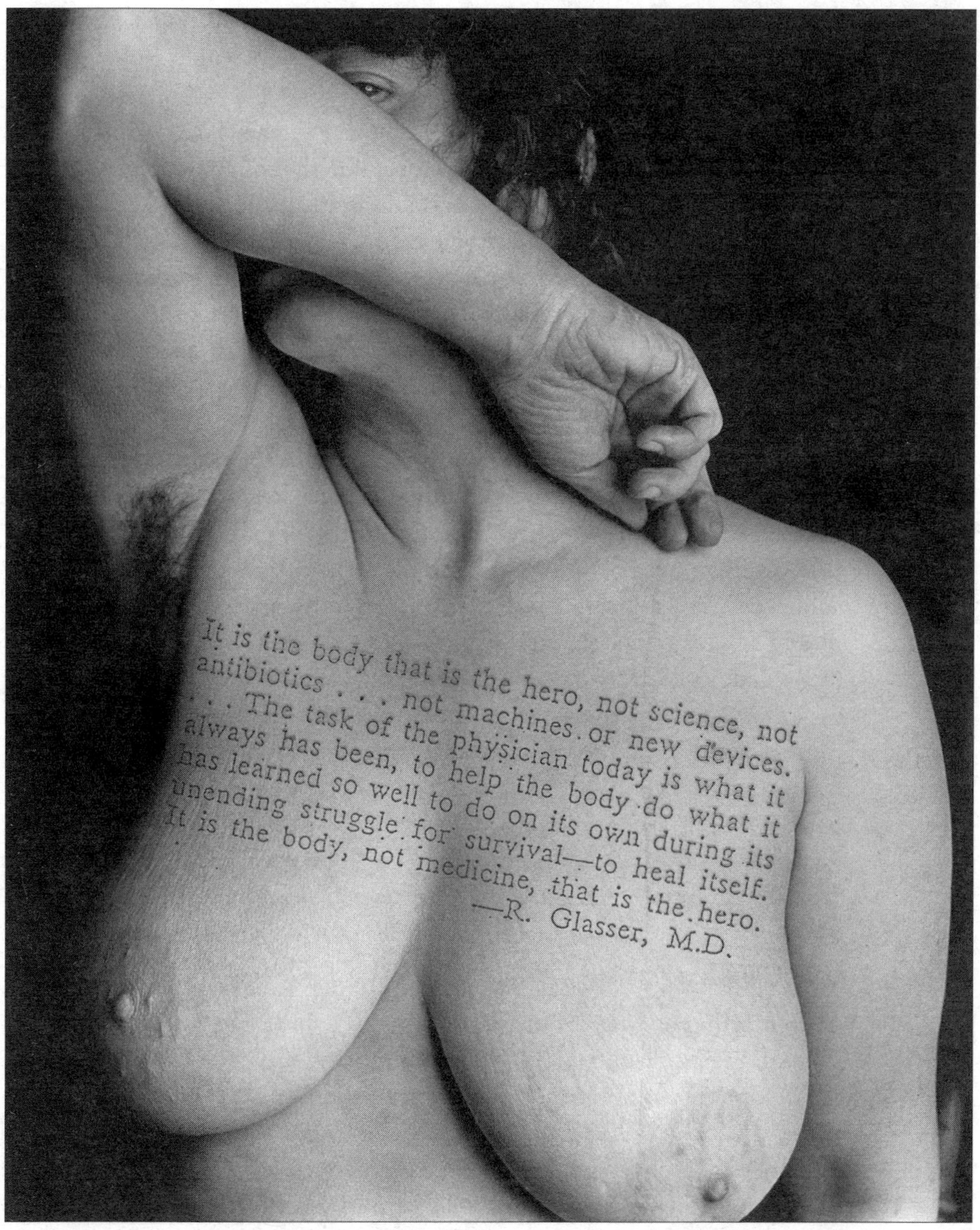

Image 1: *The Body from The Cancer Project, 1975/1983 (Jo Spence/Terry Dennett). Courtesy of Terry Dennett and the Jo Spence Archive.*

Spence's long-term collaborator, points out, "Jo insisted that we consider the politics of hidden suffering, that which is 'private' and outside the public gaze."[6]

After meeting at a co-counselling session in 1983, Spence and Martin began to work together. Addressing cultural taboos of class, gender, sexuality and sexual orientation, illness and family relations, they created imaginative and often daring self-portraits through photographic collaboration. Spence and Martin interwove personal and historical narratives, enabling identifications from marginalized perspectives. They gave themselves permission to play, to allow raw emotions to emerge and to direct the process of looking and being looked at. Their photographs were constructed to reveal what is absent in the face of dominant mythologies of the family.

Using memory and existing family photographs to tap feelings that eluded the idealized images of their childhoods, Spence and Martin performed re-enactments, which unveiled hidden stories. Together, they challenged "the family romance" through reframing some of their own childhood and adolescent experiences. Concentrating on the parent–child relationship through play-acting, they visualised roles they had assumed as children, like "Daddy's Little Girl." In addition, they experimented with "becoming" their mothers, dressing-up, copying familiar gestures and mimicking expressions. This approach enabled them to gain a more realistic view of family dynamics, while at the same time they developed empathy for their parents and a rapprochement towards their former "childhood selves." Needless to say, it is not easy to name, let alone photograph, that which is "visually unsayable,"[7] and therein lies the challenge of phototherapy.

OUR OWN EXPERIMENTATION

After meeting at Rosy Martin's workshop, we began exploring a range of themes, including silence and voice; authority; responsibility; gender stereotypes; and our shifting identities in relation to family and other institutional contexts. The process we use challenges us to express our issues visually or symbolically, disrupting our reliance on words. We use rituals, such as the consecration of shared space and setting aside time for each of us to talk, to create a framework for self-expression and to open ourselves to experience. As Stephanie describes it: "Julia's presence, including incisive questioning and strategic reflecting-back, brings out feelings and validates my experience, feeding a sense that this is my space to take."

We usually follow some combination of the steps outlined here:

1. Sometimes, the extent of our formality is that we take turns sharing and listening, talking through an issue with attention to how it might be visually represented. Brainstorming possible images is a good way into a story, as is working with keywords or sentences. The act of naming is powerful and humbling as it helps us move beyond idiosyncratic explanations and isolation.

2. We often select artefacts, props and costumes and explore situations through role-playing. Spence and Martin's practice was greatly influenced by the work of psychoanalyst D.W. Winnicott and the Brazilian popular theatre practitioner Augusto Boal, who believed that play has an essential function in the therapeutic process, allowing "what if" or "as-if" scenarios to be explored creatively.[8] Once a scenario has been acted out, the divide between fantasy and reality becomes blurred, opening up possibilities for further exploration or change. In his workshops, Boal uses a wide range of devices such as getting participants to tell a story and stopping them at a key moment to have them exaggerate the mood of that moment as a mask.

We sometimes experiment with using masks as a distancing technique, removing first stage reality and symbolically transforming ourselves: "You temporarily become the other, the object, the mother, the helper, the animal."[9] In an early session, Stephanie photographed Julia wearing first a crown, then a tiger mask. Julia reflects back: "I wanted to explore female archetypes like the 'good girl/wild woman' dichotomy and also express a desire to be more daring in the face of family expectations. In this guise I could play out both aspects of my personality and gain strength from the tiger mask." (See Image 2.)

3. Some of our sessions begin by looking at an existing photograph. In their role as *aide-mémoires*, images stimulate the telling of stories and act as a substitute where words fail. Images provide a "material connection to the past,"[10] invoking the presence of people and places. A photograph infuses almost all levels of memory. Unlike a memory anchored in thought, a photograph is tactile, making physical and mental connection possible. The shock of recognition, which we may experience when looking at a

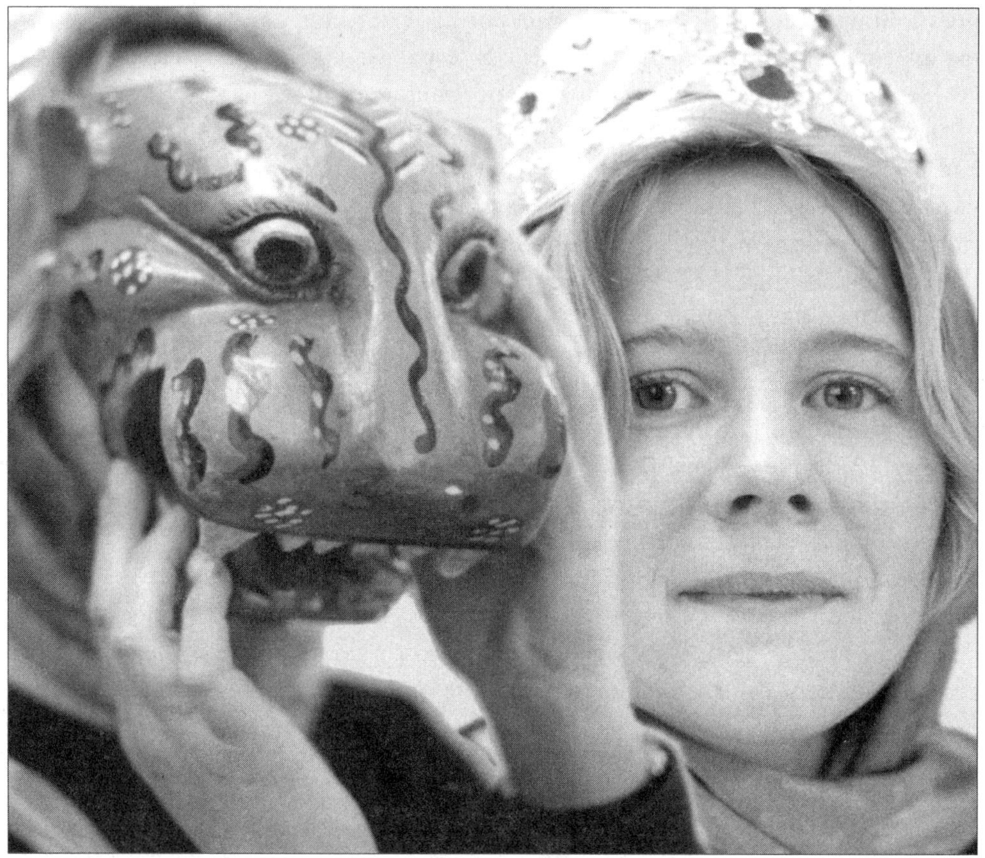

Image 2: *Female Archetypes, 1996 (Stephanie Conway/Julia Winckler).*

photograph taken during a difficult time in our lives, makes it possible for us to feel that we have been transported back in time. We can reawaken dormant emotions, using them as guides into a story.

4. We take photographs at key moments: at the beginning and end, when the facilitator (the listener) witnesses a crucial moment or at the request of the sitter (the speaker). The images we get from a session constitute raw material with open-ended meanings. They can serve as both documentary evidence (something we can refer back to) and cultural inscription (a basis for constructing meaning). "The photography sessions are not about 'capturing' the image; they are about seeking to make it happen … so

that the body ... may then be seen as performing rather than essentially containing those meanings."[11]

5. Over the years we sometimes revisit images from previous sessions and discover overarching themes. Our visual archive has become an alternative family album, offering dissonant visions to the stories we normally tell. The photographs become representative moments, reminding us of where we are still stuck or how we have moved on. They become psychic support in a continual process of identity construction and "containers of memory" that can be tapped into later with fresh perspectives. These images, unlike snapshots, are marked less by their significance in space/time and more by the way we use them to name issues and evoke contexts. Stephanie illustrates this in the following example (see Image 3):

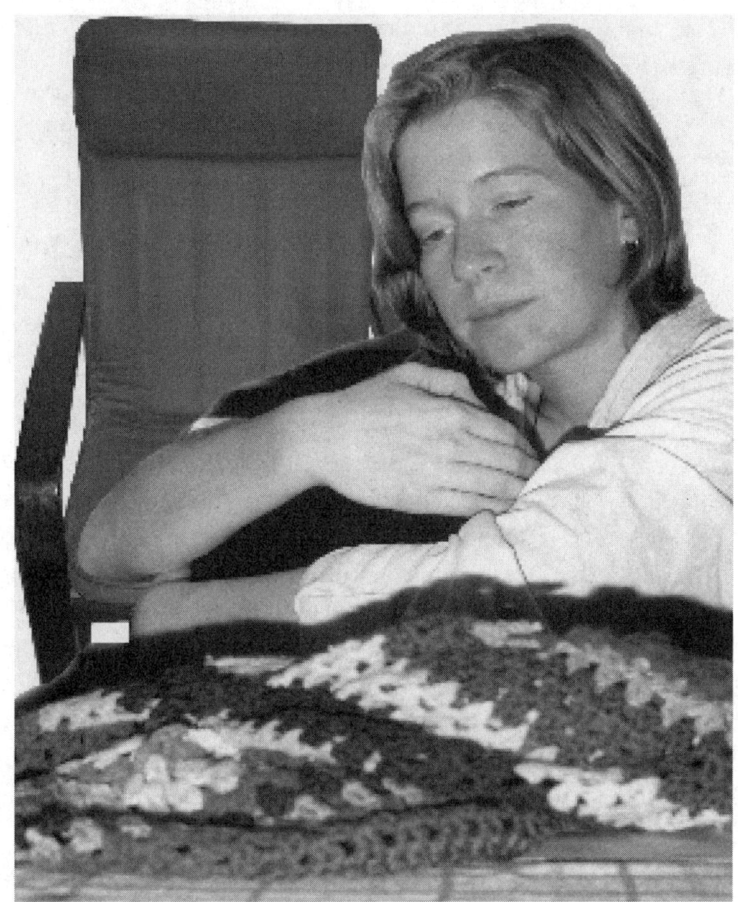

Image 3: ***Projections and Reclamations, 2004 (Stephanie Conway/Julia Winckler).***

> In my first session with Julia, I constructed a "dinner table" scene, using different symbolic objects to represent each family member. At the time, the photograph of me, holding my "security blanket," represented my struggle to find a voice as the youngest child amidst parental conflict and sibling rivalry. I used the phototherapy session to explore the process of becoming the child, physically and emotionally identifying with her. Re-enacting my child-self for the camera evokes the hidden story in a way that the happy snapshots of me as a child do not. While snapshots can

capture raw emotion, re-experiencing a childhood moment allows me to recognize how I still carry my past with me. The image tells a story that is neither fixed in time nor static: I can have compassion for my child-self and still realize as an adult that I can change the script.

Two Phototherapy Stories

During our most recent session, in June 2004, we both addressed the theme of "letting go" in different ways. Below we each make preliminary interpretations of the issues and images that emerged.

STEPHANIE: *WHAT DOES IT MEAN TO LET GO?*

I envisioned the photo collages (see Images 3 and 4) after exploring, in a session with Julia, my relationship with the therapist I had been seeing since my mother's death. The paradoxical nature of desire and fear shaped much of my therapy. The T-shirt represents my desire to get help, absurdist text mediating the challenge of asking for what I want. My body language is open but I hide behind the shirt, afraid of being seen. I want my therapist to see me, for me to feel understood and reflected back (or "mirrored"). But to be seen involves a kind of surrender, a letting go into relationship and self-acceptance. What is the risk of exposure?

Re-experiencing the *form* of a phototherapy session with Julia was as revealing as the content. After eight months of weekly psychotherapy, constrained by unidirectional sharing and my difficulty with being the object of the therapeutic gaze, it was a relief to be vulnerable in the presence of a friend in a context based on mutual sharing. In session, Julia and I role-played the therapist–client relationship and explored its power dynamics. She challenged me: "If you didn't believe I had that power, I wouldn't have it." The super-imposed eyes highlight my internalization of authority, projected onto my therapist as the "all-seeing eye," positioned to name or judge. But they also represent the challenge of looking back, seeing for myself, from within.

In therapy I faced the psychic task of separation. The chair photographed was my mother's, where she sat in her own work as a therapist. It evokes her absence, my loss. There is also a material connection to a very similar chair I sat in during therapy, which enabled both identification with my mother and awareness of its limits. I recognize that I am of my mother; I carry her

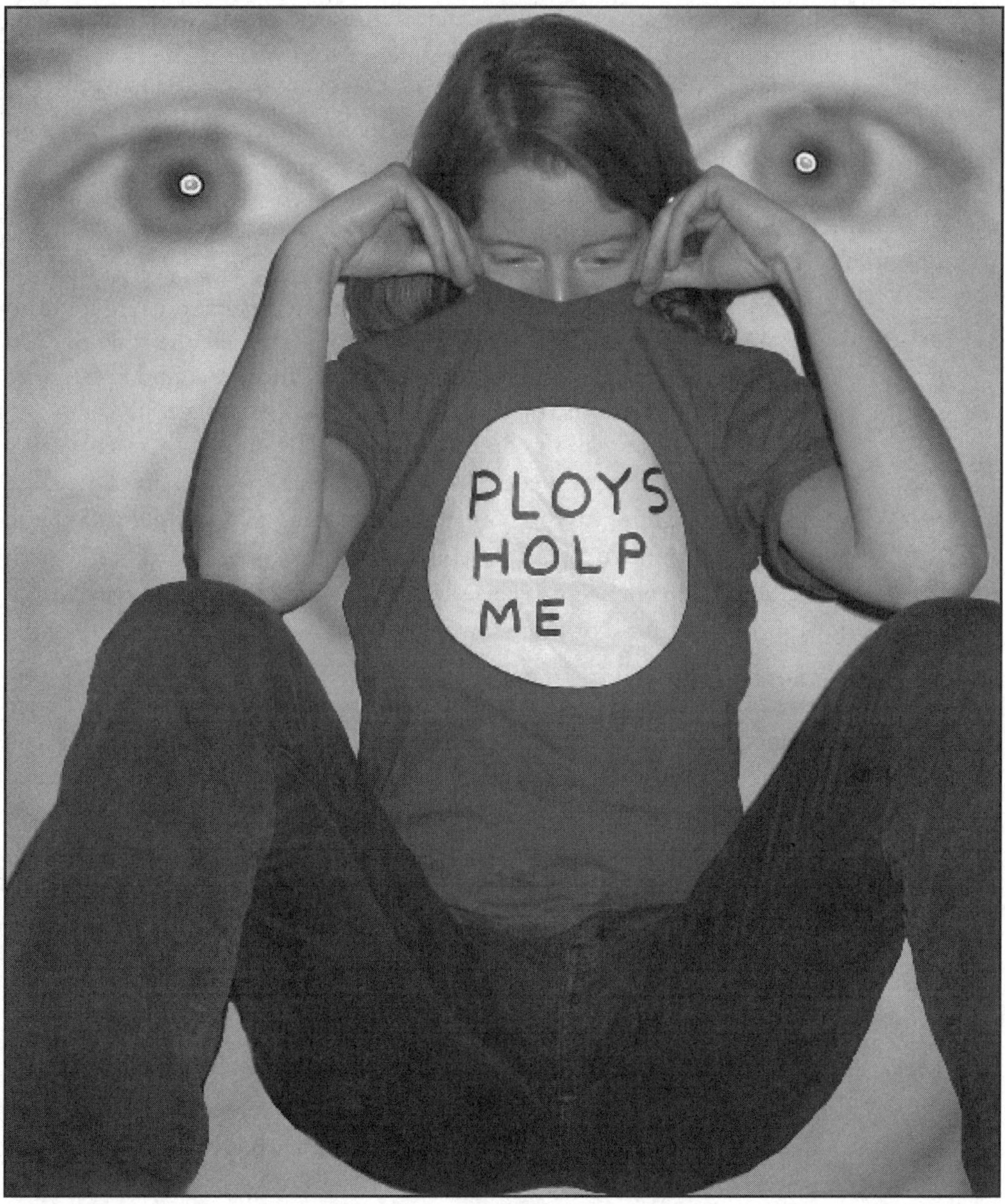

Image 4: *What Does It Mean To Let Go? 1996/2004 (Stephanie Conway/Julia Winckler).*

within me as she once carried me. Yet, in life as in death, we must separate from our mothers — a letting go into being who we are. The image of me in the foreground was taken in the 1996 session described above when I photographed my "family dinner table." It reappears with the chair, connecting my childhood losses with my current grief.

JULIA: *WHAT HAPPENS TO ENERGY?*

A collage made up of a portrait of me covering my face, overlaid with a tree trunk split in two and the question "What happens to energy?" sums up the mood of the session, which explored my sense at the time of "just getting by." The image is about feeling depleted and tired, and wanting to withdraw and go inwards (by covering my face). (See Image 5.)

We explored the way my body, rather than being an ally, was "letting me down" in crucial moments. I have a tendency to over-intellectualize things, and to ignore my body's needs for as long as I can get away with it. Asking questions such as "Do you take enough time to feel and experience?" Stephanie opened up spaces for me to go deeper into physical sensations. I became aware of moments when I was talking and even breathing faster. I remembered situations that were energizing or depleting. Often, the same activities (e.g., teaching or creating artwork) can give and take away energy. As the session unfolded I began to let go, moving deeper into experiences, almost reliving them.

Persistent in her questioning, Stephanie picked up sentences I had left unfinished, or repeated words to me. An attentive listener, she noticed inconsistencies in my narrative. A turning point of the session was when she reminded me that "we are our bodies," and that I was trying to gain control over "it" when "it" is me. Learning to nurture body and soul are essential for self-preservation.

Creativity dries up when we are tired. The background image of a dead tree trunk cut in two represents this. The image was taken six years ago at the verge of a relationship break-up, and just prior to embarking on a new phase in my life. I decided to merge this image with the portrait taken by Stephanie in session. Visual fragments collapse into one another in the layered image, pulling together different times and places and pointing to a sense of continuity. The "there then" and the "here now" become one in the composite image.

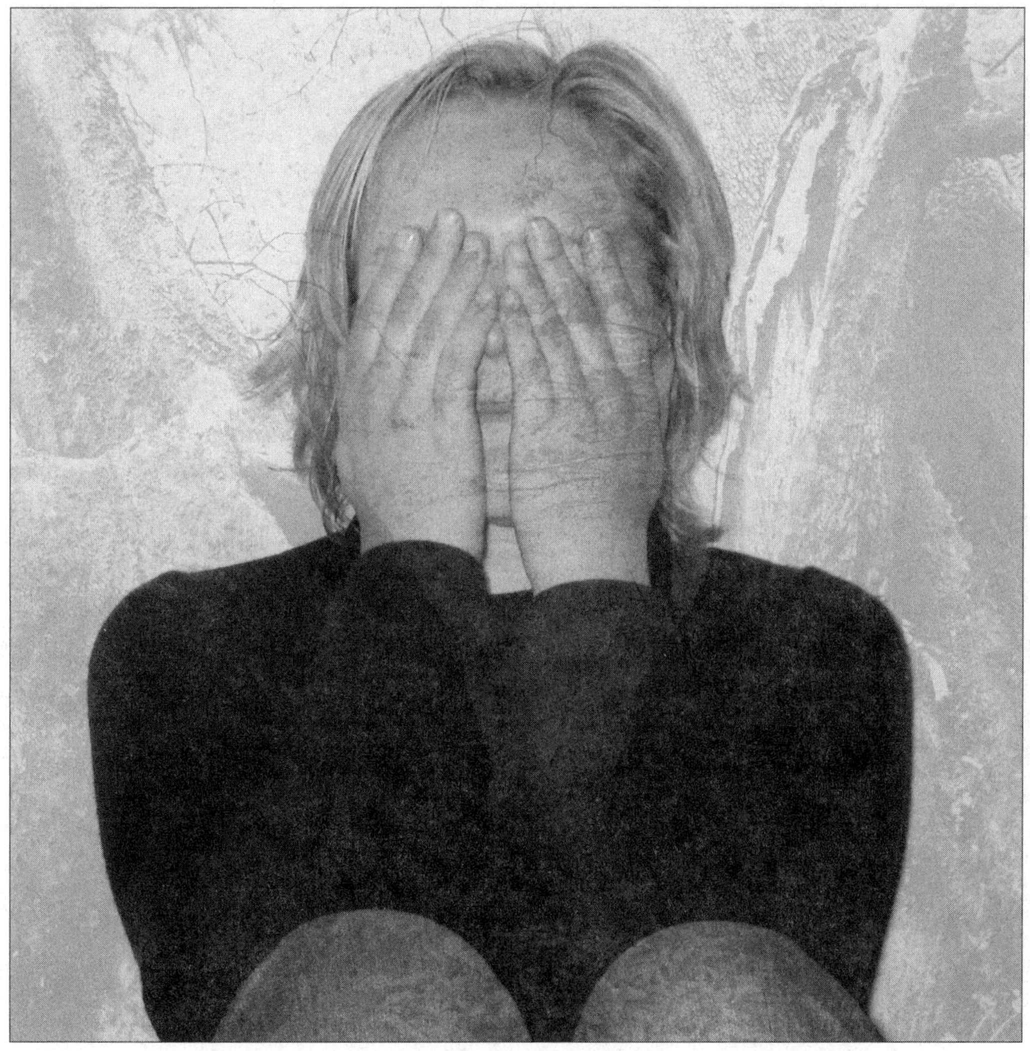

Image 5: *What Happens to Energy? 1998/2004 (Stephanie Conway/Julia Winckler).*

The second image to come out of the session was taken on Mont Royal in Montreal the day after the session. (See Image 6.) I felt the energy of the trees and the heat of the late afternoon sun in the park, and tried to visualize a more balanced life. This image now also is a reminder of our time spent together in Montreal, but it took on more poignancy after Stephanie

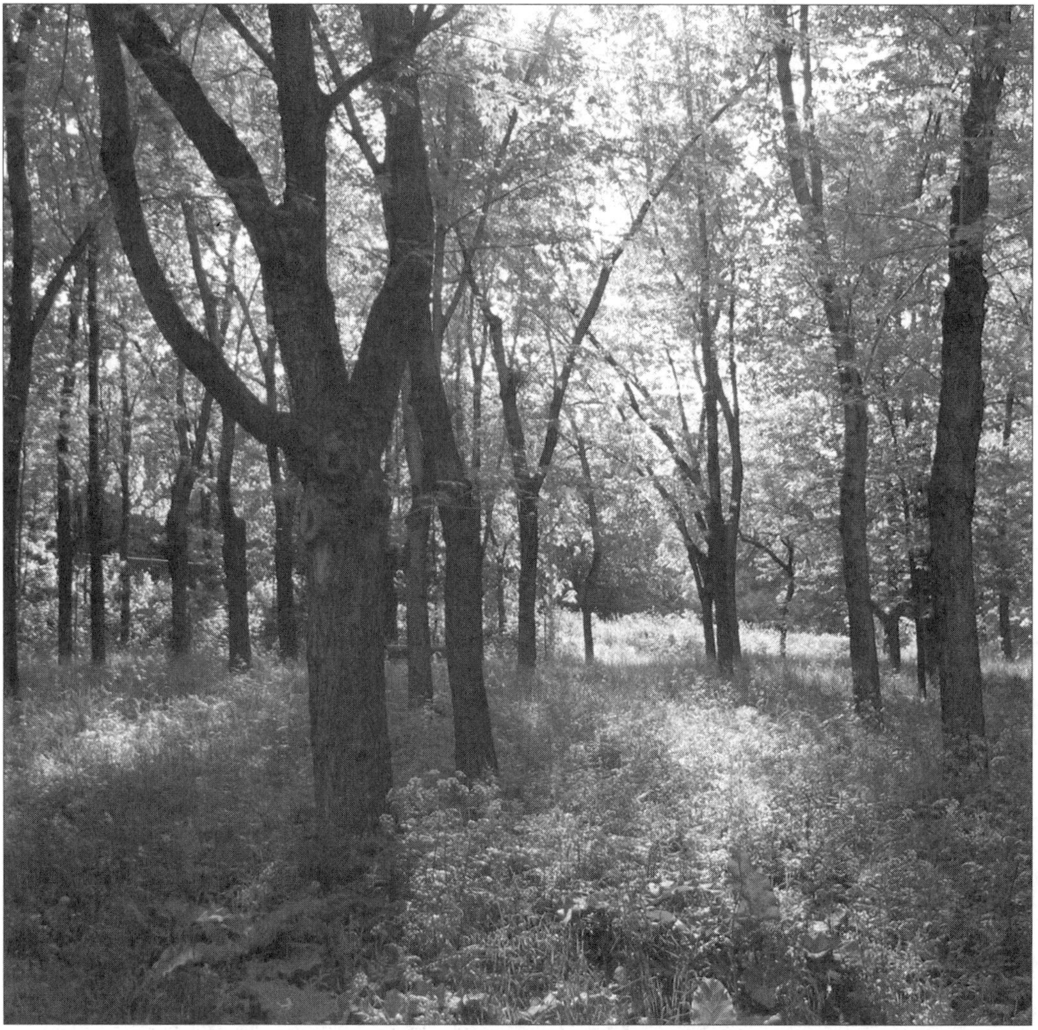

Image 6: *Light, 2004 (Stephanie Conway/Julia Winckler).*

responded to it: "When I saw the image of light coming through the trees in the city where I live and where my mother lived and died under the title 'What Happens to Energy?' I felt my mother's spirit. "

Unsettling Practice

In this essay, we have attempted to foreground our own explorations in phototherapy. However, the images we have chosen to illustrate our own therapeutic process require explanation for an audience to *read* them. What is gained or lost when we privilege the therapeutic process as healing over constructing photographic images for an audience? How would our process change if we prioritized aesthetics?

In our most recent session we have, for the first time, paid more attention to what we want the images to "say." Whereas in the past we looked at machine-processed snapshots or developed and printed negatives in the darkroom, this time we revisited the images on screen and adjusted them digitally. This process made the images more constructed, with more conscious attention to composition and framing. The computer screen acted as a mirror (projecting back at us the images taken during the session) while also creating distance, as the physicality of the images was removed. The meaning of the images became more fluid and negotiable, as we selected and prioritized certain parts while leaving out others. For the first time, we have included other images as layers and reused images from previous sessions. Deciding which images to combine brought new stories to light and helped us anchor existing themes, ultimately bringing more depth to the images.

In our practice with phototherapy we have re-enacted, remodelled or redefined images and scenes from our family albums and have experimented with photo-theatre. As we continue our working practice, we would like to explore further the role of fantasy, the visual enactment of "what if" scenarios and their roots in the unconscious. With our emphasis on analytic insight we have often neglected the awareness that comes with being in the moment. A session we did in 1998 at a theatre using costumes and props best exemplifies the difference in process. We began by improvising without identifying issues first and played spontaneously. The resulting photographs were richly encoded and continue to be revealing without our attempts to anchor their meaning. In one of those photos included here (see Image 7), we are foregrounded wearing capes, a stark branch behind us, then a shrinking perspective down a long hallway, with chequered floors. The photo has a magical quality, inviting the viewer into a fantasy realm, an organic construction, where we celebrate the body, shared experience and spontaneous expression. "Life is the soul's breathing in, spontaneity its breathing out."[12]

Breath takes us back to the body as the conduit of our practice. To be embodied is to take the risk of "being seen" and then accepting what we see. As a political praxis, phototherapy brings private moments of insight into a shared space of recognition. When we focus on the particularity of how our stories are embodied we improve our chances of speaking to the general. The underlying ethic is one of *allowing* without imposing meaning: something or someone will always be "other" to us and differing meanings emerge over time/space. The self-knowledge that phototherapy engages with is not about dealing with our issues in order to emerge as fully formed subjects in the public realm. It is about acting-out and using our creative energies to open up new ways of knowing that we recognize

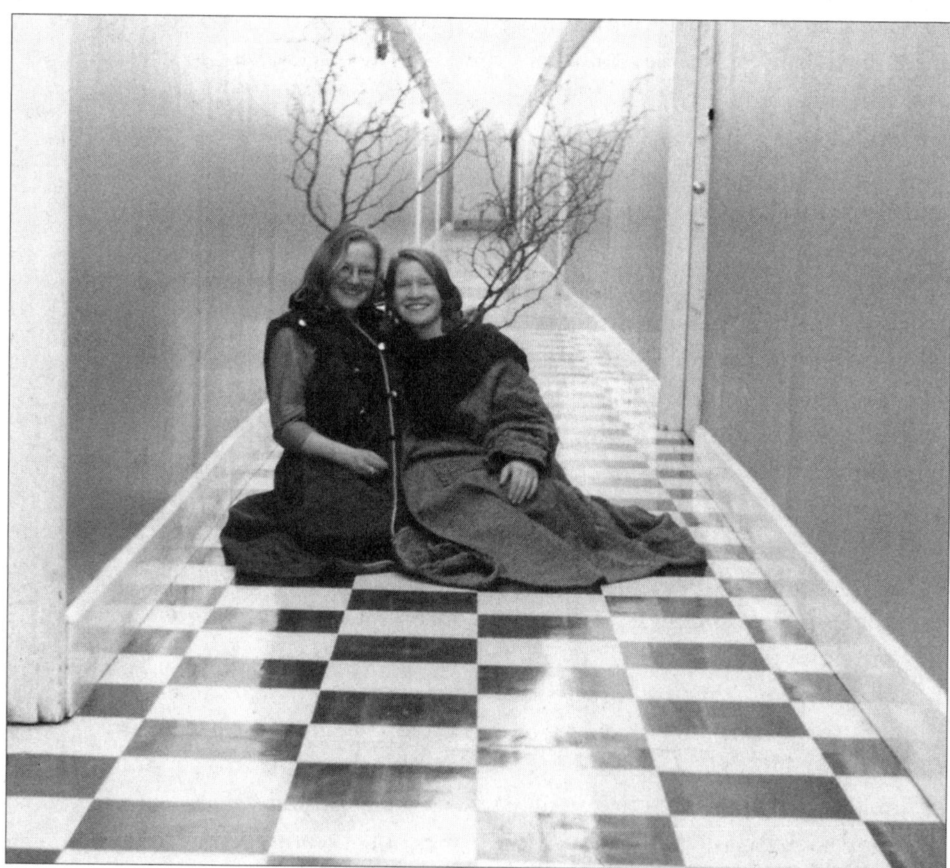

Image 7: *Theatre, 1998 (Stephanie Conway/Julia Winckler).*

as limited, contingent and cyclical. "New knowledge is really often old knowledge found in places new to the seeker."[13] The stories we tell in a phototherapy session feel new to us and the images speak to the moment when this new insight came into focus. But this clarity is disguised as an essence, only to dissolve into the constituent elements of fresh stories. While insights and photographic meanings are ephemeral, phototherapy practice gives meaning to the now as part of a much broader process of connection and integration.

NOTES

We dedicate this chapter to Terry Dennett, Jo Spence and Keith Kennedy.

1. Marion Milner, *On Not Being Able to Paint* (London: Heinemann, 1977), 123.

2. A fascinating link between photography and the therapeutic process was identified by German cultural critic Walter Benjamin in 1928 when he discussed the ways that camera technology makes it possible to reveal processes otherwise invisible to the human eye. This is similar to a therapeutic intervention, which can bring deeply buried knowledge to light. "The camera introduces us to unconscious optics as does psychoanalysis to unconscious impulses." Walter Benjamin, "The Work of Art in the Age of Mechanical Reproduction," in *Illuminations* (New York: Schocken, 1969), 236–237.

3. Jo Spence, *Cultural Sniping: The Art of Transgression* (London: Routledge, 1995), 150.

4. Jo Spence, *Putting Myself in the Picture* (Seattle: The Real Comet Press, 1998), 118. For a detailed description of Spence's therapeutic camera explorations, see Terry Dennett, "The Wounded Photographer: The Genesis of Jo Spence's Camera Therapy," *Afterimage* (Nov/Dec 2001), 26–27.

5. Spence, *Putting Myself in the Picture*, 162.

6. Terry Dennett, interview by authors, London, UK, 1996.

7. Spence, *Putting Myself in the Picture*, 121.

8. See D.W. Winnicott, *Playing and Reality* (New York: Routledge, 1982); Augusto Boal, *The Rainbow of Desire* (London: Routledge, 1995); Mady Schutzman and Jan Cohen-Cruz, eds., *Playing Boal: Theatre, Therapy, Activism* (London: Routledge, 1994).

9. Dennett interview.

10. Roland Barthes, *Camera Lucida: Reflections on Photography* (London: Fontana, 1984), 88.

11. Rosy Martin, "You (Never) Can Tell: Phototherapy, Memory, and Subjectivity," *Blackflash* 14, no. 3 (Fall 1996), 6.

12. J.L. Moreno, *The Theatre of Spontaneity* (New York: Beacon, 1970), 71.

13. Augusto Boal, personal communication at Theatre Workshop, Toronto, 1997.

CHAPTER 17

You Are My Sunshine:

REFUGEE PARTICIPATION IN PERFORMANCE

Heather Lash

THE VERY FIRST THING REQUIRED OF REFUGEES UPON ARRIVAL IN CANADA is a narrative. They must relate the story of what brought them here in great detail on the Personal Information Form, which is the cornerstone of the application process. Lawyers and psychologists require the story, as well as doctors and counsellors. Then there are the optional tellings, for example, to the volunteer with whom they've been matched in a befriending program, or to the curious face of a sympathetic civil society hungry for models of resilience and for evidence that *Life is,* in fact, *Beautiful.*[1] Already on the scene are arts practitioners of all sorts. We include performance art therapists, folks preparing educational film and video presentations, facilitators of collectives that create popular theatre for public education and arts-inclined activists who engage in all of the above. I suppose I fall into this last category.

I am tremendously skeptical about "therapeutic" arts practices with refugees. It's not just because of the risk of reinscribing oppression and trauma through the eliciting of autobiographical stories; it's that from the beginning it seems offensive to propound "the healing power of art" in the face of what some people have gone through. When a woman tells me about getting her kneecaps smashed off by her own government, or being left in a pit of dead bodies for days, can I seriously suggest that "our" Western art forms have anything to offer her? No, because first, there is the problem of ethnocentrism, of privileged philanthropists who are of the opinion that making art is good for people, playing out their paternalistic and naive fantasies. And second, "our" heritage is the way of seeing, the way of being, the way of organizing human activity, which is in large part responsible for the brutal situations these people must heal from.

Nevertheless, instead of dispensing with arts practices altogether, we need to bring the utmost humility to the project of reorienting ourselves within them. We need to be with other people's stories in a way that embodies the principles of testimonial work, rather than those of spectacle, even if the event is not literally or strictly testimony.

Spectacle is never concerned with social justice. This is evident in the way most mainstream artistic representations fail to deal with the root causes or complexities of the tragedies they represent. When trauma is simply on display, a spectator may be intimately affected — for example, when we cry at the movies — but may not be moved to act. Spectacle does not await my invitation or response in order to be complete. By reducing the story and characters to a coherent narrative with familiar forms and stereotypes or essences, spectacle addresses itself to a generic consumer and asks nothing of *me* in particular.

Testimony, on the other hand, does not even exist without me as its witness. It is an unfinished project, in the same way an object must be received to be called a gift. It demands my response; it announces the need for justice in public, in community. What it offers is counsel, but specifically to *me*; it implicates *me*.[2] This interpersonal involvement provides some insurance against voyeurism and other abuses to which theatre tends to lend itself. Now, I'd like to tell you a story about a theatrical experience that involved, guided and challenged me; it counselled me.

BALANCING POWER DYNAMICS

I have long been a volunteer at the Canadian Centre for Victims of Torture (CCVT), whose services include group and individual counselling, English as a Second Language classes and access to doctors and lawyers specializing in cases concerning torture. Throughout the spring of 2002, I was involved in a theatrical project with the CCVT that culminated in a public presentation in late June at a fancy event with bigwigs from the United Nations and our minister of immigration. Later that year, we took it to York University as a public education piece for future social workers. Directly following that presentation, we facilitated a role-play workshop with the audience in the tradition of Augusto Boal (the Brazilian whose "theatre of the oppressed" techniques transform those watching into "spect-actors" who jump into the scene).

The show, called *Chasing Shadow*, was mounted by the director Wolfgang Vachon, myself, another volunteer and three CCVT clients. It is debatable whether doing community theatre can strictly be called activism, but there is plenty of interesting overlap in the discussions generated by both. Preparation for this piece raised questions as to how principles from critical theory and activism can inform an art-making process; in particular, is the quality of the process to be emphasized over the final product? and vice versa? Ultimately, this theatre experience embodied many of the values we strive for in more explicitly "political" work.

The process of creating *Chasing Shadow* took shape as we went along; none of us had known one another beforehand, and we had no model to reference. By improvising together in this way, each participant's worth was entirely and equally honoured; this was the project's greatest success. The three clients[3] were in every way participants and in no way "subjects" of our research. Their status as "insiders" was, nonetheless, critical to the rhyme and reason of the project: we were making a show about the experience of migration, incarceration, torture, shelters … a narrative of trauma and healing.

Well, it wasn't as clear as all that. First of all, what exactly is meant here by "insider"? There are different configurations of the "insider/outsider" distinction, that turn on different criteria. Being an insider provides familiarity and knowledge, two major sources of power. Being an outsider is often disempowering and alienating, like any experience of "not knowing the ropes." Yet, in the end, we found this distinction muddled by contraction and crossover. When I interviewed Wolfgang about the process,[4] he "felt very much like an outsider" among all of us because he was the newest to the CCVT community. Among the three of us volunteers, there was an affinity; both Wolfgang and I had a background in theatre, and we were both in grad school, so we had a shared understanding. Then there was gender. The female client was the only woman present when Wolfgang rehearsed with just the clients, while the two male clients shared a country of origin and language. Yet the female client was the only one with professional performance experience, so there was some shared vocabulary between her and Wolfgang. Age also came into play, leaving the older man, whose English-language skills were also the weakest, quite marginalized. Wolfgang found the whole notion of insider/outsider "very limiting … It's too easy to say 'insider/outsider' without breaking that down into what exactly you mean and what the specific context is," he said.

Although each relationship does have a unique power dynamic, language is always a paramount site of authority. Rehearsing, interacting and performing in English presented our single biggest challenge, one that complicated our every move towards meaningful and uncoerced consensus. This did not, however, result in a straightforward power struggle, but rather blockages and confusion. We were even unable to have an explicit discussion together that was critical of the philosophy or theory that framed the process. In such a scenario, care must be taken to honour the experience, wisdom and adulthood of each participant. How, though, does that respect manifest itself?

For example, Wolfgang reported that his acting directions were frequently misunderstood, but he needed to step back and respect just how the clients were translating his directions for themselves.

> I often didn't know whether they didn't understand the direction, didn't like the direction, or just didn't care … Sometimes, I would ask a question; they would respond; I would say, "No, no, no, that's not what I asked"; they would say, "Hold on," and they would eventually answer the question I asked, but in a way that I just wasn't expecting at all. And they understood what I said but they took it in their own way …

In giving instructions and directions, a balance must be achieved between giving people too much credit and not giving them enough.

The same principle applies to decision-making power. In this process, the clients had most of it, especially when it came to content. Wolfgang never imposed a shape onto the script. The clients very much controlled what the show looked like, and that was *nothing* like the original script described above. Wolfgang found they were "very clear that they did not want to do something that ever named torture, ever talked about torture or prison or anything like that, which is what I was intending. So we left it."

He had several drafts of the script rejected as he tried to reflect the clients' desires and recognize their needs. What we presented resulted directly from the agency of the clients: *Chasing Shadow* wound up being a satirical, playful piece that depicts a young man who comes to Canada in search of his lost horse, and most of the show is spent poking vicious and delightful fun at Canadian refugee settlement systems.

I am compelled, however, to question what might be considered giving participants a *disproportionate* amount of control. How much is too much? In non-community settings — "regular" alternative theatre, if you will — there are plenty of moments when a good director can and does say, "Just wear the damn horse head at the end of the show, okay?" Letting participants totally run things can express just as bad a faith as any other condescension.

Wolfgang said that although the process was as participatory as possible, "without a doubt … I allowed myself to have the final say." He chose to be a more controlling director once the script existed and the show approached: "I think people *like* to be directed, people like to feel safe and secure, like to have that sense of containment, and it goes back to a huge background and variety of reasons." Of course, he wanted people to feel comfortable, "and part of that was taking on the role of the director, telling them what worked, what didn't … working with language and pronunciation."

The above mentioned "background and variety of reasons" introduced the tricky theme of *the expert*. We were, after all, creating a piece that observed our Western theatrical conventions. Imagine us, for example, when we only had a week until the curtain rose on our show. In moments of anxiety, habit dominates. When you combine oppressive cultural conditioning with a process as nervous-making as mounting a show, it becomes far easier for everyone to play the same roles as they have historically: experts and their followers.

The expert need not only be a person. Our theatrical conventions are dominant cultural forms. They are hegemonic. You have to have a stage, characters, dialogue, a narrative arc, music at the end. Those things, unfortunately, legitimize theatre; those things make it a "real play," perhaps especially in the minds of the clients. People wanting, maybe passionately, to prove themselves and "do things right" in a new culture are going to resist letting go of those conventions. Wolfgang wanted them to experiment with more non-verbal work, but "they insisted on having a script, they insisted on text, they insisted on speaking." Even if the volunteers intended to place far more emphasis on process than product, the clients wanted to do a *show*. Their desire for immediate returns (making the audience laugh) made itself evident and would have to co-exist with our desire for long-term transformation (ending global imperialism, fighting evil, etc.). Besides, we all wanted to use cultural codes that could be understood by the spectators; we wanted our comedy to be funny!

And though the final production had its moments, it was not perfect, nor was that its goal in any case. Community theatre and mainstream theatre are different. The latter denies the political nature of its goals by virtue of its supposed neutrality; as such it can afford the time, money and energy needed to make perfection a priority. Conversely, community theatre, as Wolfgang put it, "takes participants as the foundation; it's about giving voice, it's that time is taken, that the process is action and reflection, that praxis, that cyclical way of working." The ethical and educational dimensions (and the sheer playfulness) of a community theatre process might override whatever would make for the ideal product. And this kind of play somehow works on the folks doing it. Just as meaningful change can happen at the extreme borders or on the margins of systems and cultures, imperceptible shifts are also going on in the consciousness of each individual engaged in these loving activities.

Balanced Relationships

Despite all the challenges described here, there was an emotional and energetic harmony among the six of us volunteers and clients, and the tensions were only the garden variety that arise in *any* context of preparing a staged presentation. This harmony meant that at no time were the clients turned into instruments of the volunteers' development; there were genuine relationships among us. Such relationships develop when people are encouraged to bring themselves as whole people to a process. It happens when a facilitator or director is aware that he or she is part of what is to be examined and transformed. When I asked Wolfgang to talk about the danger of romanticizing healing (and I meant the clients'), he shrugged and replied, "I healed."

People can feel it. There is a discomfort (even if it's not articulated) when people's realities are disrespected or appropriated; people know when they are being used. Even if they have become accustomed to it, even if it asks them to reproduce roles they are very familiar with. When this kind of violation is absent, the solidarity and ease are also palpable, making possible the real communication that lies at the heart of praxis. We need to speak from the heart, resisting the use of truisms or catchphrases, and this requires trust. But more important than the participants' trust in the facilitator is the trust the facilitator has in the people with whom she or he works: Paulo Freire said that a real humanist can be identified more by her or his trust in the people than by a thousand actions in their favour without that trust. Trust demands a quieting of the ego, a sort of giving over to an intelligent and uncontrollable world, one full of potentials we cannot yet imagine.

Such a surrender has no time for a voyeuristic need to "find out," for the opinion that we *can* "know" another's pain, or for the egotistical impulse to comprehend. Com-prehension means to take everything into your hands; we "grasp" or "capture" a reality in language, in narrative. The deep and complex other person confronting you, however, is lost to you (and so is the opportunity to learn that they offer you) the moment you think you 'get' them. We must instead leave space for mysteries that remain undisclosed, for private details not meant to be shared, and art has the capacity to leave this silence intact. Poetic language, movement or images offer a way to express nasty and painful experiences, and even contradictions. Art has the power to hold paradoxical truths, like an egg in each hand. It can do this in that it can bypass rationality; stories are free from the requirement to be linear or coherent or even "true." This rescues arts practices from much of our (justified) criticism and suspicion; it makes up for all the risks.

A Final Story

I was working at CCVT, at a later time, in another context. I was putting together a display for a big public education event at Metro Hall, the civic centre in downtown Toronto. On the floor of a tiny office, I was arranging several harrowing images of torture. I was being extremely critical; I couldn't make a spectacle out of them, no, and they definitely had to be tactful and understated, had to make the viewer do most of the work. This is not daydreaming. The noise in my head is more like sustained interrogation, thinking of the master's thesis I was writing vis-à-vis this display, and exactly who and what was this Metro Hall thing for anyway? An opportunity to righteously spread the word that *Life is* not *Beautiful*? Had I checked in with my body I would have found it contracted, my forehead harsh and grooved. This is not vigilance. It's more like anger, as if all the services for refugees in this city were ethical debacles.

I am interrupted by the sound coming from the ESL classroom next door, by the voices of people who have *lived* the experiences I am so wary of representing in my little display; displaced Kurds, Somalis, Afghanis and Rwandans, whose shattered and wobbly bodies drag them here on weekday afternoons, to learn this alphabet together, sometimes in the same class as enemies from home. They are practising English by singing "You Are My Sunshine." One of the voices — an old man's — slightly out of tune and also the most confident, rises above the others. They all swell with enthusiasm near the end, imperfect and giggling, imploring all to please not to take their sunshine away.

What a fool I am. I sit, gluestick in hand, wondering who in the hell I think I am to take feel-good Hollywood movies away from those who clearly appreciate them, suddenly weeping fat and unacademic tears. I feel not like a "witness" (in all the responsibility that introduces) to this, but rather like a rabbit, caught in the headlights, frozen and quaking before possible responses, made still by a rib-cracking love.

Not all services for refugees are totally misguided, nor are all the arts practitioners. This happy fact is the natural result of people working together, living together, doing daily things together. People do all these things imperfectly; but over long periods of time, we get used to each other, inevitably encounter one another as real individuals and begin to share ourselves with one another. Face to face in this way, we begin to tell our stories, but only ever begin. Parts of the story will always be missing, and even in all its glory the sunshine won't illuminate everything.

Because not everything is for display.

NOTES

1. I return again and again in my writing to this 1997 film as an example of artistic romanticization of trauma and its "anti-activism." Such films finish on a note of closure, which is anathema to mobilization or even to seeing present-day parallels with and reverberations of, in this case, the Holocaust.

2. Please see the work on testimony done by Roger I. Simon, in particular the brilliant *Remembrance as Praxis and the Ethics of the Inter-Human*, co-written with Mario DiPaolantonio and Mark Clamen, published in the online journal *Culture Machine*, no. 4 (February 2002), available at http://culturemachine.tees.ac.uk/frm_f1.htm.

3. In observance of both CCVT protocol and common sense, they will remain anonymous. For the purposes of this discussion, I will refer to them as the older man, the younger man and the woman.

4. Every direct quotation in this chapter is from Wolfgang Vachon, interview by author, Toronto, ON, July 2002.

Contributors

Deborah Barndt worked for over twenty years as a community-based educator, photographer, and activist in the U.S., Canada and Latin America before joining York University's Faculty of Environmental Studies in 1993, where she is a teacher and co-learner with the other contributors to this volume.

Lee Bensted completed her MA in Education from the Ontario Institute for Studies in Education/University of Toronto in 2005. Her graduate work explored the importance of collaborative art-making and storytelling to social and environmental justice education. She is currently working on a community arts and education project in Vancouver's False Creek Watershed and creating salmon murals with BC school children through the Stream of Dreams Mural Society. Lee's artistic passions include photography, silk-screening, encaustic painting and fashioning costumes for just about any occasion!

Salima Bhimani holds a Master Degree in Environmental Studies, a Bachelor of Arts in Anthropology and Women's Studies and a Bachelor of Education. Salima's work with NGOs, government agencies and community organizations, internationally and locally has been in international development, education, women's issues and human rights, youth issues, cultural development, representation and the media, social justice issues, interfaith dialogue, art and spirituality for social justice, and equity/diversity issues. She has published *Majalis Al-Ilm: Sessions of Knowledge. Reclaiming and Representing the Lives of Muslim Women*, and is the founding director of the NGO group Muslim Women's Collective.

Leah Burns is a multidisciplinary artist who works in collaboration with communities to address issues of health and environmental sustainability. She is currently undertaking doctoral studies in connection with the Centre for Arts-Informed Research at the Ontario Institute for Studies in Education/University of Toronto.

chris cavanagh is a popular educator, storyteller, writer and artist. He is a co-founder and member of the Catalyst Centre popular education worker co-op (www.catalystcentre.ca) and has worked in many coalition-building efforts (anti-apartheid, Nicaraguan solidarity, Native sovereignty, anti-racism and more). He designs curricula and facilitates trainings in popular education, popular arts production, participatory democracy and community organizing.

HEATHER CHETWYND has been working in voice, music and education since the mid-1970s. As a professional singer, she has studied locally and in Cuba and has performed in Latin America, the United States and Canada. In her master's studies, Heather researched the relationship between voice, learning and processes of change, and began her journey into voice exploration. She has worked as an English as a Second Language teacher since 1982. As a result of her interest in voice, Heather now focuses on accent reduction, voice training and intercultural communications in her business, Voice to Word Consulting.

STEPHANIE CONWAY teaches in the Department of Humanities at Champlain College in Montreal. She has taught courses in visual culture, education and social change, mythology and environmental studies. Stephanie is currently enjoying the challenges of new motherhood. She hopes, at some point, to integrate her experiences with phototherapy into professional therapeutic training and practice.

GABRIELLE ETCHEVERRY is a freelance Spanish–English translator and a co-publisher at Split Quotation/La Cita Trunca, an independent publisher of English- and Spanish-language poetry and prose based in Ottawa, Ontario. She holds a Master of Communication and Cultural Studies from York University (Toronto) where she studied Chilean small-press production in Canada. In addition to presenting conference papers on ethnic minority literary production in Canada, Gabrielle has published articles on this subject in Canadian and Mexican cultural magazines.

PARISS GARRAMONE is a doctoral student in the Faculty of Education at York University. Her work focuses on sustainability education, and particularly explores the role of art in sustainability curriculum. Pariss has presented talks and workshops on her zine project, *Her Hand Made Forest*, both internationally and in Canada.

HEATHER HERMANT is a Toronto-based spoken word performer. She has worked as a journalist, teacher and community artist in Canada and abroad, and lived in Budapest, Hungary, from 1997 to 2003. Heather completed her Master in Environmental Studies at York University in 2006 with a focus on arts-based strategies for mediation, for which she produced a documentary entitled *Everything Which Was Familiar* about the project she was involved with in Bosnia.

Maggie Hutcheson is a graduate student in the Faculty of Environmental Studies at York University. Her current research focuses of the reclamation of urban spaces through collaborative cultural productions, and her ongoing activist and artistic practices continue to fuel her commitment to working in the intersections of art-making and social change.

Yukyung Kim-Cho is a graduate of the Master of Environmental Studies Program at York University. Her areas of interest are female migrants and arts-informed feminist research on women's activisms. She has been part of the women's rights movements for thirteen years, particularly in the area of violence against women, in South Korea and Canada. Her cultural productions include "Cheonggye Creek Artist" (She and I, Seoul), "Journeys" (English Internet radio show, International Broadcast for Migrants in Korea) and "In Memory of Dec. 6" (Toronto). Copies of her self-published jamming book, *Jamming with Women's Rights Activists in East Asia*, are available from the Toronto Women's Bookstore and or by contacting Yukyung at ykimcho@pancakehouse.org.

Melanie Kramer completed her Master in Environmental Studies at York University and her Master of Landscape Architecture at the University of Toronto. She plans to combine her interests in urban interventions, food growing, ecology, writing and design to find innovative ways to infuse urban environments with creative energy and living green spaces. She recently published an article in Issue 02 of the online journal *vague terrain*, available at www.vagueterrain.net.

Petra Kukacka has worked on several projects in her home town of Toronto as well as in parts of Mexico that have challenged her to think about creativity and self-knowledge. She continues to live in Toronto, cultivating an amateur cactus collection and playing in a local punk-rock band.

Heather Lash lives in Toronto and recently had a baby. Her thesis for her Master in Environmental Studies was called "Ethics, Narrative and Refugee Issues." She works in refugee advocacy and public education, and also engages in performance art, spoken word performance and puppetry, but her first love is writing.

Jacinda Mack is an indigenous graduate student from the Nuxalk Nation on the Northwest Coast. In 2006, she completed her master's thesis at York University, including a video documentary on Nuxalk sovereignty and social change. Publications include poetry and book reviews in *Redwire* Magazine and *BC Studies Journal*. She currently resides with her son, Orden, and their eight cats in Cmetem, a small Native community of the Secwepemc Nation.

Christine McKenzie has been a curious journeyer, popular educator and activist in and around Latin America, the Caribbean and Canada over the past ten years. She is forever indebted to those she writes about here, who taught her many lessons on the way to receiving her Master in Environmental Studies from York University.

Oona Padgham lives, works and agitates in Toronto. She co-ordinates a social housing apartment building in Kensington Market for people who were homeless and/or coming out of the shelter system. Oona has been active in No One Is Illegal (Toronto) and the "Status for All — Don't Ask Don't Tell" Campaign. She has completed her Master in Environmental Studies at York University and tries to incorporate art into as much of her life as possible.

Aileen Penner is a a writer, artist and activist with a passion for wild Pacific salmon. She holds a Master in Environmental Studies from York University and lives in Vancouver, BC.

Sau Wai Tai's main medium of artistic expression is installation art through which she collaborates with communities, places and materials to open up dialogues about the state of our being and our society. Her works draw attention to the connection between the social-political-ecological environment and disadvantaged groups. Some of her works have been published in *Undercurrent* Magazine. She also facilitates workshops and contributes to Chinese newspapers.

Julia Winckler is a German-Canadian artist. Her work has been exhibited in the UK, France, Germany, Taiwan and Canada. She uses photography, sound and video to explore personal, collective and cultural memories and real and imagined journeys. Recent projects include "Traces" and "Two Sisters." She is currently developing two new interactive projects: "Retracing Heinrich Barth" explores the journey of a nineteenth-century explorer in West Africa, and "My Canadian Pilgrimage" revisits an unusual 1929 pilgrimage to Canada. She has received support from the Arts Council South East, UK, and the Canada and Ontario Arts Council for the Arts. Julia teaches in the BA Communication and Digital Media and the BA Photography courses at the University of Brighton, UK.

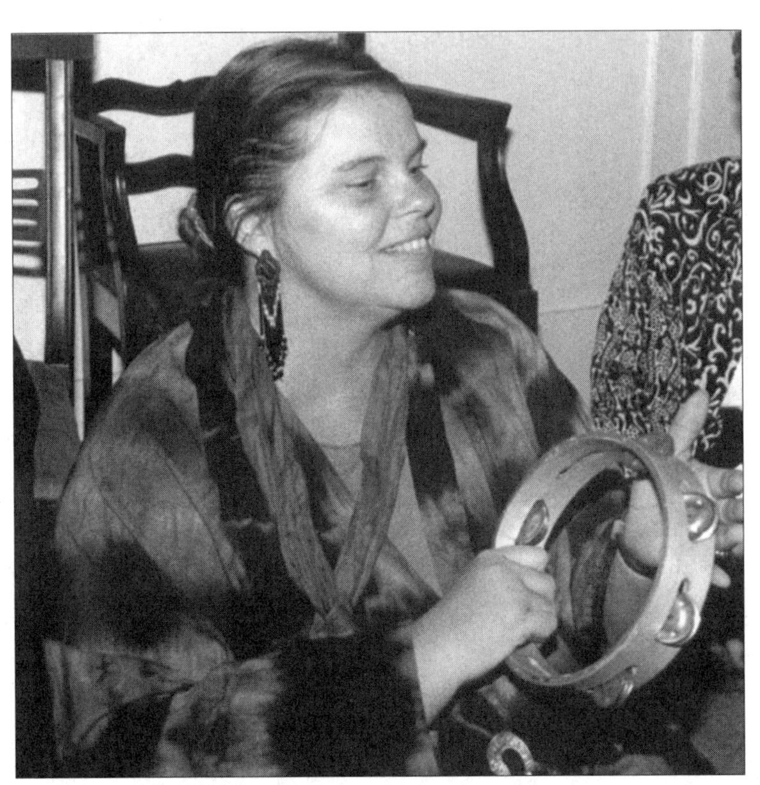

Dedication

Always be passionately aware ...
that you could be completely wrong.
— dian marino

dian marino (1941-1993), educator, artist, activist and storyteller extraordinaire, wrote her name in lower case letters, and word-processing software constantly tries to turn the "d" into "D", conforming with the programmed convention of starting 'proper' names with the upper case. But dian could not be programmed nor packaged — not by computer software, not by university authorities, not by her closest friends and family.

In her years of teaching at the Faculty of Environmental Studies in the 1980s and early 1990s, dian created a space for the wild and unpredictable — for a unique combination of critical questioning and creative expression, challenge and humour. Tales abound of dian filling the hallways with looms and other hands-on projects. The day after she died of breast cancer in 1993, FES students plastered the walls and ceilings, in classrooms and bathroom stalls, with heart stickers, honouring her favourite symbol and the immense love, generosity and playfulness she shared with her students and colleagues.

When friends compiled her written and visual art work into a volume, *Wild Garden: Art, Education and the Culture of Resistance,* in 1997, colleagues at FES decided to name the Wild Garden Media Centre in her honour. It is in this context that most of the contributors to this book met each other and crafted their own challenging creations, individual and collective. dian's trickster spirit is present in FES today and peeks through these pages. For many of us, she has been an important mentor in spreading the wild fire of art as activism.

Contributors have agreed that all royalties from this publication will go to the dian marino fund, a source of support to future FES students "who creatively use multi-media tools of inquiry and modes of communication to critically explore environmental issues," and are "committed to environmental and social justice."

Other titles from Sumach Press

A Recognition of Being: Reconstructing Native Womanhood
Kim Anderson

Back to the Drawing Board: African-Canadian Feminisms
Edited by Njoki Nathane Wane, Katerina Deliovsky and Erica Lawson

Battle Cries: Justice for Kids with Special Needs
Miriam Edelson

Doing IT: Women Working in Information Technology
Krista Scott-Dixon

Fuelling Body, Mind and Spirit: A Balanced Approach to Healthy Eating
Miriam Hoffer

Growing Up Degrassi: Television, Identity and Youth Cultures
Edited by Michele Byers

Madeleine Parent: Activist
Edited by Andrée Lévèsque

My Breasts, My Choice: Journeys Through Surgery
Barbara Brown, Maureen Aslin & Betsy Carey

Remembering Women Murdered by Men: Memorials Across Canada
The Cultural Memory Group

Strong Women Stories: Native Vision and Community Survival
Edited by Kim Anderson and Bonita Lawrence

Turbo Chicks: Talking Young Feminisms
Edited by Allyson Mitchell, Lisa Bryn Rundle and Lara Karaian

Women in the Office: Transitions in a Global Economy
Ann Eyerman

The Women's Daybook
With images by Canadian photographers

Women's Bodies/Women's Lives: Women, Health, Well-Being and Body Image
Edited by Baukje Miedema, Janet Stoppard and Vivienne Anderson

Writing Your Way: Creating a Personal Journal
Ellen Jaffe

Check Out our Great Fiction and Books for Young Adults at

www.sumachpress.com